IMAGES
*of America*

# FRANKFORT

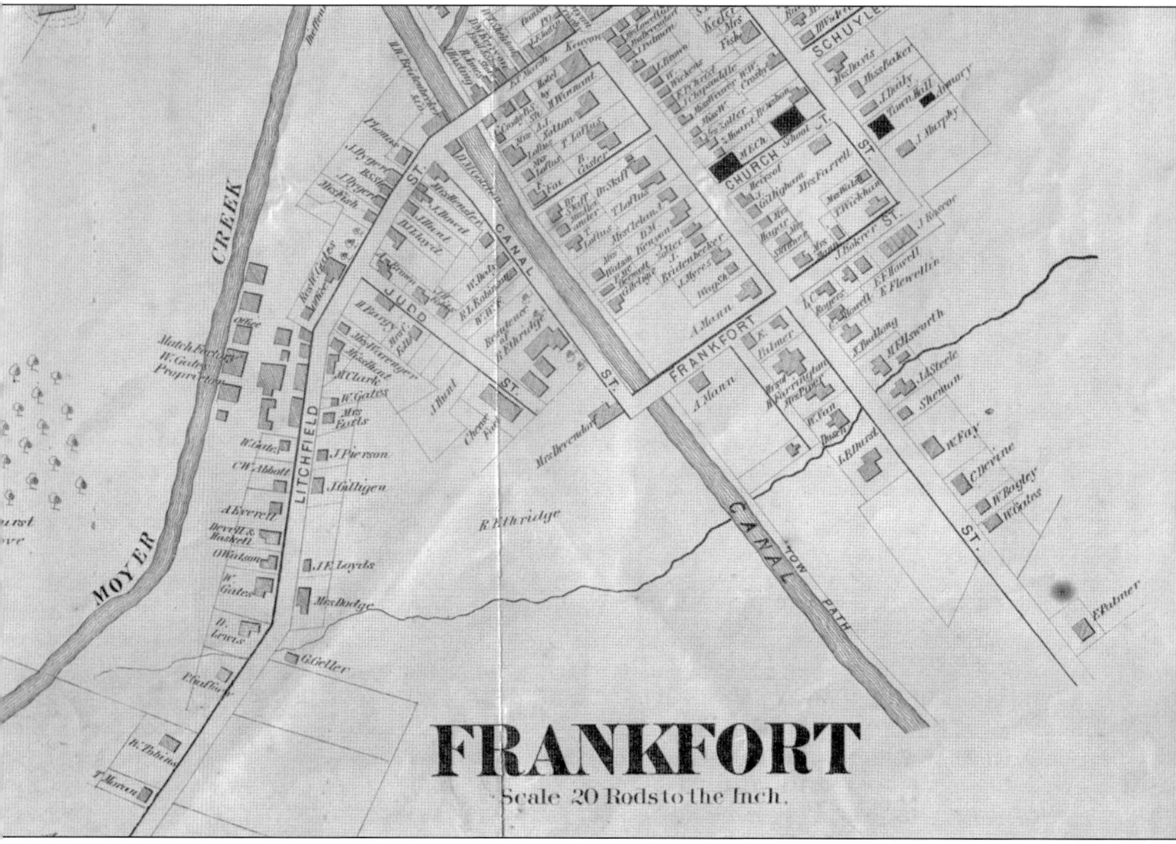


**Village Map, 1868.** This map shows a bustling and growing community along Moyer Creek and the Erie Canal, illustrating the growth of the community in the mid-1800s. The map includes Litchfield, Main, Frankfort, and Church Streets, as well as the Gates Match Factory along the creek, the towpath along the canal, the Methodist Episcopal church, Church Street School, and the residences along the village streets. (Courtesy of the Herkimer County Historical Society.)

**On the Cover:** The Balloon Farm is one of Frankfort's most notable landmarks, drawing attention from spectators and aeronautical enthusiasts from across the United States. (Courtesy of the Herkimer County Historical Society.)

IMAGES
*of America*

# FRANKFORT

Susan R. Perkins and Caryl A. Hopson

ARCADIA
PUBLISHING

ISBN 978-1-4671-2055-5

Published by Arcadia Publishing
Charleston, South Carolina

Printed in the United States of America

Library of Congress Control Number: 2013937221

For all general information, please contact Arcadia Publishing:
Telephone 843-853-2070
Fax 843-853-0044
E-mail sales@arcadiapublishing.com
For customer service and orders:
Toll-Free 1-888-313-2665

Visit us on the Internet at www.arcadiapublishing.com

*This book is dedicated to all of the residents of Frankfort, past and present.*

# Contents

# ACKNOWLEDGMENTS

This book was a community effort, and there are so many people to thank for their contributions. We could not go very far without our dependable volunteers at the Herkimer County Historical Society who assisted us with the book: Mary Haefele and her husband, Chuck, who knocked on some doors for us; Ben Stovall; Steve Knight; Linda Pratt; Sharon Rolchigo; and Jeff Steele.

Thank you to those who contributed photographs for the book: Peg Bianchi, Tom Bracken, Betsy Cirelli, Jacquelyn Conners, Carole Crimmins, William Ferguson, the Frankfort Fire Department, the Frankfort Free Library, the Frankfort Hill Volunteer Fire Company, Beverly Ferguson Gado, Lillian Gaherty, Dominick and Mary Green, Jody Grippe, the estate of Joseph J. and Mary Alice Grippe, Mary Haefele, Gerry Elthorp and the Herkimer County Fair, Eunice Hanson, Marilyn Hughes, Dorine Jenkins, Rob Juteau, Eugene and Eileen Kipper, Rev. Alfred Lamanna, JoAnn and Theresa Maneen, LaVergne McMurray, Steve McMurray, Keith McNally, the National Baseball Hall of Fame Library, the Oneida County Historical Society, Joseph Oriolo, Our Lady Queen of Apostles Church, Frank Palumbo, Donald Roberts, Marilyn Salvaggio, Dave Sanders, Frank Spina, Angela Thurston, Eva Tripple, the Village of Frankfort, Chad Wohler, and Rita Yashinski.

We asked a lot of people for their assistance in identifying photographs and providing information. Thanks go out to the following for their help: George Bianchi; Peg Bianchi; Providence Bono; Chuck Conigilaro of the Frankfort Fire Department; Carole Crimmins; Dominick DiNardo; Dick Farrell; William Ferguson; Christine Russell of the Frankfort Free Library; Beverly Ferguson Gado; Jody Grippe; Nancy Hamlin; Eunice Hanson; Mary Iocovozzi; Eugene Kipper; Jean Kull; Rev. Alfred Lamanna; Carol Lavalla; JoAnn Maneen; LaVergne McMurray; Steve McMurray; Keith McNally; Brian Howard, Carl Saporito, and Frank Tomaino of the Oneida County Historical Society; Arnold Riggs, Donald Roberts, and the St. Francis Society members; Mike Scalise; Sam Salamone; Marilyn Salvaggio; Roe Salvaggio; Thane Sanzo; Henry Seeger Jr.; Frank Spina; Mayor Frank Moracco, clerk Karlee Tamburro, and treasurer Doreen Fiorentino of the Village of Frankfort; Angela Thurston; Joseph Tocco; Daniel Tripple; Patti Viti of Our Lady Queen of Apostles; George Weiss; Chad Wohler; and Anne Whitney Yarnall. A special thank you to Bill Ferguson, Jody Grippe, Chuck and Mary Haefele, Eunice Hanson, Keith McNally, Donald Roberts, Angela Thurston, and Chad Wohler for going above and beyond to help us with this book.

Unless otherwise noted, all images are courtesy of the Herkimer County Historical Society archives.

# Introduction

We are honored to present this book during the village of Frankfort's sesquicentennial celebration year in 2013. The majority of the photographs featured in this book come from people in the community who have shared them with us, of both the village and town of Frankfort. Each image tells a story that deserves to be shared about the community's history, the people who made a life here, and the events that took place, all of which led us to where we are today. This quote by author Pearl Buck is appropriate: "If you want to understand today, you have to search yesterday."

Along the journey of putting this book together, we have met so many wonderful people who reside in the community of Frankfort. There was not one person we approached for assistance who did not greet us in a friendly manner, and more than one went above and beyond in searching for photographs and information. This book, then, is a production of community effort.

The land that comprises the town of Frankfort was originally settled by Palatine Germans. A portion of the land was the Burnetsfield Patent, which was signed on April 30, 1725, by Gov. William Burnet, giving Palatines 100 acres lying north and south of the Mohawk River between what are now Frankfort and Little Falls. Jacob Folts (Folz), the first settler, had lot No. 3 in the patent. The Town of Frankfort was formed on February 5, 1796. The Mohawk River bounds the town to the north, along with the town of German Flatts to the east, the town of Litchfield to the south, and Oneida County to the west. The town received its name from Lawrence Frank, one of the early settlers.

The Erie Canal's opening in 1825 brought improved transportation, and travelers streamed through the valley. As the population grew and dispersed throughout the town, small hamlets sprang up. The community of East Frankfort, located one mile east of the village, was built up through the efforts of a Vermont native, Hon. Archibald McGowan, who came here in the mid-1850s and built a dry dock and a general store. The area became known as McGowansville. Another community was Frankfort Center, which was once known as Howard's Bush after James and Patience Balch Howard, who purchased close to 70 acres in that area in the early 1800s. The Howards built their home on the corner of what is now Gates Road. The name lasted until the late 1850s.

On May 4, 1863, an act was passed by the New York legislature incorporating the Village of Frankfort. A board of trustees was elected under this charter, which included J.W. Bridenbecker (president), A.W. Sheldon, Isaac Piper, M. Golden, and Samuel Hoard. The population of the village at the time was 1,337.

Gates Match Factory founder William Gates started experimenting with the making of friction matches in Frankfort in 1844 and started a business. In 1854, he patented a continuous match-making machine, and, by 1870, it had grown in to a large establishment on Litchfield Street along Moyer Creek. Gates's patented invention of a match-making machine produced millions of matches annually. His son sold the business to Diamond Match Company of Oswego in 1893. The site of the factory is now Lehman Park.

The advent of the street railroad, or trolley line, reached Frankfort in 1872. In the 1880s, the West Shore Railroad and the Railroad Shops brought more people to the village, where they found jobs and settled down. It was a boom when the shops came to town, and it was disheartening when they left not two decades later, in 1897. However, this did not stop the progressive streak of business in the village, because the vacant shops attracted new industry. The Railroad Shop paint shop became the Michigan Condensed Milk Company. The foundry and office building were occupied by the Central Hudson Railroad Company. The blacksmith shop became Pratt Chuck, and the erection shop became the Continental Tool Company. The latter industry eventually provided one of Frankfort's biggest companies, the Union Fork & Hoe Company. In the 1900s, the village was ripe with businesses that sold their products all around the country and even to other countries.

The village gained an international reputation in the 1880s and 1890s when Charles "Carl" Myers and his wife, Carlotta, turned William Gates's mansion into an aerodrome for the manufacturing and launching of their hot air balloons and sky ships. Crowds gathered from near and far to see the ascents. Today, visitors still come from far and wide to visit the area, although now they go across the street from the Balloon Farm to the Herkimer County Fairgrounds. The Herkimer County Fair itself is held every year in mid-August. It first started in the village of Herkimer, but it withered away in the wake of World War I. A modest, farm-oriented fair was revived in Frankfort in 1949. Today, it has grown into one of the area's most popular summer attractions.

Although there are no photographs of the Olive Branch Lodge No. 40 of Free and Accepted Masons in this book, it warrants mention because it was the only Masonic lodge in the county that has maintained an uninterrupted existence since it was chartered, in 1812, by Grand Master DeWitt Clinton. The lodge merged with the Ilion Masonic Lodge in 1997.

One-room schools abounded, as they did in every community, before centralization took place, combining local school districts. Thanks to local community members who have preserved them, many photographs still exist of those one-room schools. While there are photographs of Frankfort Hill District School No. 10, it is also a living photograph to this day, thanks to the Frankfort Hill Historical Society, which undertook a major campaign to save the school and turn it into a museum showing what one-room schools looked like in their day. The historical society is even working with local educators to bring students to visit the school and spend a day experiencing firsthand what education was like in the 1800s.

Musical talent abounded in Frankfort, with two champion bands: the Frankfort Kiwanis Band and the Starlighters Drum and Bugle Corps, as well as Joe Grippe and His Top Hatters. The area's vocal talent was later reflected in the bicentennial choir that was created to celebrate the country's 200th anniversary in 1976 and went on to perform in Washington, DC.

Community is also reflected in the churches that were built and the organizations that were founded that are seen in this book. We would like to thank everyone, again, for their contributions to this book, and we hope that they enjoy this walk down memory lane.

# *One*

# Notable People

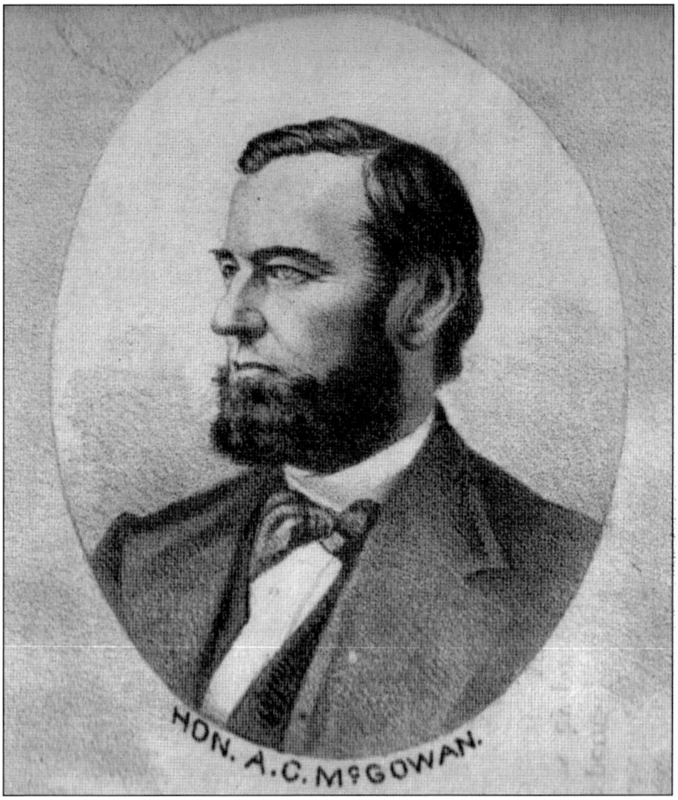


**Hon. Archibald McGowan.** Hon. Archibald McGowan (1820–1893), born in Vermont, made his own way at a young age and came to Frankfort in 1854, where he helped establish East Frankfort, which was once known as McGowansville. He was a merchant, boatbuilder, and farmer who represented Frankfort on the board of supervisors. He served as a state assemblyman in 1862 and 1865 and in the state senate in 1871 and 1873.

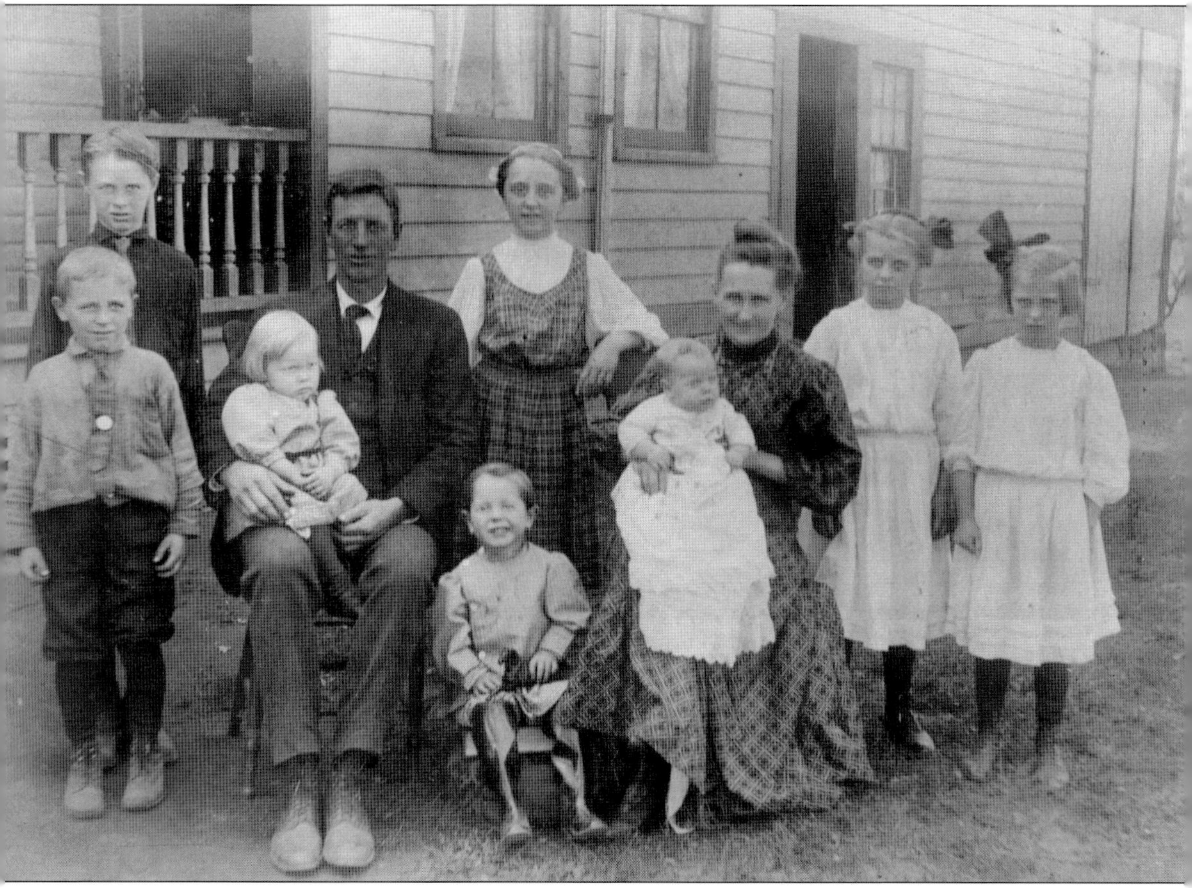

**James D. Ferguson.** James Day Ferguson II (1871–1930) was a large property owner and farmer who resided on the land farmed by his ancestors, early settlers of Frankfort. Ferguson Creek and Ferguson Road bear their name. Samuel Ferguson, along with his son James G., came from Oneida County to Frankfort about 1795. James G. married Christina Day, and their second son, James D. (1829–1903), continued the family farm, combining farming with stock raising and the operation of boats on the Erie Canal, with boats carrying general merchandise between Buffalo and New York City. James D. married Elizabeth Davis, and their son, James D. II, is seen here with his family, from left to right, (first row) James D. III, Raymond, James D. II, Harold, Dora (holding baby Donald), Marjorie, and Helen; (standing in back) Frankie and Mary. (Courtesy of William Ferguson.)

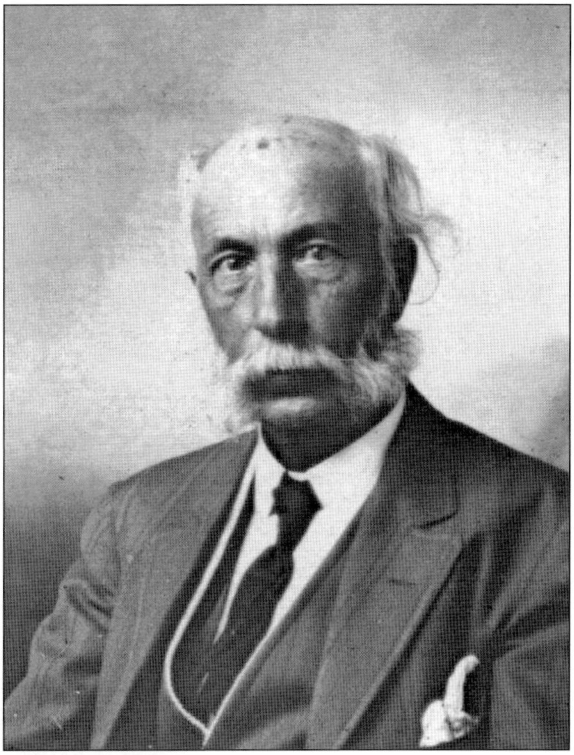

**CARL AND CARLOTTA MYERS.** Charles "Carl" Myers (1842–1925) was born in Fort Herkimer but grew up in Mohawk. As a young man, he developed his scientific interest in telegraphy, electricity, and photography. He married Mary "Carlotta" Hawley (1850–1932) in 1871 in Hornell, New York. A few years later, they moved to Mohawk. They shared a passion for aeronautics and became well known for their balloon ascensions. Carlotta made her first public ascension on July 4, 1880, before a crowd of 15,000 at Little Falls. In 1881, their daughter Elizabeth "Aerial" Myers was born. In 1889, the Myerses purchased the former Gates mansion in Frankfort. He is noted for his work for the US government with hydrogen balloons used for meteorology and for the Army and Navy with balloons used for signaling purposes and monitoring movements of war vessels. (Both, courtesy of JoAnn and Theresa Maneen.)

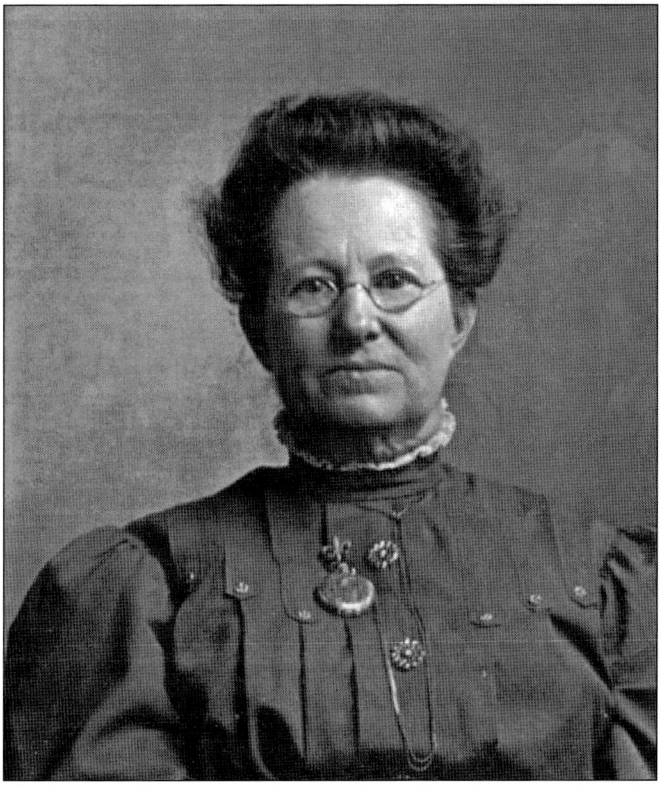

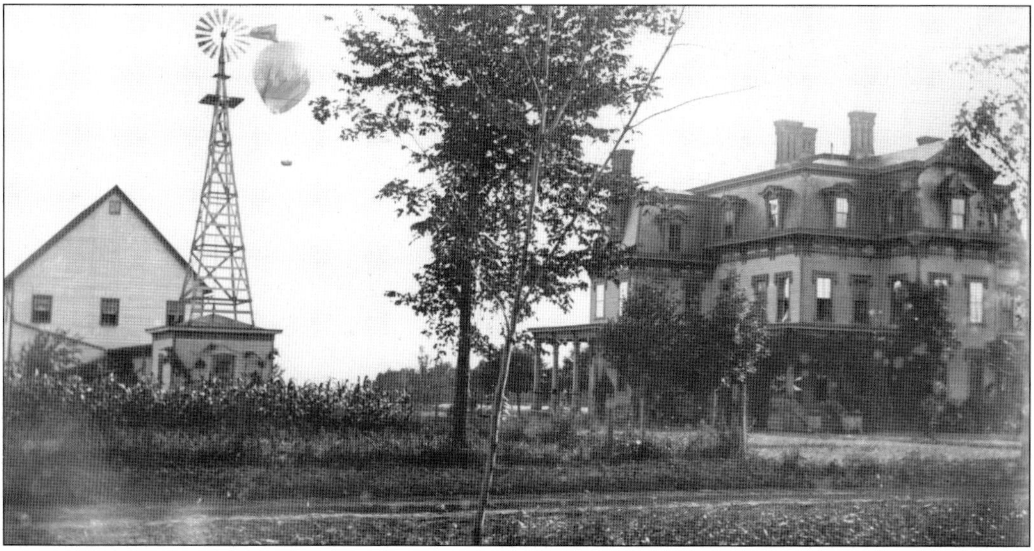

**BALLOON FARM.** This Victorian-style mansion, the home of Carl and Carlotta Myers, is best known as the Balloon Farm. It was originally built in 1883 by Frederick Gates (1848–1942), son of the founder of the Gates Match Factory. In 1889, the Myerses purchased the spacious mansion on Cemetery Street. They used the lower two floors for family quarters and entertaining. The third floor became a factory, with a chemical laboratory, a machine shop, carpentry equipment, and sewing shops. Here, the couple invented and manufactured aeronautical equipment and instrument-carrying balloons used in meteorological experiments. In 1919, they moved to Atlanta to live with their daughter Elizabeth Wing. JoAnn and Theresa Maneen purchased the property at auction in 1994. Today, it is operated as a bed-and-breakfast. It was added to the State and National Registers of Historic Places in 1997 and 1998. (Both, courtesy of JoAnn and Theresa Maneen.)

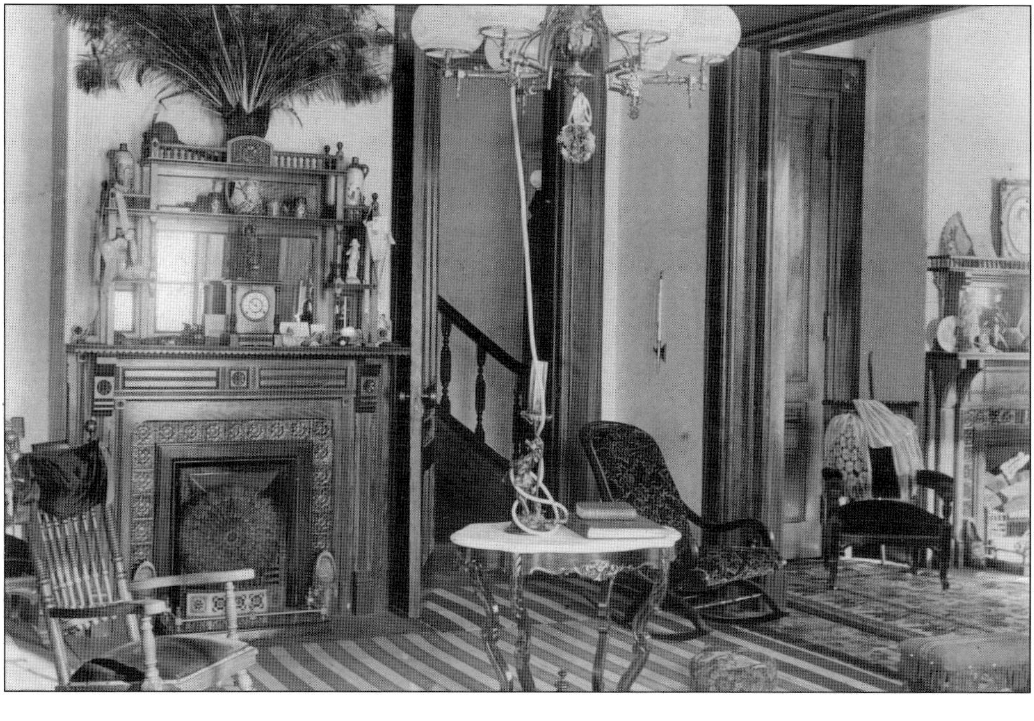

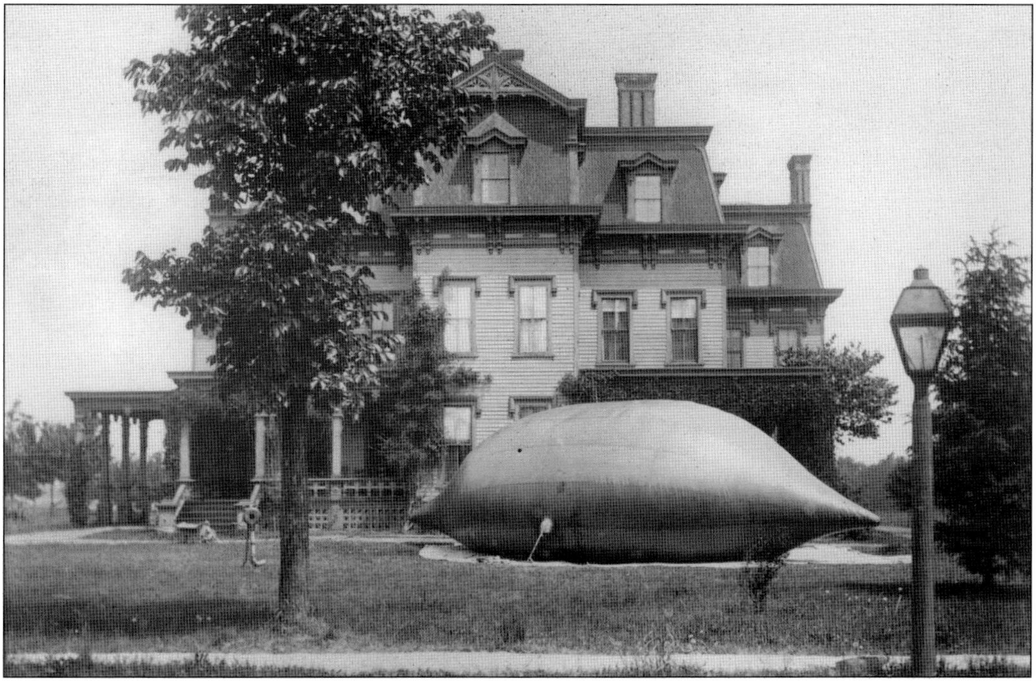

**EXPERIMENTS ATTRACT ONLOOKERS.** A new motor airship was designed by T.C. Benbow (1864–1932) of Montana, who brought his design to the Myerses for their assistance in developing the flying machine in 1903. The gas bag section of the airship was 74 feet in length and could hold 14,000 cubic feet of hydrogen gas. The lifting power of the ship was produced by setting fans in motion and by cams controlling the motion of the pins. The power for operating the fans, four of which were on each corner, was furnished by two double-cylinder gasoline engines. The car of the ship was suspended by a cable and hung from the center. A trial of the ship drew thousands of spectators, with Benbow entering the car of his ship and raising it to a height of 75 feet in the air. (Both, courtesy of JoAnn and Theresa Maneen.)

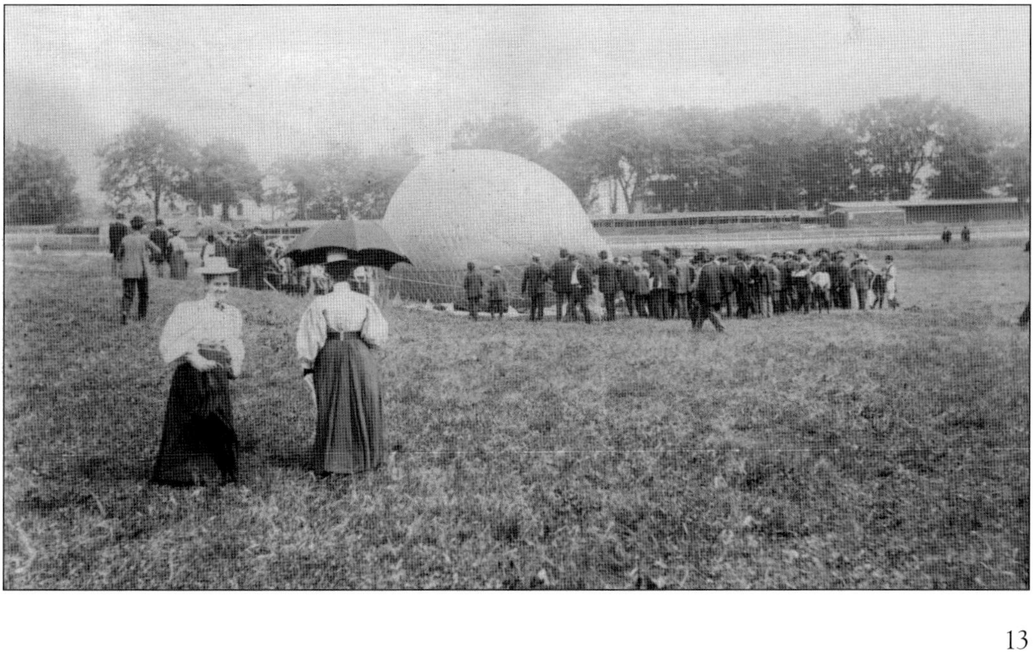

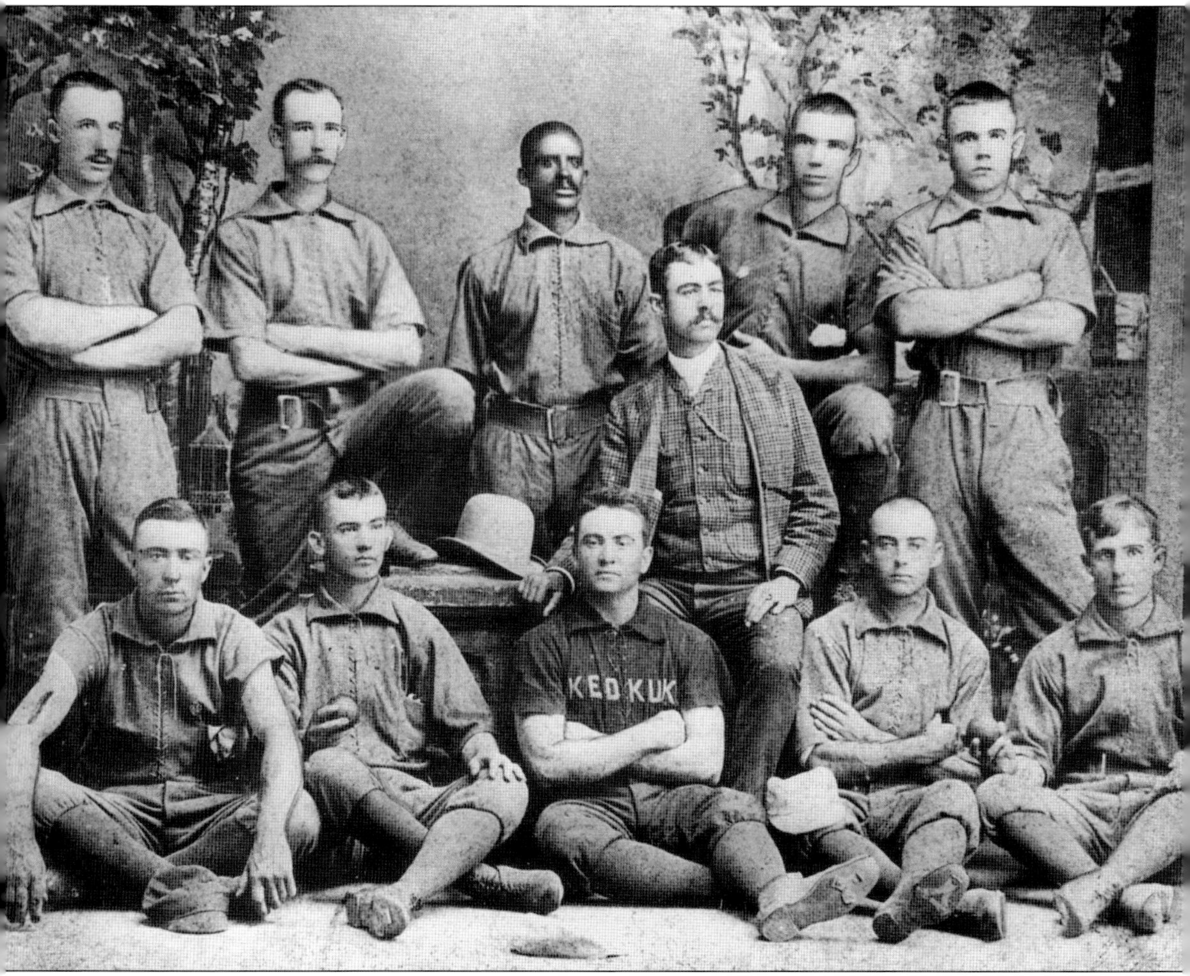


**Bud Fowler.** John W. Jackson Jr. (1858–1913), also known as Bud Fowler, was born in Fort Plain to John and Mary Lansing Jackson. The family had moved to Cooperstown by 1860. Fowler (second row, center) is recognized as the first African American player in organized baseball. He played for over 20 years in the 1800s, despite facing racial discrimination. He started playing amateur ball in 1878 in Massachusetts and then continued his professional career, playing for minor-league teams throughout the United States. In 1894, he organized and managed an all-black team, the Page Fence Giants, and had a successful season touring the Midwest. In 1900, he organized another team, the Black Tourists, in Columbus, Ohio, playing black and white teams. Fowler died on February 26, 1913, at the home of his sister, Mrs. John Odom (Harriet), in Frankfort and is buried in Oak View Cemetery. In 1987, the Society of American Baseball Research purchased a headstone and placed it on his unmarked grave. It reads, "John W. Jackson: 'Bud Fowler, Black Baseball Pioneer.' " (Courtesy of the National Baseball Hall of Fame Library.)

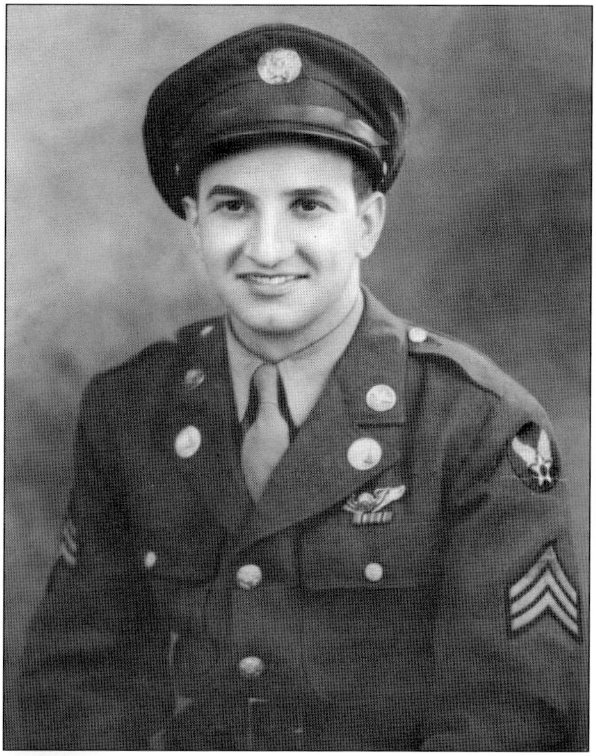

**Sgt. Paul James Spina.** When Paul Spina (1916–1978), the son of John and Jennie Spina, enlisted in the Air Force in March 1942, he was taking on the adventure of a lifetime. On November 9 of that year, he and a six-man crew of the Air Transport Command crashed on the Greenland Ice Cap while searching for a missing plane. They were able to live in makeshift quarters made from the tail of the broken fuselage, but they had limited food, no heat, and no lights. One of the crew rigged up the radio for communication and their position was located. Food and supplies were dropped by parachute, along with letters from his mother, who never lost hope. It was too dangerous to land a plane for rescue, so a dogsled rescue was attempted, but it failed. They were finally rescued in April 1943. (Both, courtesy of Frank Spina.)

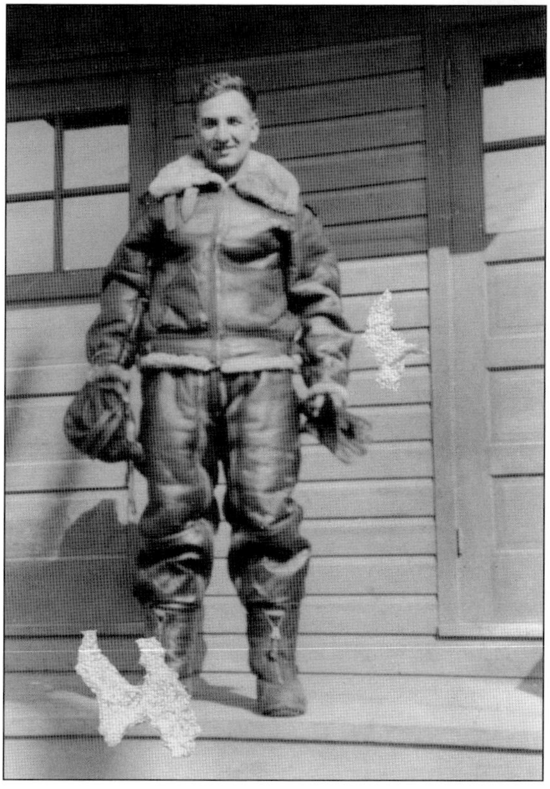

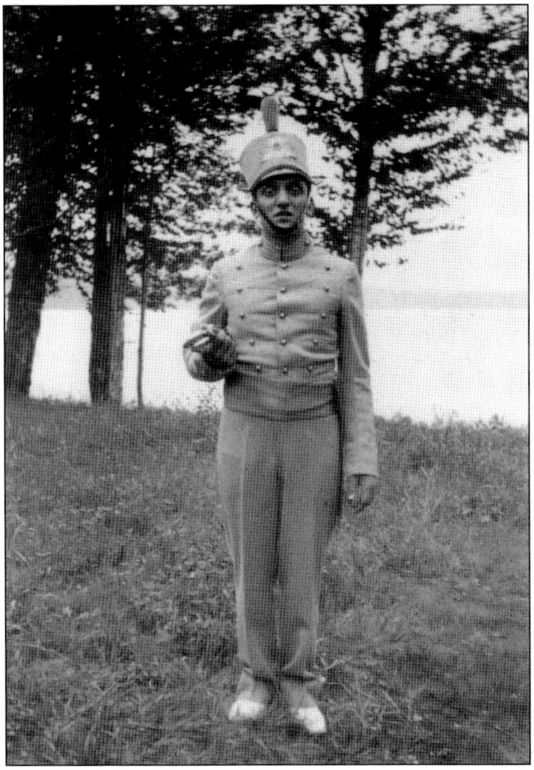

**Joseph Thurston.** Born into a musical family, the son of James and Eleanor Gumina Thurston, Joseph Thurston (1927–1994) carried on his family's love for music in a big way by organizing Frankfort's first junior drum corps. He was an avid trumpet player himself and played with the Red Band, the Ilion Firemen's Band, the Blackhawks, the Frankfort Kiwanis Band, and the Fort Schuyler Band. In September 1959, he and 10 committee members started the Starlighters Junior Drum and Bugle Corps, which performed in countless parades and competitions around New York and Massachusetts. On September 2, 1950 (below), he married Angie Antonucci, and they had two children, James and Angela. (Both, courtesy of Angela Thurston.)

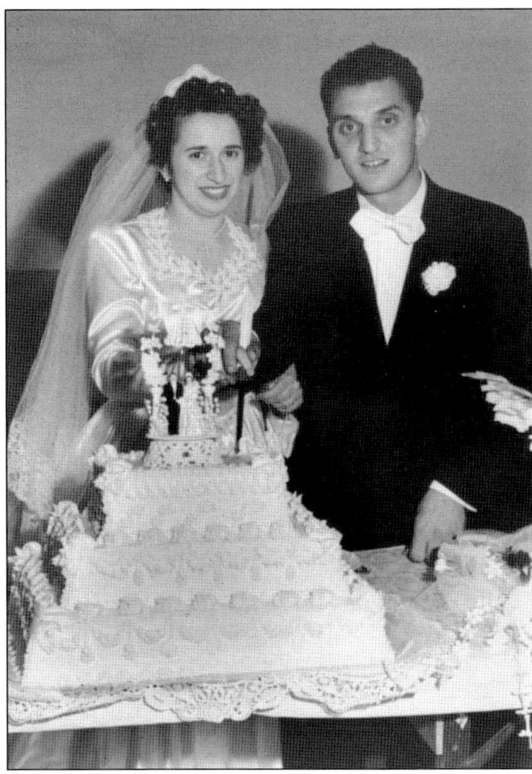

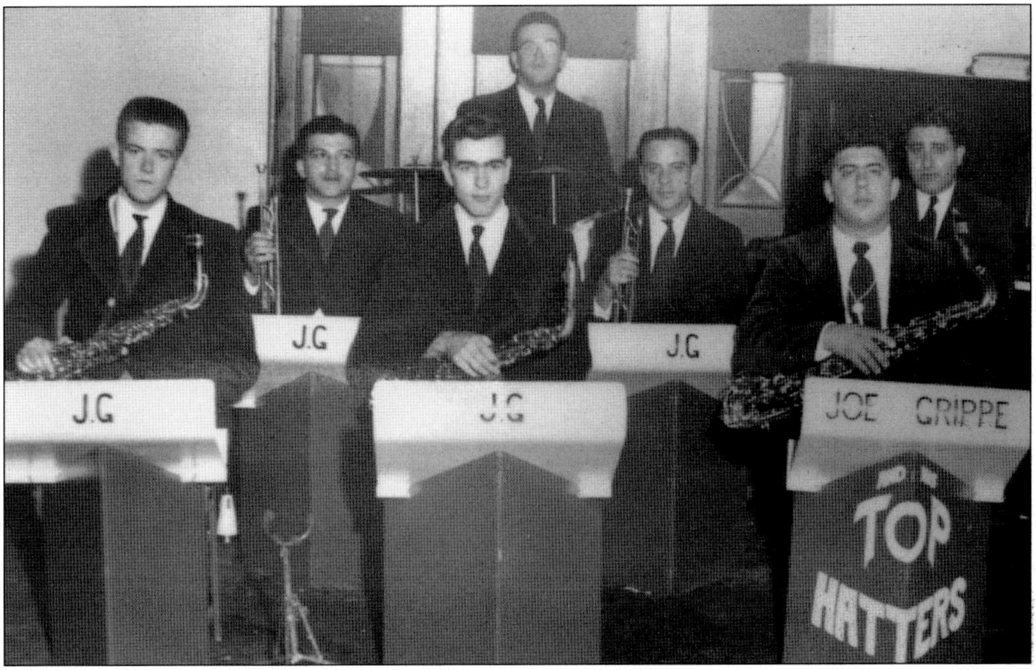


**Joe Grippe and His Top Hatters.** Joseph Grippe began his music career at the age of seven, playing clarinet. Later, he learned how to play tenor saxophone. He founded the band Joe Grippe and His Top Hatters, a popular attraction throughout the valley. They played at proms, block dances, weddings, special community events, and for war veterans in New York hospitals. Seen above in 1950 are, from left to right, Arnold Riggs (1925–), Michael Cirillo (1917–1982), Charles Warburton (1926–1999), Charles "Chubby" Dolch (1919–2001), Charles Cattat (1910–2000), Joe Grippe (1924–2010) and Dominick Fragale (1904–1972). Seen below in 1952 are, from left to right, Joe Sanzo (1908–1990), Joe Tocco (1925–), Charles Cattat, Robert Bennett, Chubby Dolch, Joe Grippe, Dominick Fragale, and Joe Piroli (c. 1921–1969), the singer. (Both, courtesy of the estate of Joseph J. and Mary Alice Grippe.)

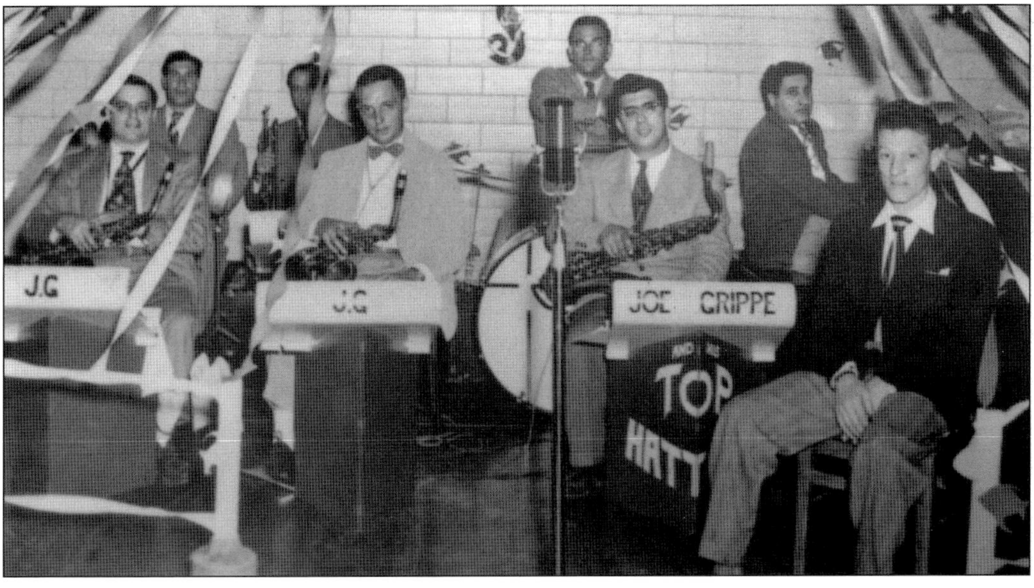

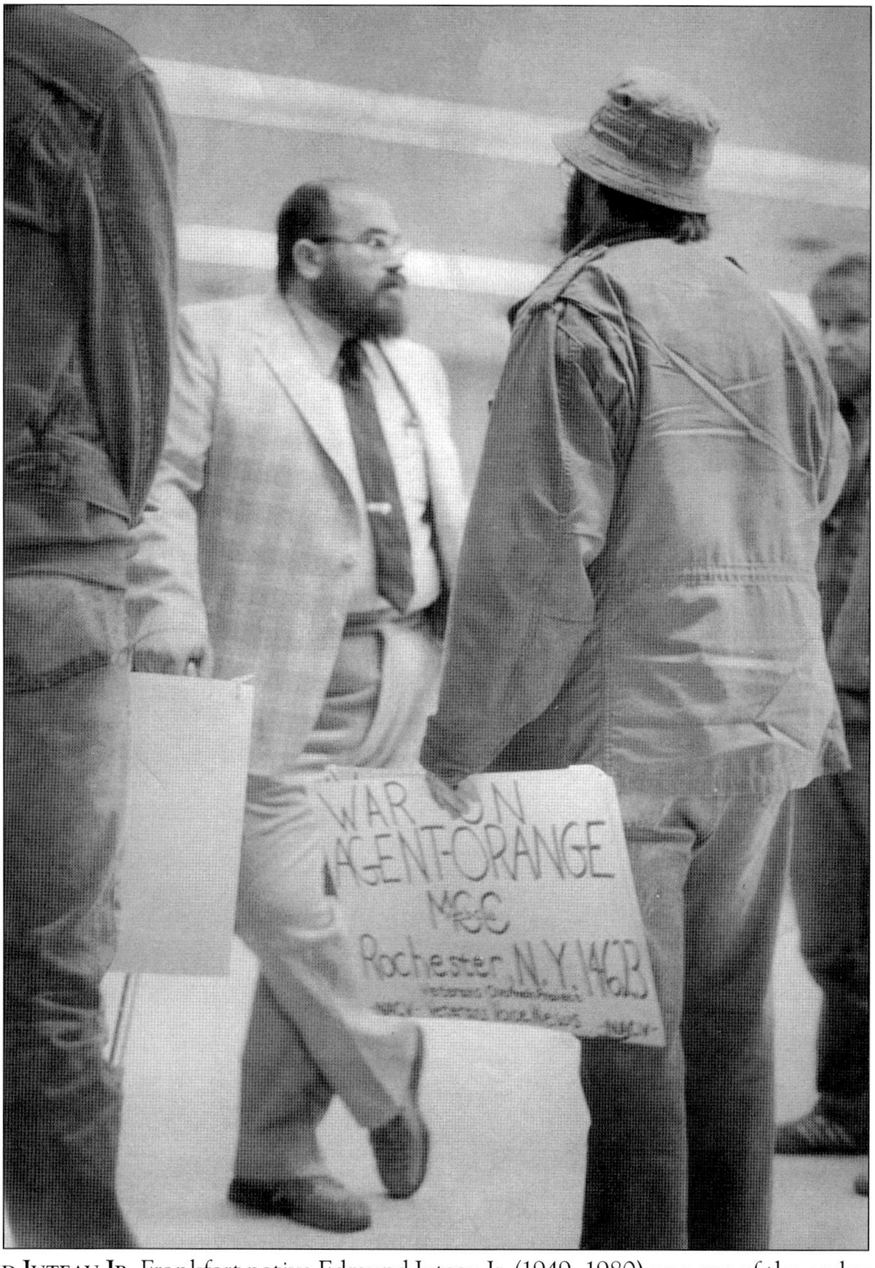


**EDMUND JUTEAU JR.** Frankfort native Edmund Juteau Jr. (1949–1980) was one of the early activists in the effort to raise awareness about the deadly effects of the defoliant Agent Orange. He was exposed to the chemical agent while serving in Vietnam with the Air Force Medical Corps and developed cancer as a result. He organized Operation Response to alert other Vietnam veterans to the health risks they had been exposed to. His campaign began locally when he organized an information day for Vietnam veterans at the Michael Pliseck VFW post in Herkimer. In 1979, he won a landmark decision to receive service-connected disability benefits from the Veterans Administration and was appointed vice president of Agent Orange Victims International. A monument was dedicated to him at Memorial Park, across from the Frankfort VFW post, in 1980. (Courtesy of Rob Juteau.)

**REV. ALFRED A. LAMANNA.** Father Lamanna served the community of Frankfort, beginning as the assistant pastor of St. Mary's in 1952 and becoming pastor in 1969, a position he held until retiring in 1994. He reflected back the warmth and hospitality shown to him by his congregation and community. Growing up in Amsterdam, he was inspired to become a priest as an altar boy at his home church of St. Michael's. He pursued theological studies at Christ the King Seminary in St. Bonaventure and was ordained in 1949. Father Lamanna was the first Catholic Youth Organization (CYO) county director, helped form the CYO basketball league, and was instrumental in bringing the US Naval Reserve Center to Frankfort in 1988. He is seen below (left) with deacon James Bower marking the 59th anniversary of his ordination. (Both, courtesy of Rev. Alfred Lamanna.)

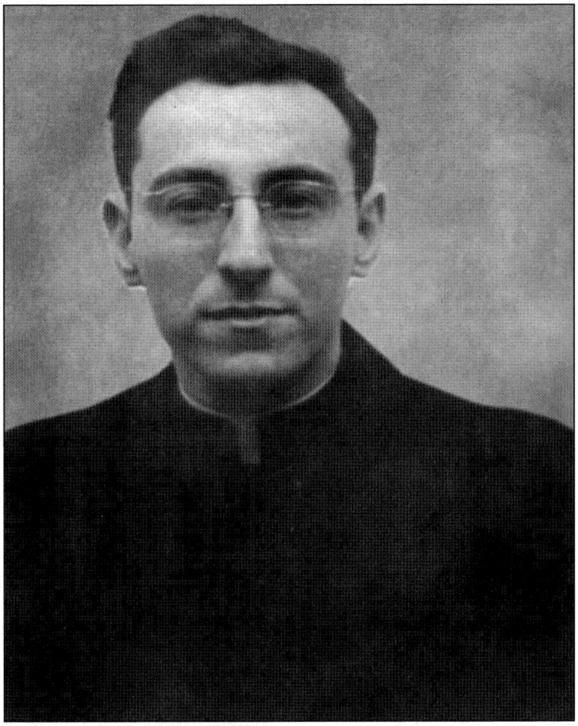

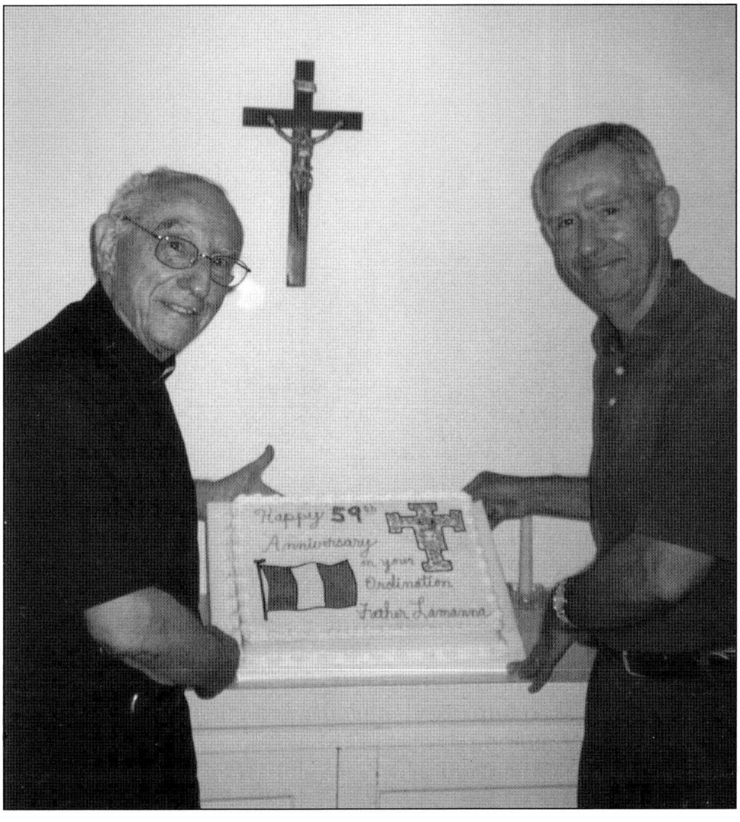

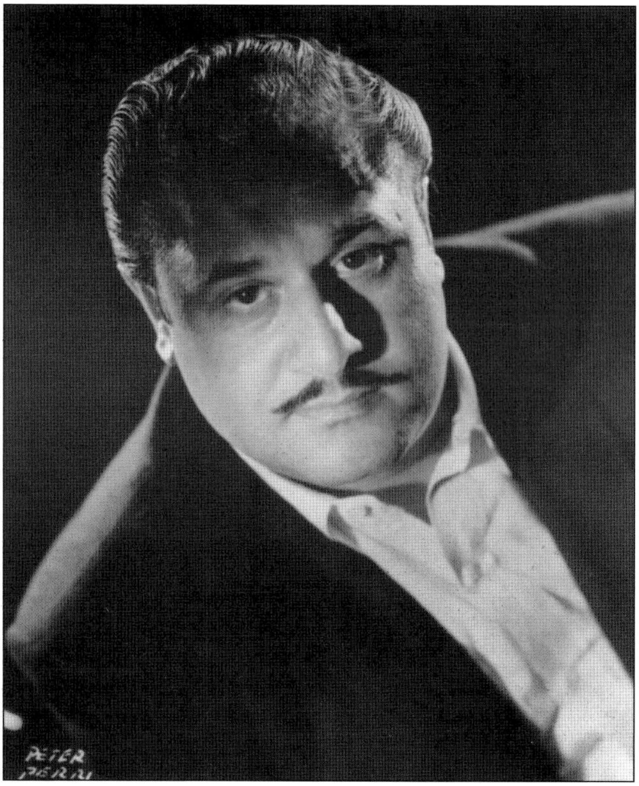


**NICHOLAS BIANCHI.** Known for his beautiful baritone voice, Bianchi (1920–1987) became a well-known opera singer but also starred in summer musical theater productions such as *Guys and Dolls* and *Happy Hunting*. He married Bette Wermine in 1964 in New York City, and they sang together in many musical comedies and concerts. He was born in Frankfort to George and Josephine Chard Bianchi. (Courtesy of Peg Bianchi.)

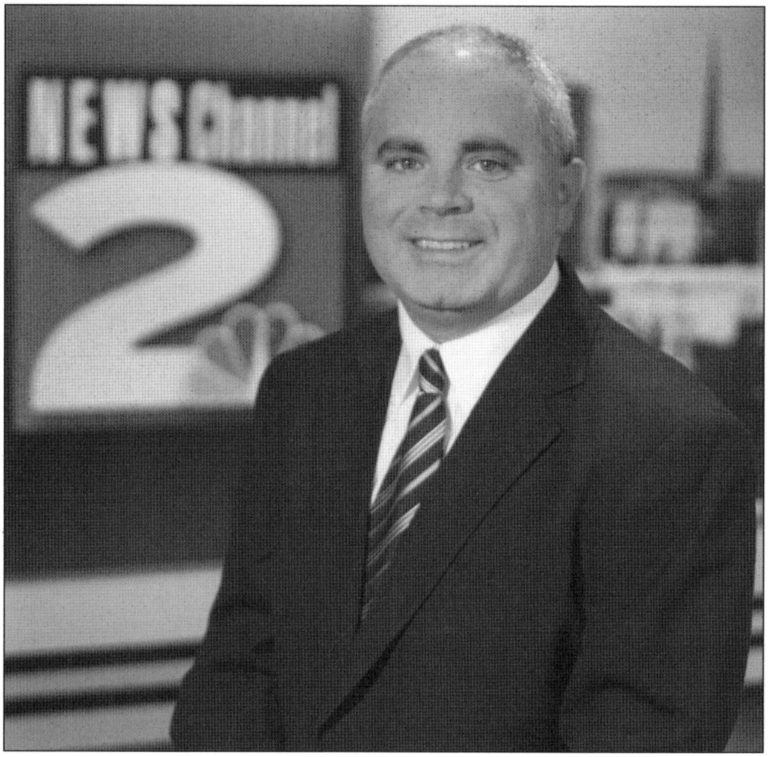


**STEVE MCMURRAY.** One of three children born in Frankfort to LaVergne and Jane McMurray, Steve McMurray graduated from the S.I. Newhouse School of Public Communications at Syracuse University and made a career in television, starting at WUTR as the sports director, news anchor, and director. He moved to WKTV in 2002 as a news anchor, became the news director in 2004, and has been the station manager since July 2012. (Courtesy of Steve McMurray.)

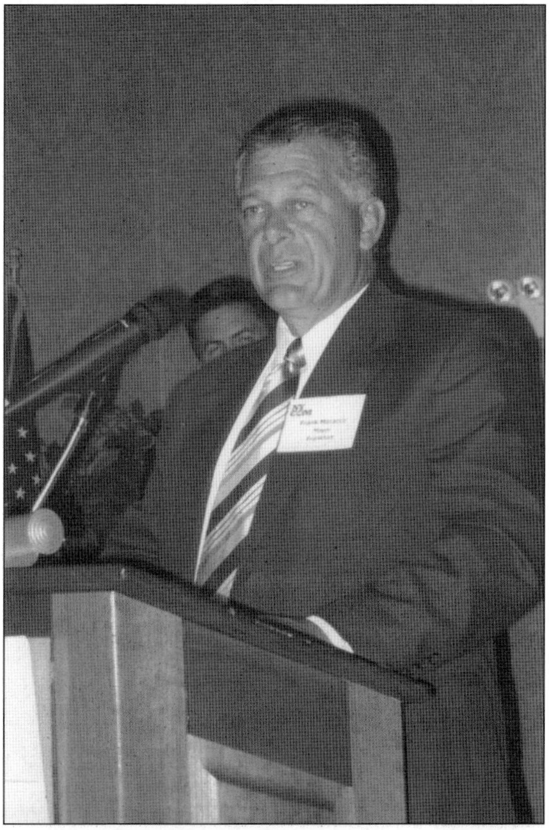

**Frank Moracco.** Working as a public servant for the community is a part of Frank Moracco's heritage, as his mother served as a village clerk in the 1990s. Moracco was first elected as a village trustee in 2002–2003 and became mayor on May 20, 2004, a position he still holds in 2013. Highlights of his mayoral career include instituting two programs in the village that received first-place awards from the New York Conference of Mayors: the village's Wi-Fi program in 2006 and, in 2011, a public water energy efficiency project involving a smart-meter water system that uses computers to read meters and send out water leakage alerts. Seen below are, from left to right, trustee Francis Spatol, superintendent of utilities Ron Vivacqua, Moracco, unidentified, trustee Anthony Fumarola, and grant writer Jeromy Silverman. (Both, courtesy of the Village of Frankfort.)

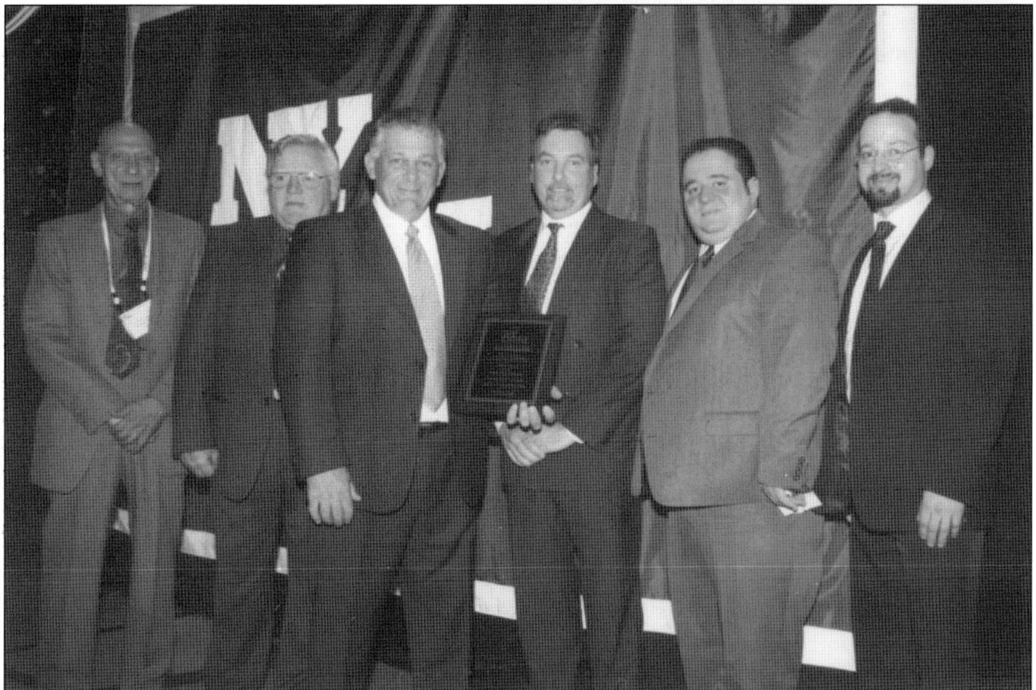

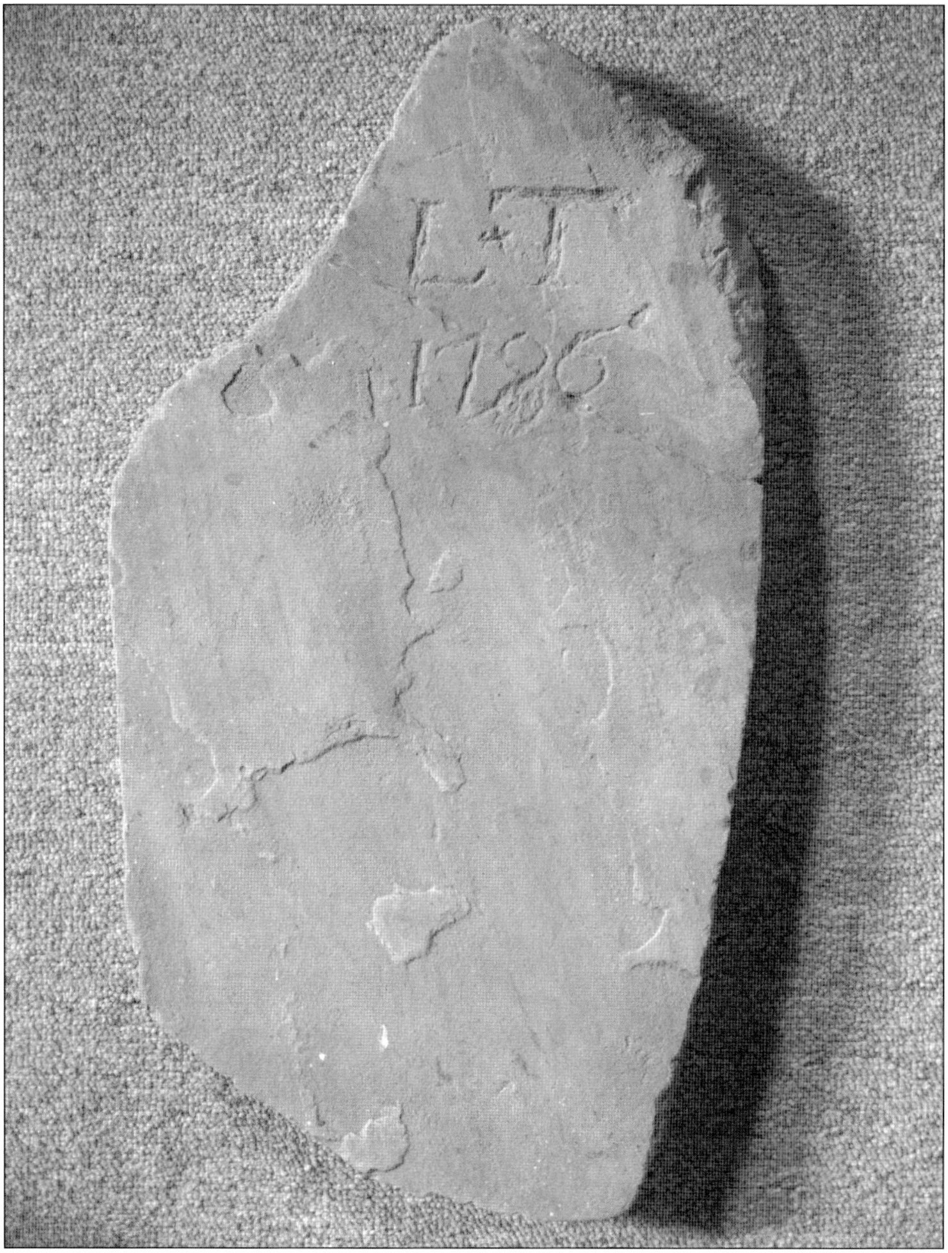

**Lucy Tucker.** The simple letters "LT" and the number "1796" are all that adorn this weathered headstone. It was rescued after the land it rested on was plowed and the stone was cut in two. Family descendant Jean Darling found it, cemented it back together, and donated it to the Herkimer County Historical Society. The headstone belonged to Lucy Tucker, who died in infancy at 18 months old in 1796. She was buried in a corner of the garden near the original dwelling on her family's property in West Frankfort. Her parents were Josiah and Lucy Dougherty Tucker. Josiah, after experiencing a lively youth as a soldier in the American Revolution and then as a sailor on a merchant ship, made his way up the Mohawk River, where he settled in Schuyler and married Lucy. After their marriage, they settled in Frankfort and began their family. Lucy was one of their first-born children.

# Two

# COMMUNITY

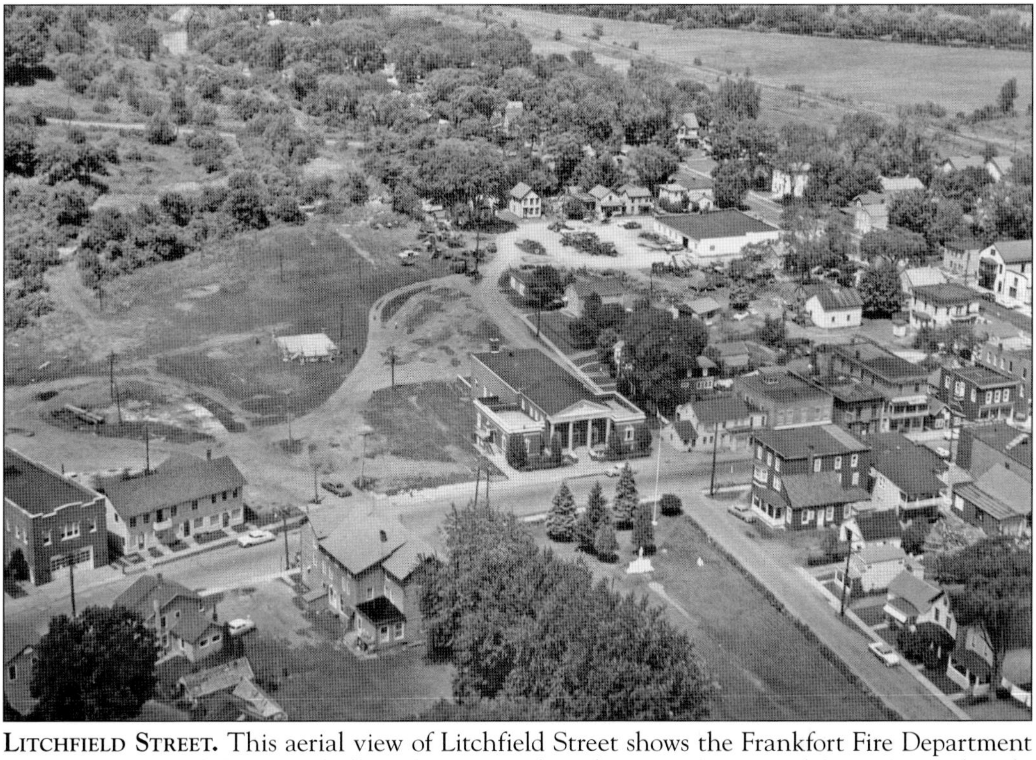

**LITCHFIELD STREET.** This aerial view of Litchfield Street shows the Frankfort Fire Department on the far left and the town hall in the center, directly across from Frankfort Memorial Park. The park's unique shape reflects an important part of the village's history, as it was once the bed of the Erie Canal.

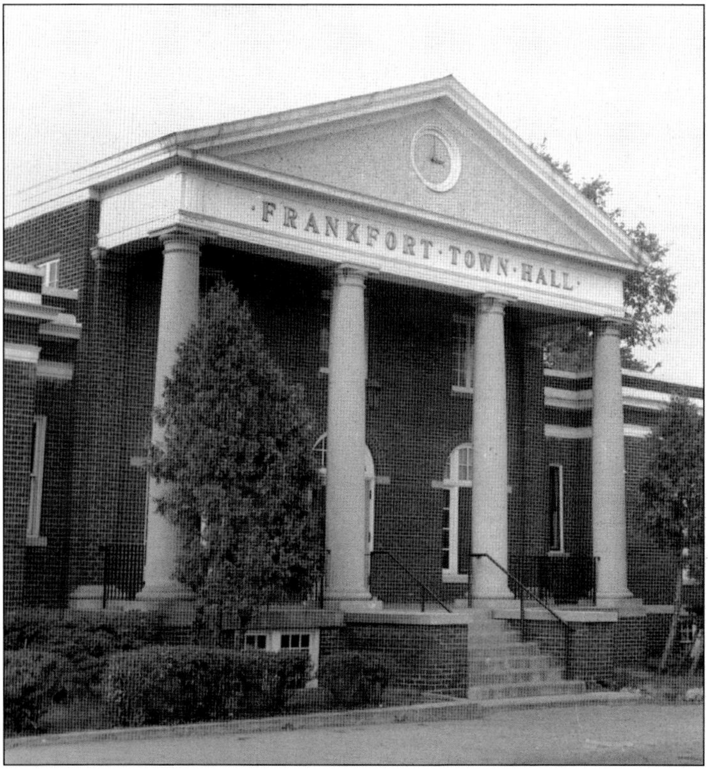


**FRANKFORT TOWN HALL.** The town hall was built as a memorial to the soldiers of World War I and dedicated on Memorial Day, 1924. The first floor housed the municipal town offices, the boardroom, and a spacious auditorium; the basement held the courtroom and the banquet hall; and the second floor held rooms for the American Legion post. It was added to the State and National Registers of Historic Places in 1999.

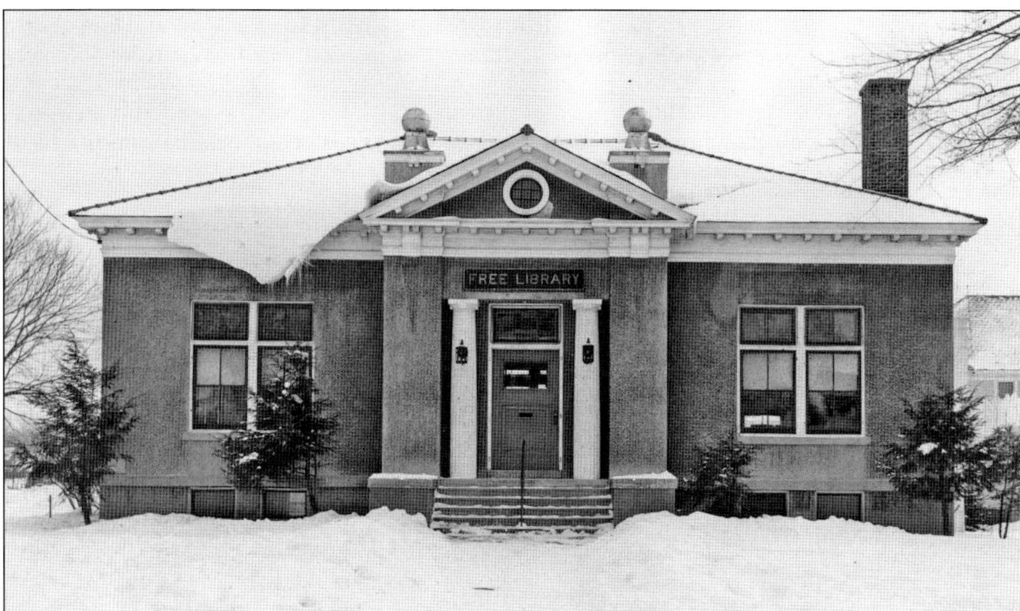


**FRANKFORT FREE LIBRARY.** The Fortnightly Club organized Frankfort's first library in 1900 and rented rooms in the Masonic block for this purpose. Minnie Cleland was the first librarian. A building fund was undertaken, and Albert N. Russell donated land for a library on Frankfort Street. A handsome new building with a stucco finish was finally built and dedicated on August 13, 1911. (Courtesy of the Frankfort Free Library.)

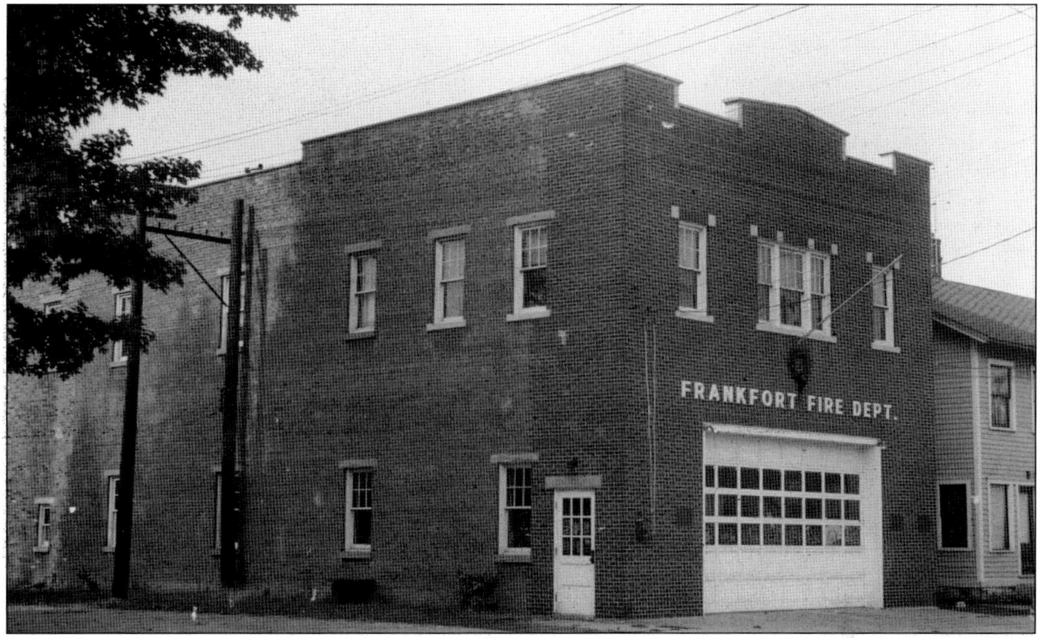


**Frankfort Fire Department.** The Frankfort Fire Department has provided fire protection service to the village since 1880, when it was chartered and became a municipal department made up of three fire companies. The first, Columbia Hose Company, formed in the early 1850s and later changed its name to Thomas Honohan Steamer and Hose Company No. 1. The second, Washington Fire Company, formed when William Gates donated an engine house and firefighting equipment in 1852. It became H.M. Wood Hose Company No. 2 in 1890. The third company organized in 1870 and became H.H. Ingham Company No. 3 in 1897. In 2003, the Frankfort Fire Company was organized, disbanding the three companies. The fire station was built on South Litchfield Street in 1886. The front portion was built in 1941 as a Works Progress Administration (WPA) project. (Below, courtesy of the Frankfort Fire Department.)

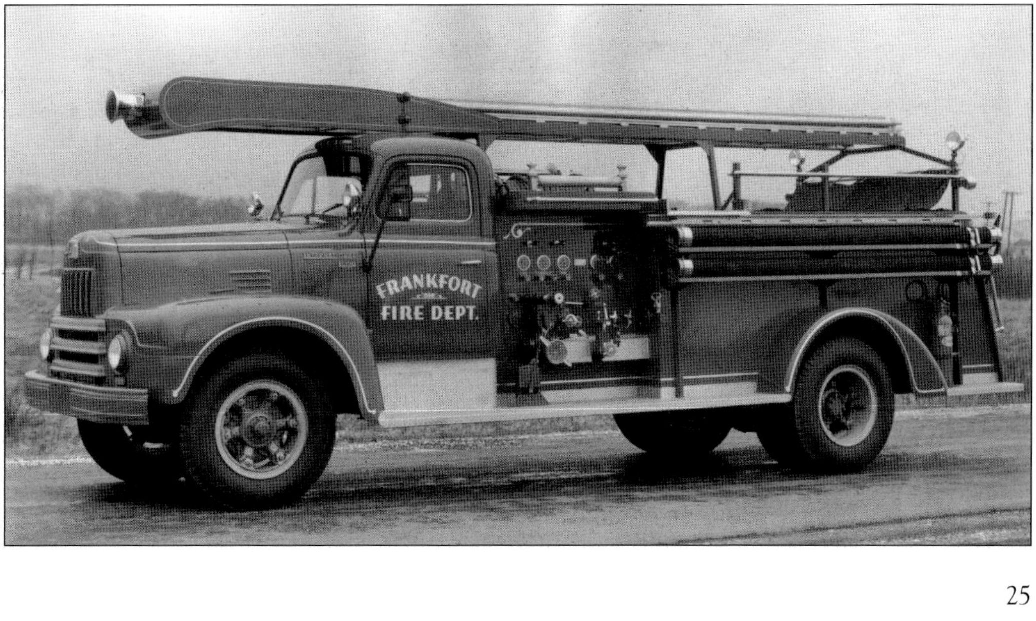

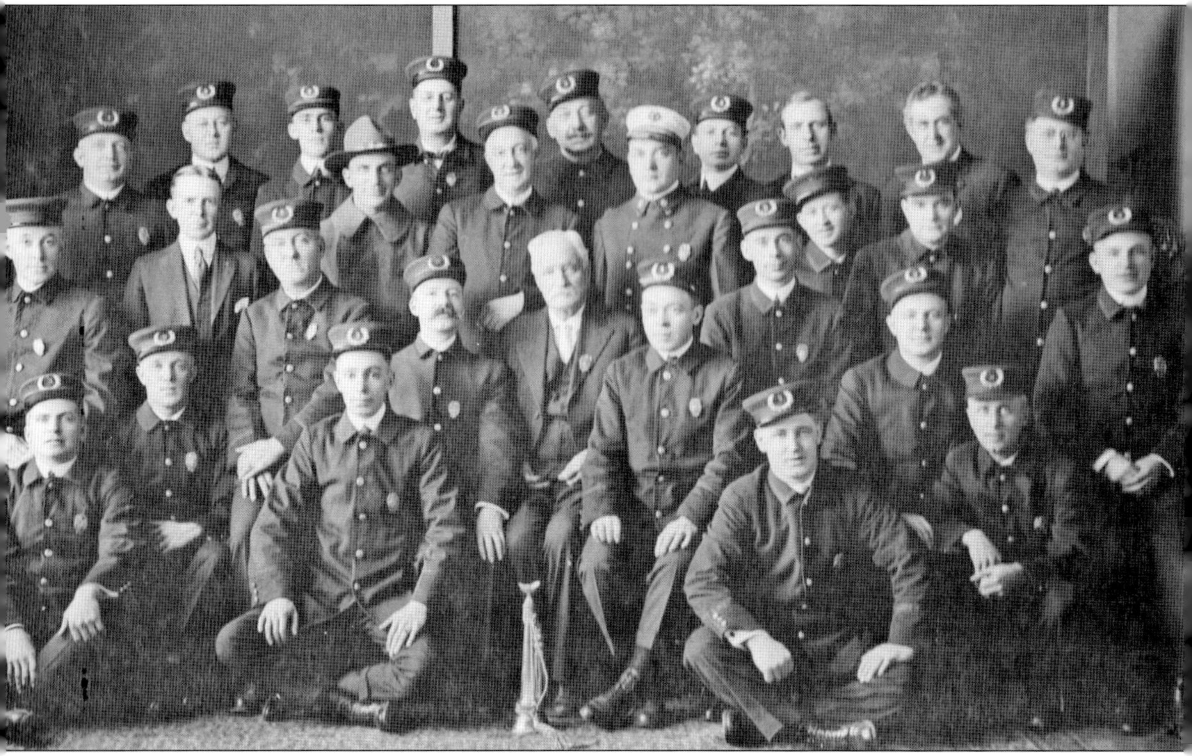

**Fire Department, 1917.** In honor of the 30th anniversary of H.H. Ingham Hose Company No. 2, founder Hamilton H. Ingham threw the members of the company a theater party at the Colonial Theater followed by a banquet at the Hotel Martin in Utica. A special trolley car was chartered for the trip to Utica. Seen here are, from left to right, (first row) John Robinson, Frank Dobbins (second lieutenant), Edward Gordon, and John Hourrigan (fire warden); (second row) Louis Vidulich, George Gordon, Herbert Lonis (president), Sam Sanford (president), Hamilton H. Ingham (honorary), Earl Matterson (captain), and Claude Johnson (first lieutenant); (third row) Arthur Seymour (treasurer), Arthur Weaver (exempt), Frank Vidulich, John Watkins, G. Arthur Limpert (chief of the Frankfort Fire Department), William Roulette, Herbert Seymour, and Louis Clauser (secretary); (fourth row) Albert Ostrander (fire police), Harry Rutherford, Frank Clayton, Jack Thomas, Frank Clarke, Samuel Williams (fire police), Charles Fenwick (exempt), Bert Sterling (exempt), and Bertram Johnson. (Courtesy of the Frankfort Fire Department.)

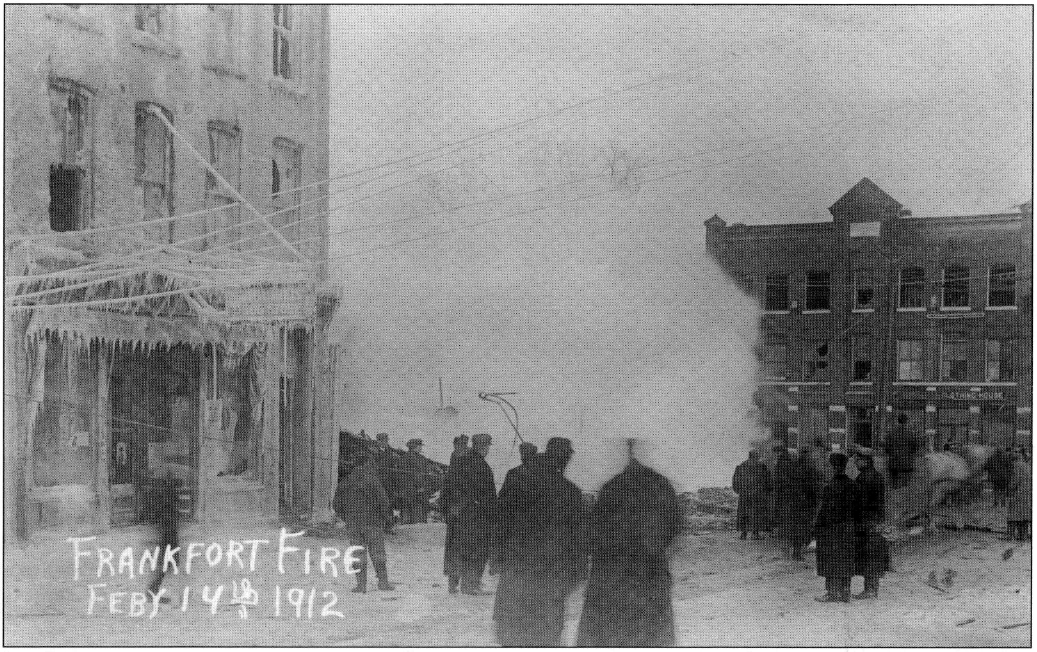


**JOSLIN BLOCK FIRE.** On February 14, 1912, a fire destroyed the Joslin Block, on the corner of West Main and Litchfield Streets. The first floor housed William Wayne's dry goods store, Conway's 5&10, Charles Rich's jewelry store, and Delia Hooper's millinery. The second floor housed the Smith & Wilbur law offices, H.H. Ingham's real estate and insurance agency, police justice Charles Loftus's office, the telephone exchange, and Maurice Williams's barge canal offices. The third floor was home to the Iron Moulders' Union and the Tryon Club. The adjacent Steele Building (below) suffered damage on the first floor, which housed William McGuire's pharmacy, and in Eddie Steele's two top-floor apartments. The Graves Block, on West Main Street (above, right), also suffered damage. (Below, courtesy of the Frankfort Fire Department.)

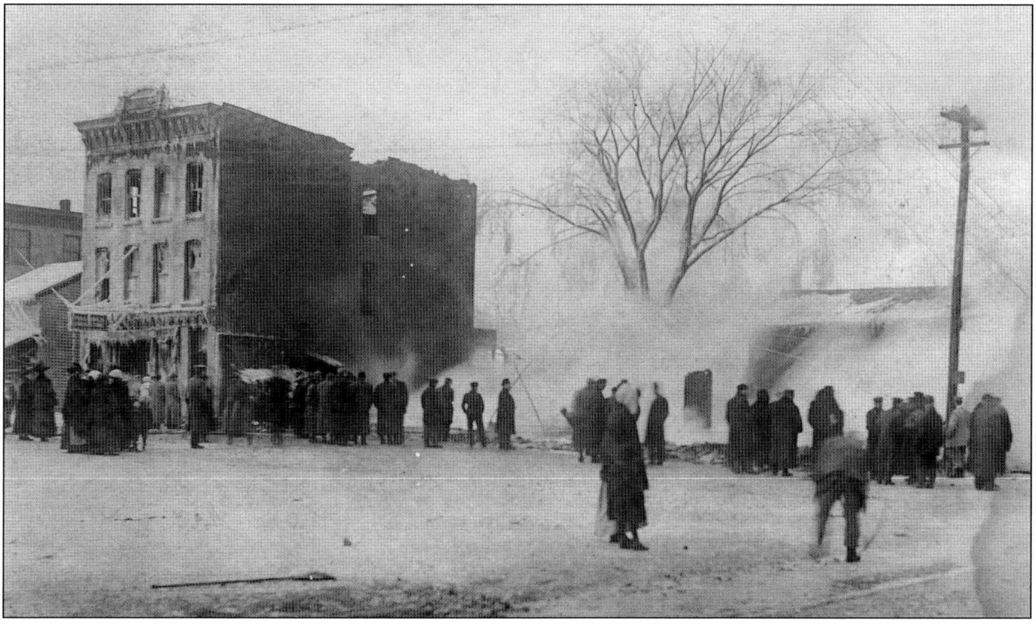

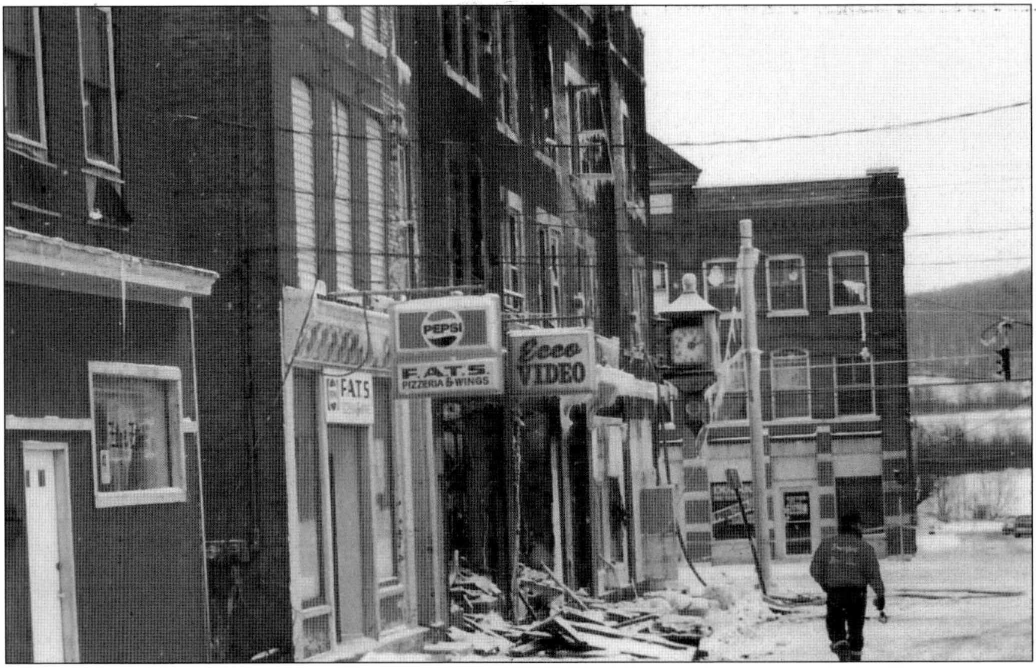


**UNION BLOCK FIRE.** Fire destroyed the three-story Union Block building, on the corner of West Main and Litchfield Streets, in the early hours of December 30, 1993. Seven fire companies assisted the Frankfort volunteer firefighters in battling the blaze. Eight families were left homeless and several businesses were destroyed by the fire, including John Bono's law office, Ecco Video, Pet's Delight, and Superior Home Health Care. A firewall prevented the fire from spreading to F.A.T.S. Pizzeria & Wings, which sustained smoke damage. The village hall, to the right of the block, escaped damage. The block was razed in 1994. The Village of Frankfort then reacquired the property and improved the site by turning it into Starlighters Park, which was dedicated in 2008. (Both, courtesy of the Frankfort Fire Department.)

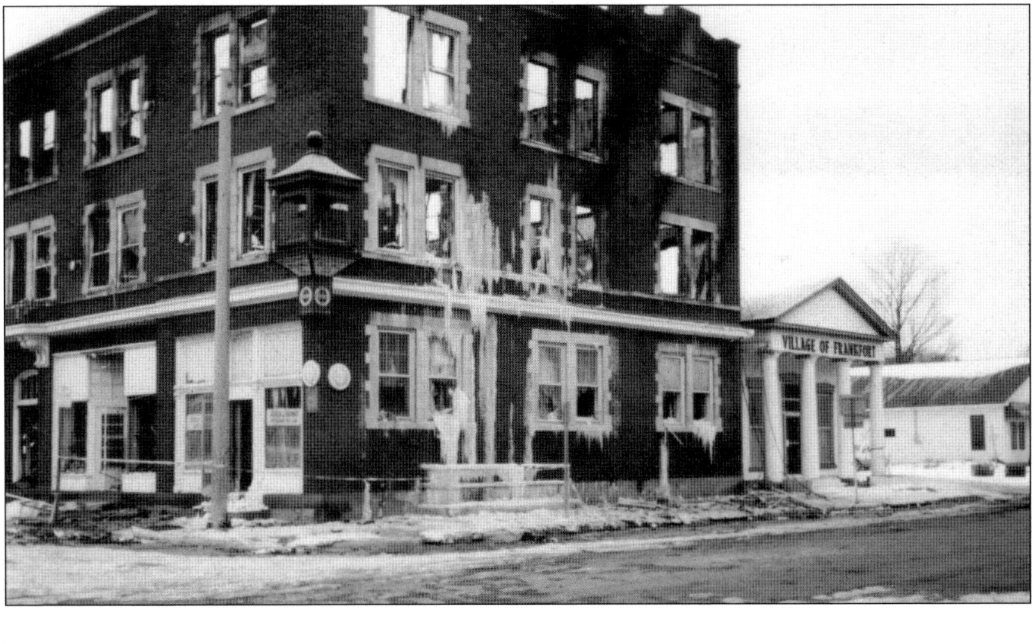

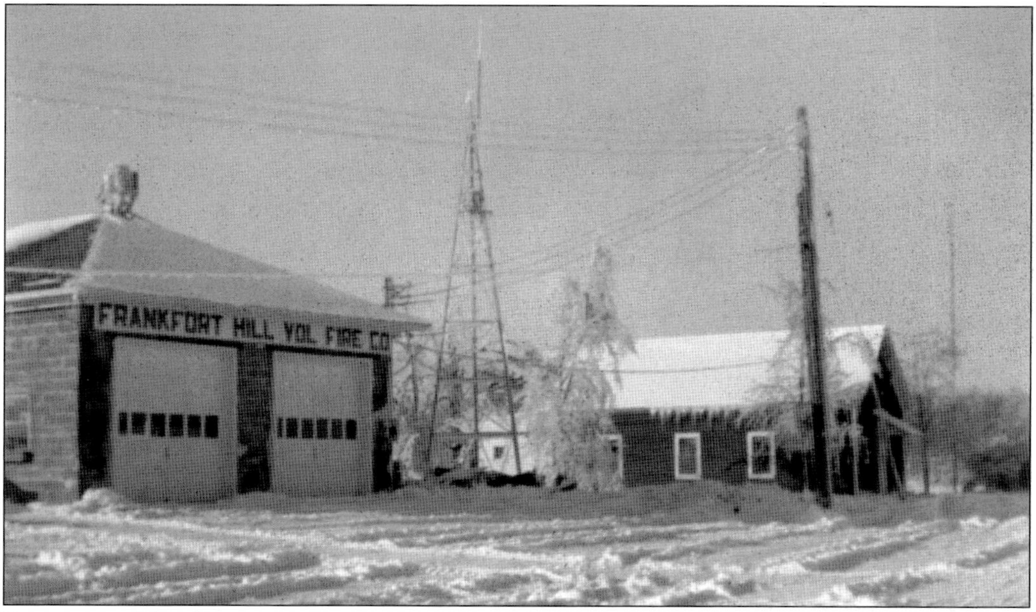


**Frankfort Hill Volunteer Fire Company.** A fire on the William Bennett farm on February 5, 1954, was the impetus to form a fire company for Frankfort Hill. A meeting was held on August 27 of that year, and ground was broken the next spring on the two-bay firehouse seen above on the corner of Albany and Higby Roads. The construction was a community effort, and funds were raised through donations and fundraisers. Chet Kane was the first president, and Joe Alukonis was the first chief. In 1962, Fire Protection District No. 4 of the Town of Frankfort was formed, with volunteer officers elected to run it. In 1967, a kitchen and meeting room was built on the back, and, in 1983, a second-story addition was built. The photograph below shows a September 11th Memorial in front of the firehouse in 2012. (Both, courtesy of the Frankfort Hill Volunteer Fire Company.)

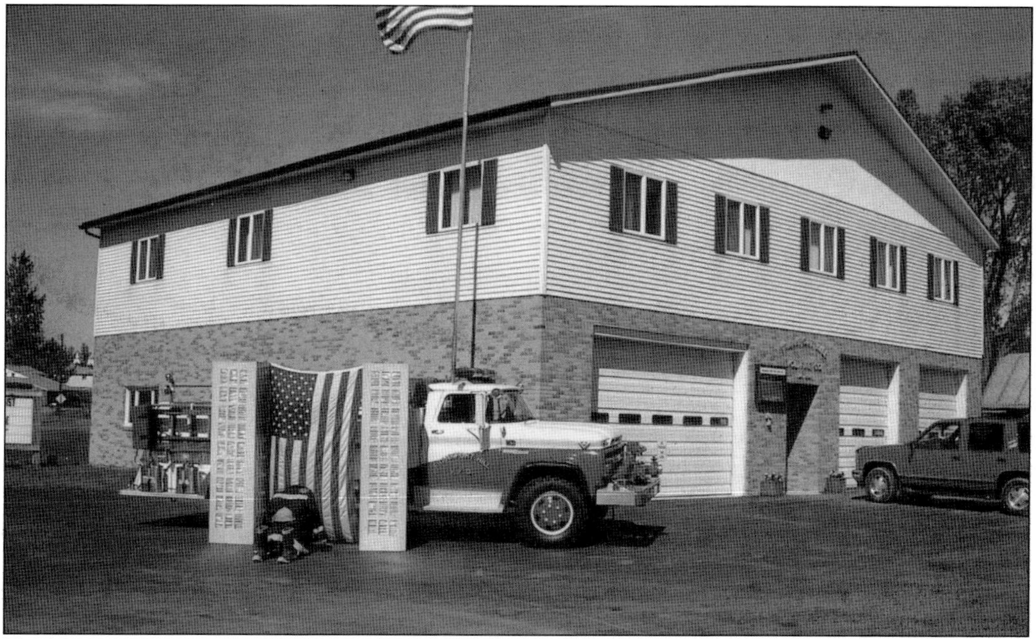

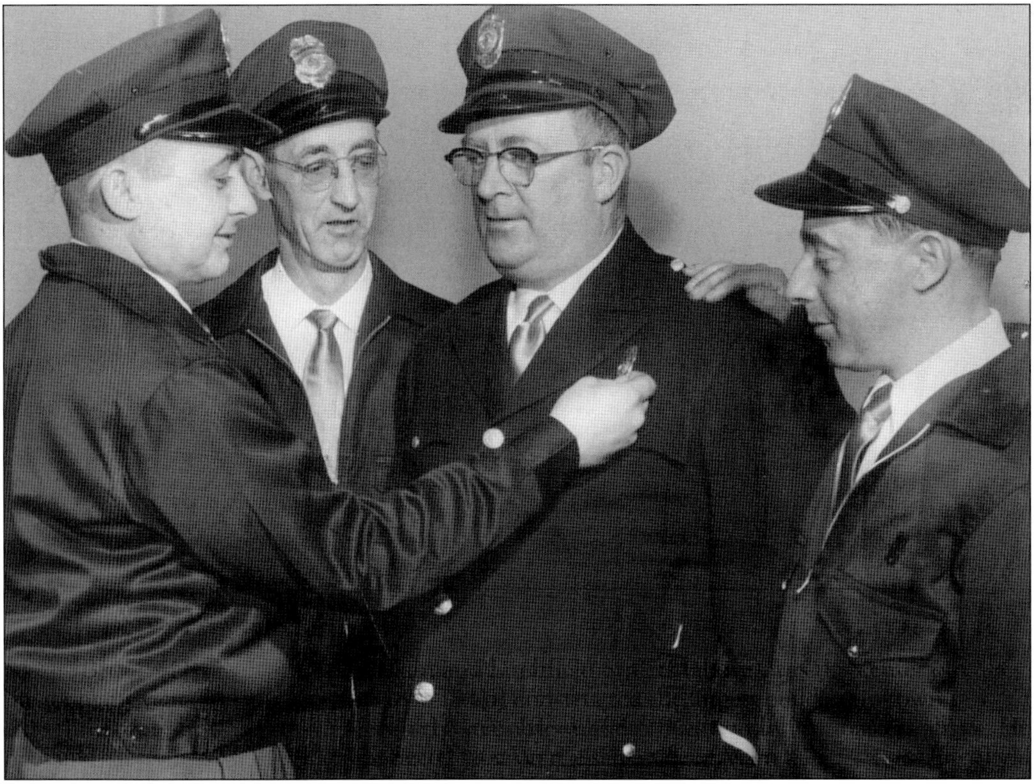

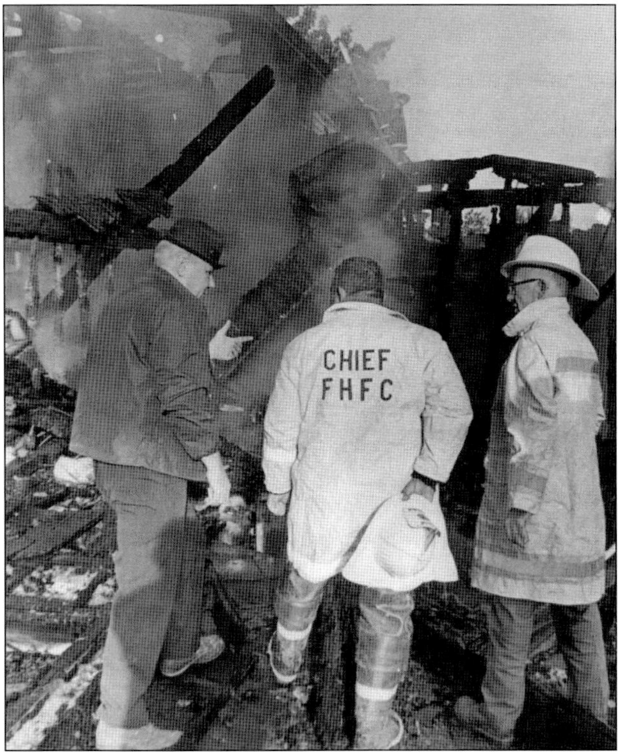


**FRANKFORT HILL FIRE COMPANY OFFICERS.** Above, in 1961, Arthur Gilloren (1910–1995) is honored for starting his third term as fire chief of the Frankfort Hill Volunteer Fire Company. He was chief from 1958 to 1967. Seen with him are, from left to right, Jack McNally, assistant chief; John Connine (1916–1990), vice president; and Lawrence Polisse (1927–2012), president. (Courtesy of the Frankfort Hill Volunteer Fire Company.)

**ON THE SCENE.** Frankfort Hill Fire Company chief Keith McNally (center), state police senior investigator Richard Gildersleeve (left), and fire coordinator Ira Allen (right) inspect the scene of a fatal fire on October 10, 1972, at the home of Clifford and Edna Austin Brown on Albany Road. (Courtesy of Frankfort Hill Volunteer Fire Company.)

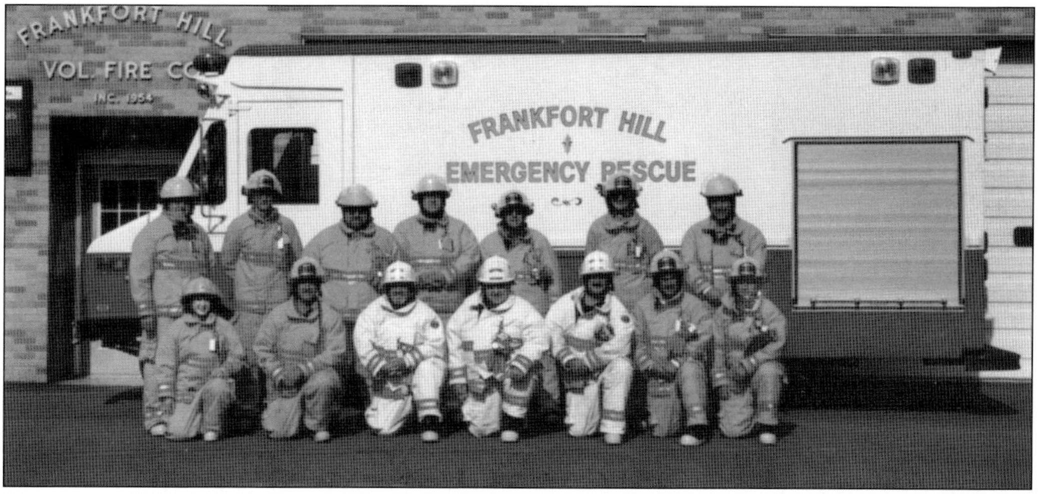


**Frankfort Hill Volunteer Firefighters, 2004.** Seen here in front of the firehouse are, from left to right, (first row) Lorrie Hale, Larry Bohling, Anthony Aurience, Keith McNally (fire chief from 1967 to 1996), Dan Dichera, Robert Moore, and Robert Farrell; (second row) Richard Presky, Mitch Dye, Mark McNally, John Leitz, Fred Christensen, Mike Talarico, and Frank Ostroski. (Courtesy of the Frankfort Hill Volunteer Fire Company.)

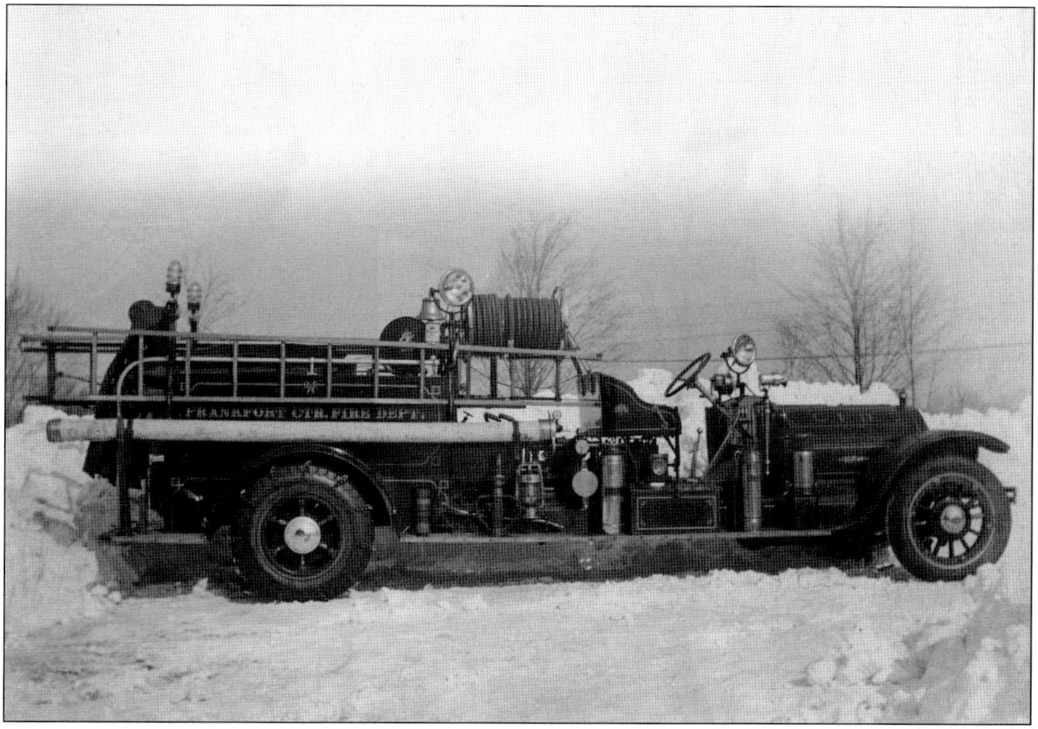

**Frankfort Center Fire Department.** The idea for the Frankfort Center Fire Department began during nightly gatherings at Fred Priest's store in 1934, and a committee was then organized to raise money for a fire department. The next year, it purchased its first fire truck, seen here, and land for a firehouse, which was completed in 1937. In 1948, the ladies auxiliary was formed, and in 1954, the Frankfort Center Volunteer Fire Department was incorporated. (Courtesy of Dorine Jenkins.)

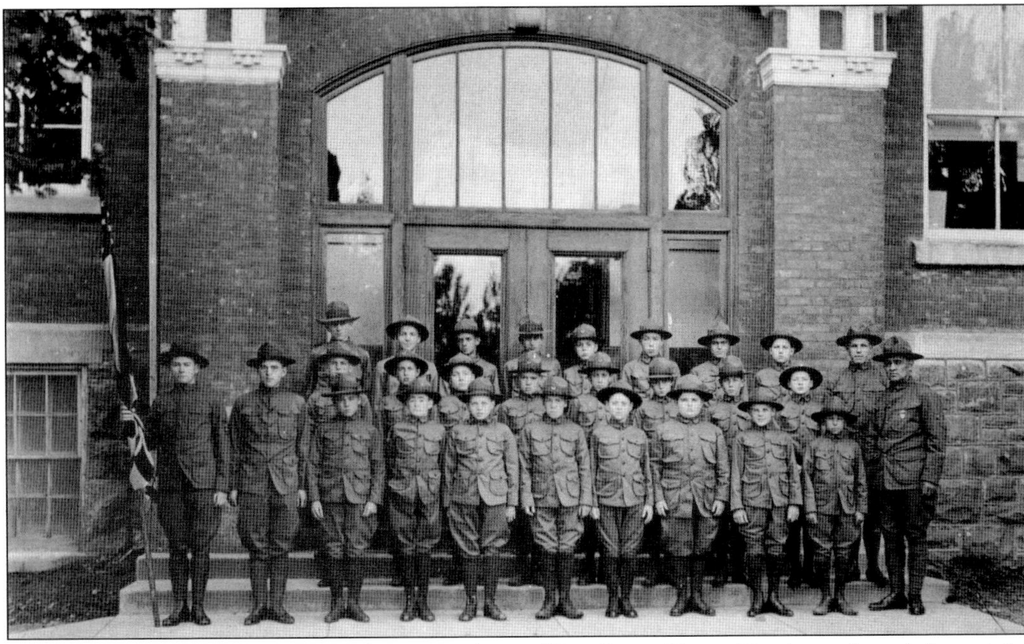

**Frankfort Boy Scouts, 1917.** These members of Boy Scout Troop No. 1 are, from left to right, (first row) Henry Skelly, Lester Krick, John Scanlon, Farrel Starling, William Simons, Forest Stacks, Floyd Krick, Thomas Skelly, Paul Graham, and Francis Chard; (second row) Robert Dennis, William Martin, James Skelly, Judson Stacks, Harold Seelback, Frank Churches, Kenneth Quillan, John Grady, and Roger Burgess; (third row) Murray Mixer, Herman Dreizler, Clyde Smith, Allen Hill, Barrie McKennon, Howard Dunn, Ellsworth Barnes, Harold Hinds, and Myron Kahler.

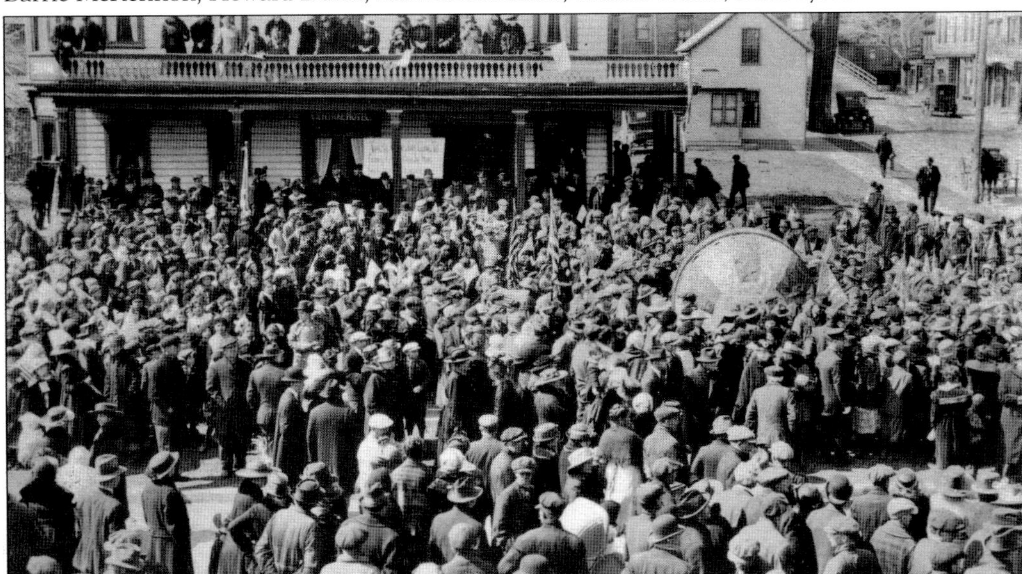

**Liberty Ball Comes to Frankfort.** A huge "liberty ball" was pushed from Buffalo to New York City during a campaign to hasten the sale of Liberty Bonds during World War I. It made its way through Frankfort amidst a crowd of people on April 19, 1918. Its arrival was greeted by the Remington Typewriter Band as the Boy Scouts pulled it from Harbor to the village square. (Courtesy of Chad Wohler.)

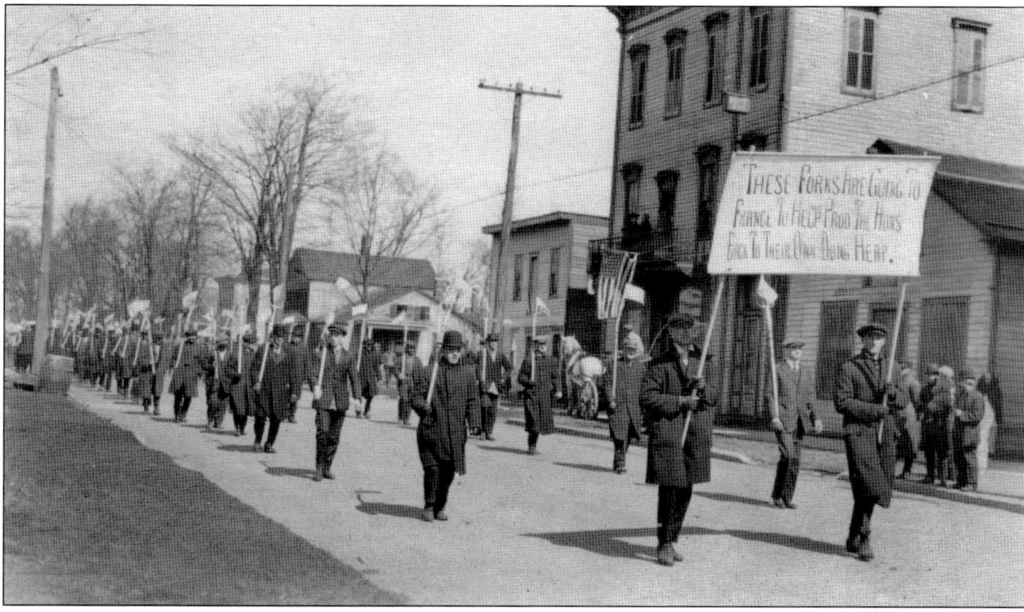


**LIBERTY BALL PARADE.** The liberty ball and liberty coach were met at the corporation line and escorted through the village by the community with much fanfare. Above, employees of the Pratt Chuck Fork & Hoe Company march down East Main Street carrying a banner that reads, "These Forks Are Going To France To Help Prod The Huns Back To Their Own Dung Heap." A total of 20 carloads of pitchforks made at the company were shipped to France at the end of April 1918. The photograph below shows the end of a contingent of Acme Road Machinery Company employees, with one of their water tanks displaying the words "To Drown The Kaiser." Schoolchildren walked behind carrying American flags and singing patriotic songs. Acme made water tanks for the forces in France. (Both, courtesy of the Frankfort Fire Department.)

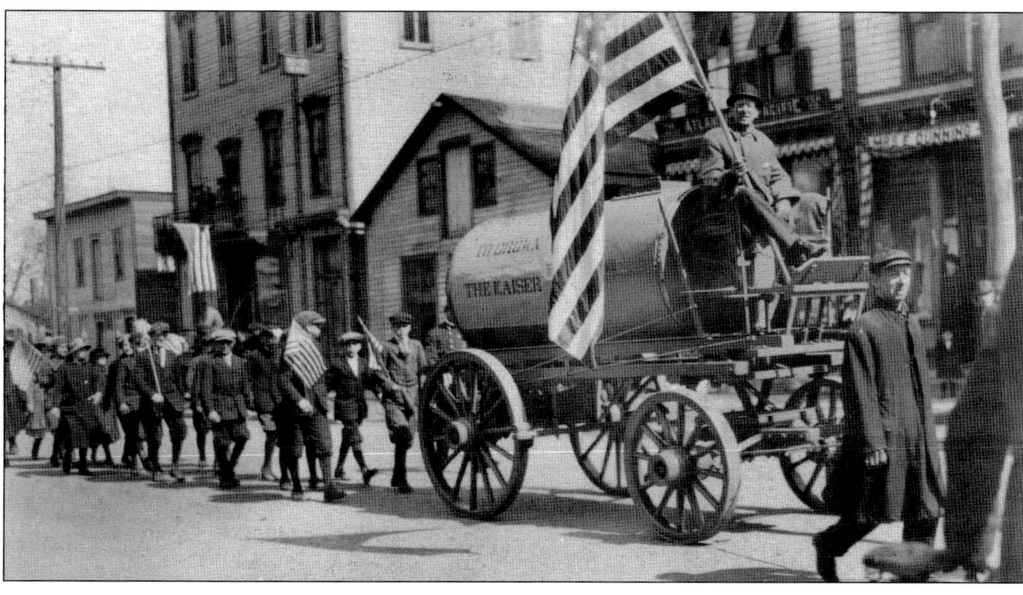

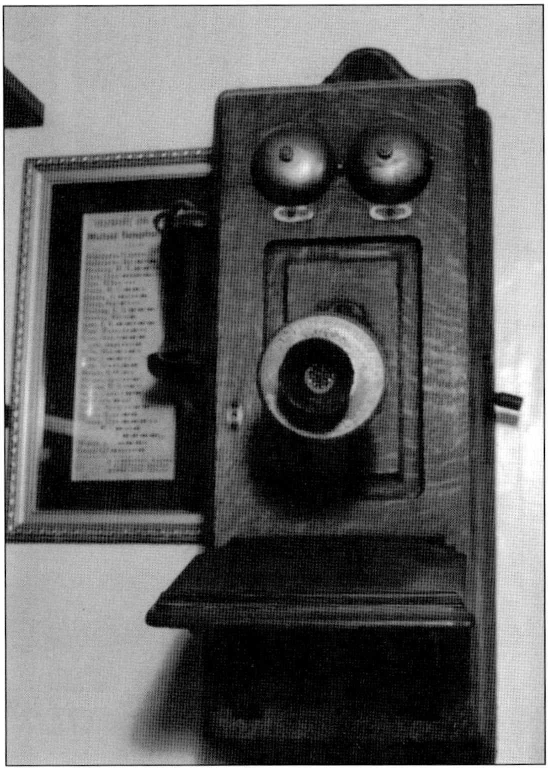

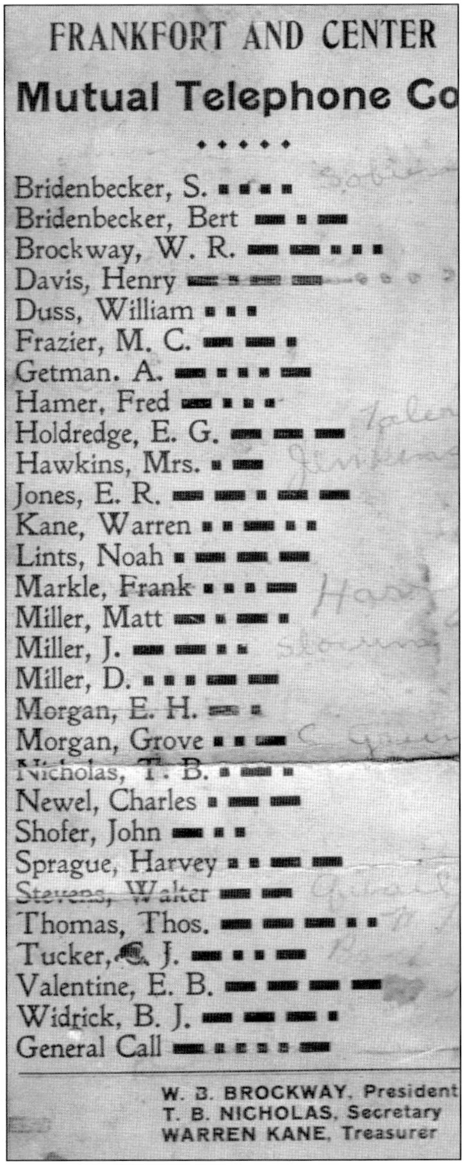

FRANKFORT AND CENTER

**Mutual Telephone Co**

Bridenbecker, S.
Bridenbecker, Bert
Brockway, W. R.
Davis, Henry
Duss, William
Frazier, M. C.
Getman. A.
Hamer, Fred
Holdredge, E. G.
Hawkins, Mrs.
Jones, E. R.
Kane, Warren
Lints, Noah
Markle, Frank
Miller, Matt
Miller, J.
Miller, D.
Morgan, E. H.
Morgan, Grove
Nicholas, T. B.
Newel, Charles
Shofer, John
Sprague, Harvey
Stevens, Walter
Thomas, Thos.
Tucker, C. J.
Valentine, E. B.
Widrick, B. J.
General Call

W. B. BROCKWAY, President
T. B. NICHOLAS, Secretary
WARREN KANE, Treasurer

**FRANKFORT CENTER PEANUT LINE.** Nothing brings a community closer than a shared telephone line. Built by a group of Frankfort Center residents in 1899, the "Peanut Line" served as a neighborhood grapevine and fire alarm system. It consisted of seven miles of line and old-fashioned wall telephones that required one to crank the handle on the right side of the box. The work of erecting the poles and stringing the wires was done by the telephone subscribers themselves. A winter storm knocked the system down in the early 1920s, and it was not restored until 1934, when the newly formed Frankfort Center Volunteer Fire Company fixed it. Seen here is one of the antique telephones that hangs in the home of Dorine Jenkins, along with a framed telephone listing of the subscribers. (Both, courtesy of Dorine Jenkins.)

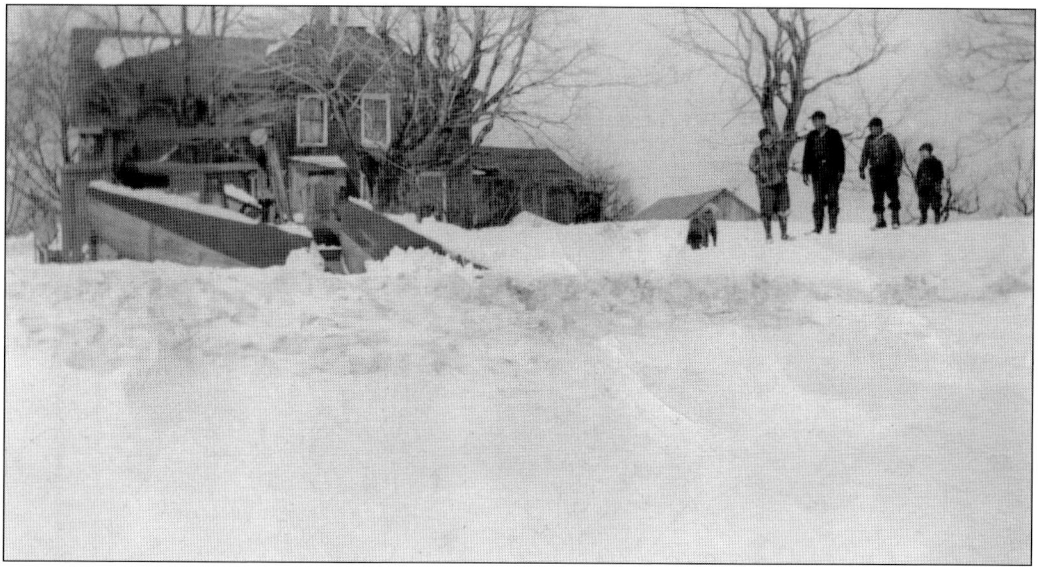

**FRANKFORT HILL SNOWSTORMS.** Plowing snow was no easy task on the heights of Frankfort Hill. In 1939, the snow was so deep that the snowplow became stuck in front of William and Edna McNally's home on Kerber Road. Seen above are, from left to right, Edna McNally, snowplow operators John Leitz and Floyd Uebler, and Keith McNally. Snow removal on Higby Road was not any better in 1945, as seen in the photograph below, which again shows Frankfort Highway Department superintendent John "Laddie" Leitz (left, 1893–1978) and Frankfort Highway Department heavy equipment operator Floyd "Stubby" Uebler (1905–1975). (Above, courtesy of Keith McNally; below, courtesy of the Frankfort Hill Volunteer Fire Company.)

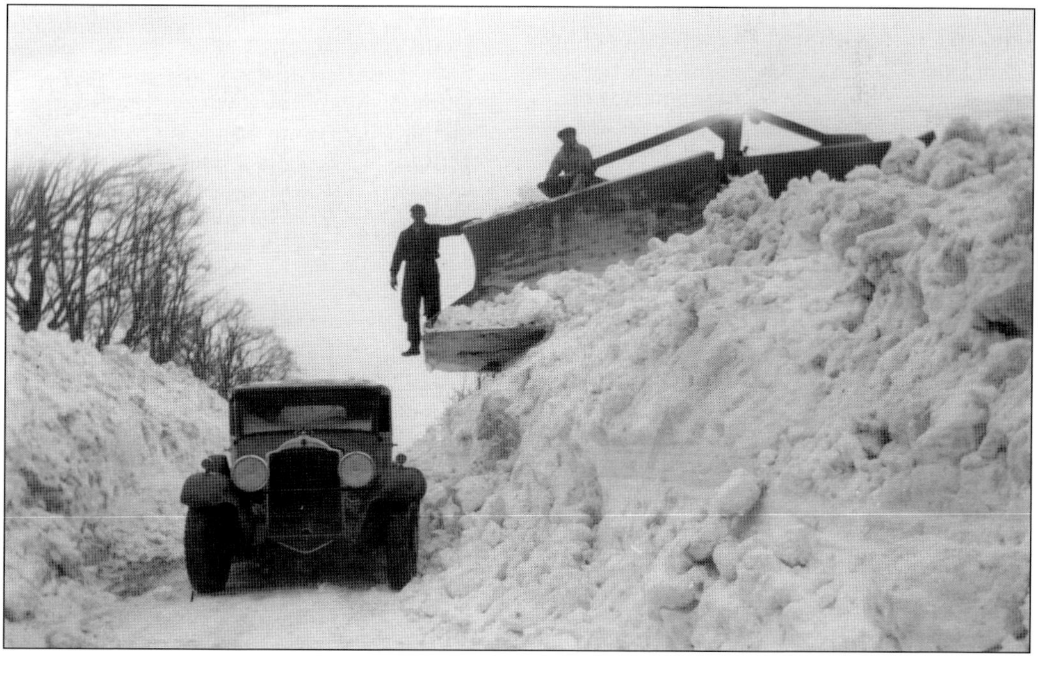

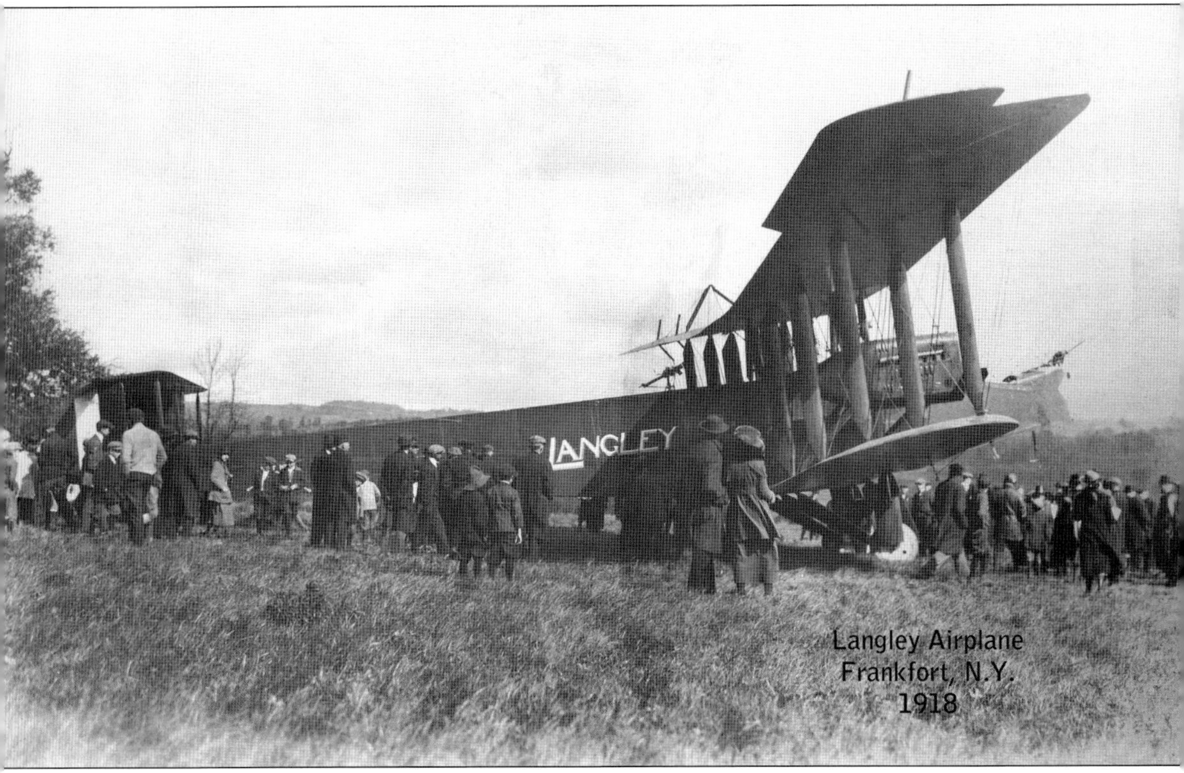


**AIRPLANE CAUSES SPECTACLE.** In 1918, it was not every day that a large plane landed in the village, or, to be precise, in Charles Harter's meadow near West Main Street. The airplane *Langley* had used up its gasoline and had to make an emergency stop in the meadow on October 15. It remained in the field until the next morning, giving thousands of onlookers a chance to stop by. The plane was built at Elizabeth, New Jersey, and was christened on July 6. The wings were 100 feet wide and the body 64 feet long. Five Lewis machine guns were carried, two in the front, two in the rear, and one at one side. There were seven in the crew: Captain Miller; Capt. Edward Waller, an Englishman; pilot Dr. Allen; E.B. Beck; B. Burnt; L. Milani; and J.A. Macafee. The local police force was called to keep the thousands who visited at a proper distance, and two soldiers from Mohawk were put on guard for the night. (Courtesy of Dave Sanders.)

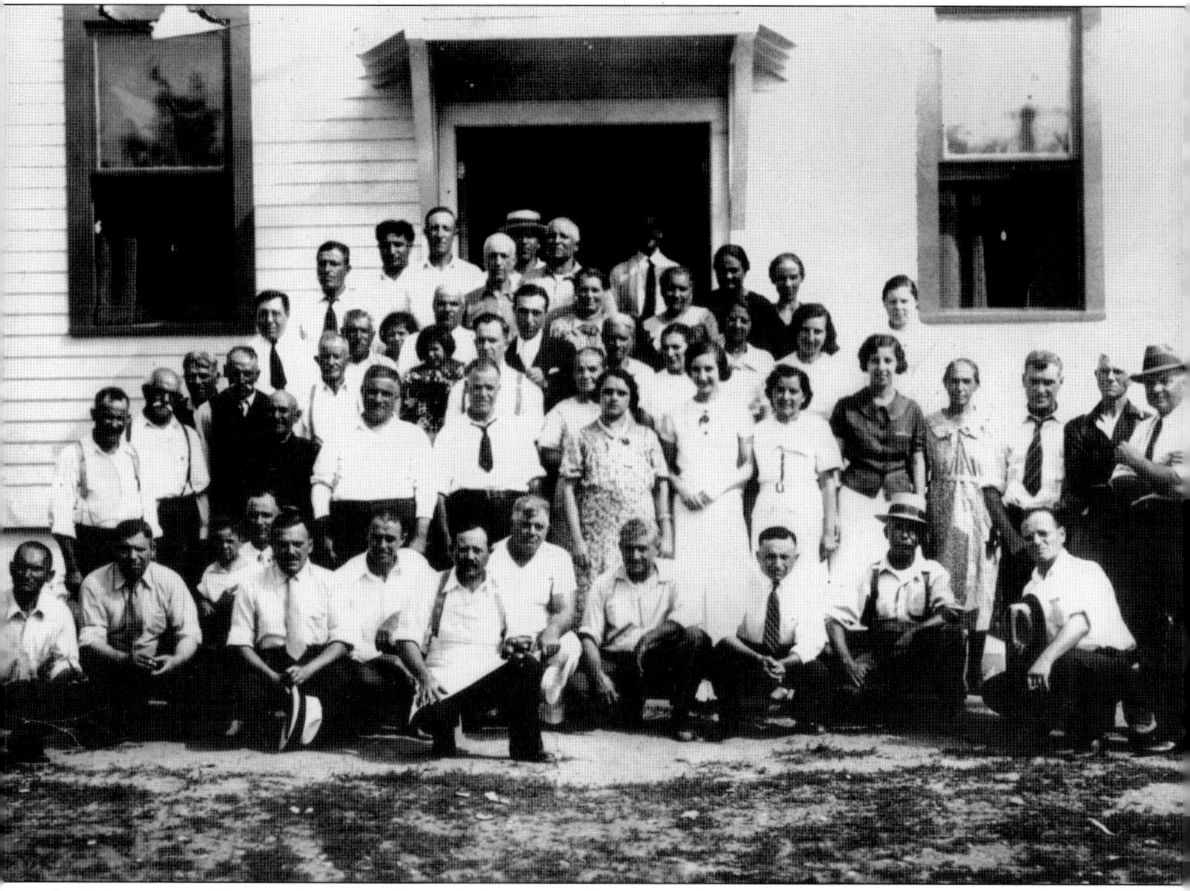

**St. Francis of Paola Society.** Founded on March 6, 1927, by emigrants from Oriolo, Italy, the St. Francis Society is the oldest of its kind in the area. This men's religious and social organization made it possible to hold onto old traditions and preserve heritage. A clubhouse was built and the organization incorporated in 1935, and a women's auxiliary was soon established. In 1980, a new clubhouse and hall were built, followed in 1985 by a pavilion. The organization is still active today, hosting the annual Italian Festival and working as a community benefactor. Some of the members in this photograph are, in no particular order, Jim DeMay, Nick Bongiorno, Joe Chippari, Frank Gatto, Fedele Vivacqua, Mr. Dunadee, Nicholas Sylvester, George Grates, Joe DeLuke, Mary Gatto, Pauline Frank, Julia Frank, Mrs. Dunadee, Tom DeJohn, James Accattato, George Dunadee, Mary Romano, Rose Chippari, Patsy Petrell, Mr. Favat, and Mamie Oriolo. (Courtesy of Betsy Cirelli.)

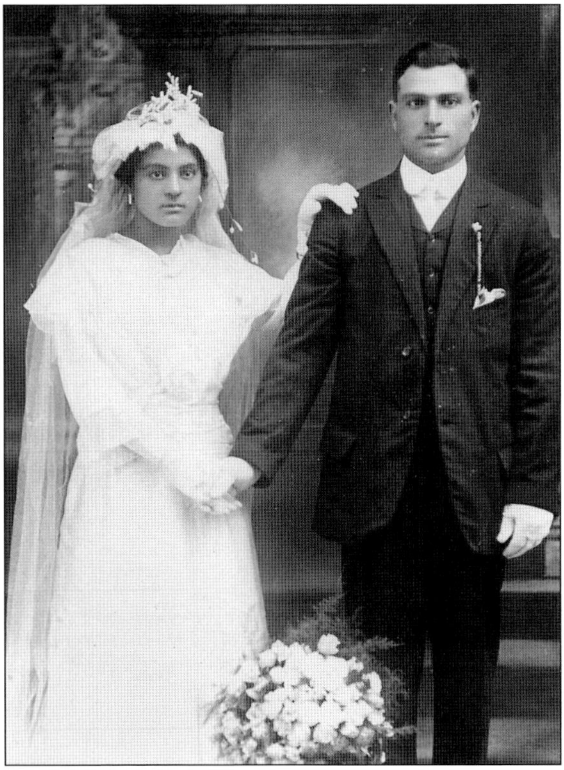

**Italian Emigrants from Oriolo.** In the early 1900s, families from the town of Oriolo, located in the Calabria region of southern Italy, settled in Frankfort to work at the many factories. Guiseppe Oriolo (1888–1929) and Maria Domenica Silvestri (1894–1973), both from Oriolo, were married on October 2, 1915, at SS. Peter and Paul Catholic Church. Approximately 50 surnames in Frankfort can be traced to emigrants from this town. (Courtesy of Joseph Oriolo.)

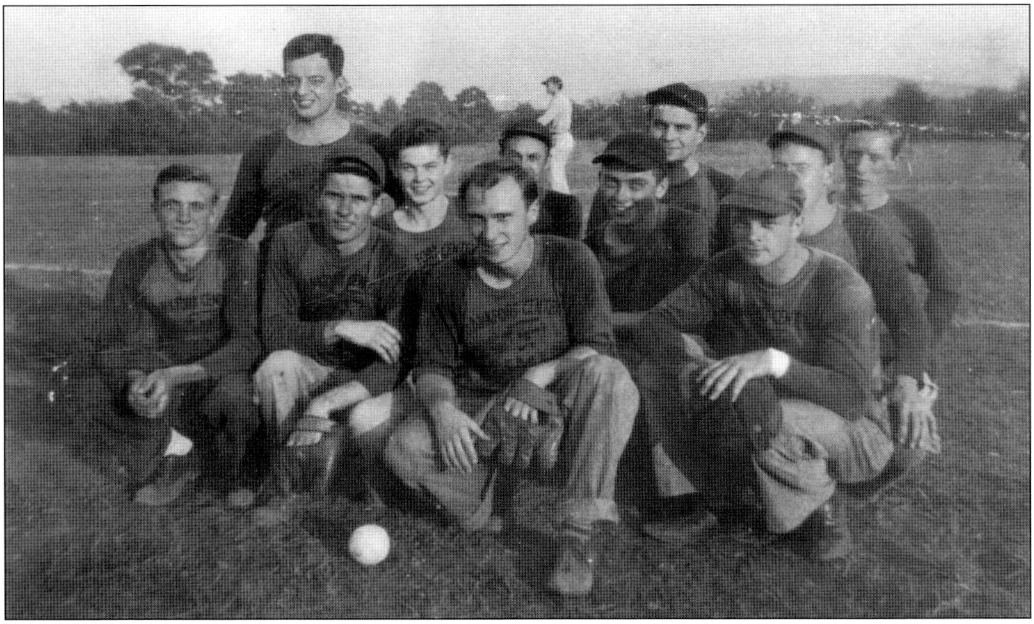

**Valley Merchants Baseball Team.** The West Frankfort Valley Merchants baseball team practiced for its Businessmen's League games in a field belonging to Edward Ferguson along Ferguson Road and old Route 5S. Seen here are, from left to right, (first row) John "Jack" Traut, Don Burdick, Bill Wendell, and Bill Hauser; (second row) Mike D'Amelio, Walt Biddlecome, unidentified, Walt Goodson, two unidentified, and ? Borden. (Courtesy of William Ferguson.)

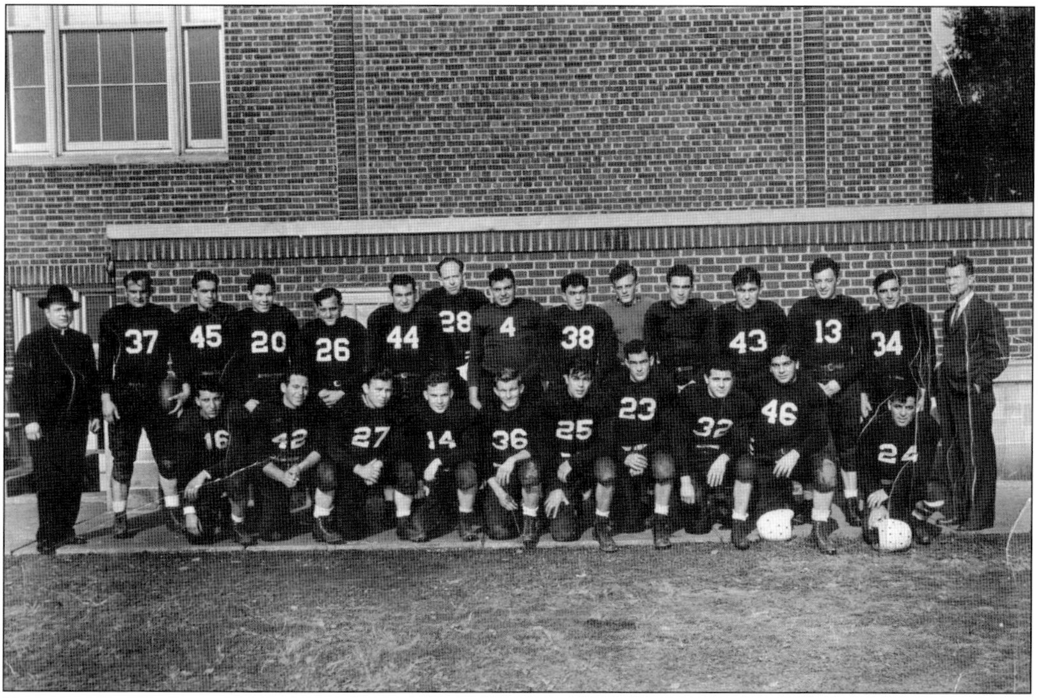

**Frankfort Veterans Semiprofessional Football Team, 1946.** This football team included, from left to right, (first row) John Pizzo, "Kuzzie" Accattato, Frank Rossi, "Roley" Yardley, Bill Busher, Nick Kattato, "Mac" Maida, Jim Piazza, Dominick Lille, and Louie Torchia; (second row) Fr. Anthony Sidoti (coach), Johnny Pizzo, John Smallwood, "Mal" Yardley, George Grates, Jack Zito, "Brick" Whiter, Tony Grippi, Frank Conte, Bill Nudo, Vito Costanza, Joe Mancuso, Mike D'Amelio, Leo Bonfardeci, and George Iocovozzi (business manager). (Courtesy of Frank Palumbo.)

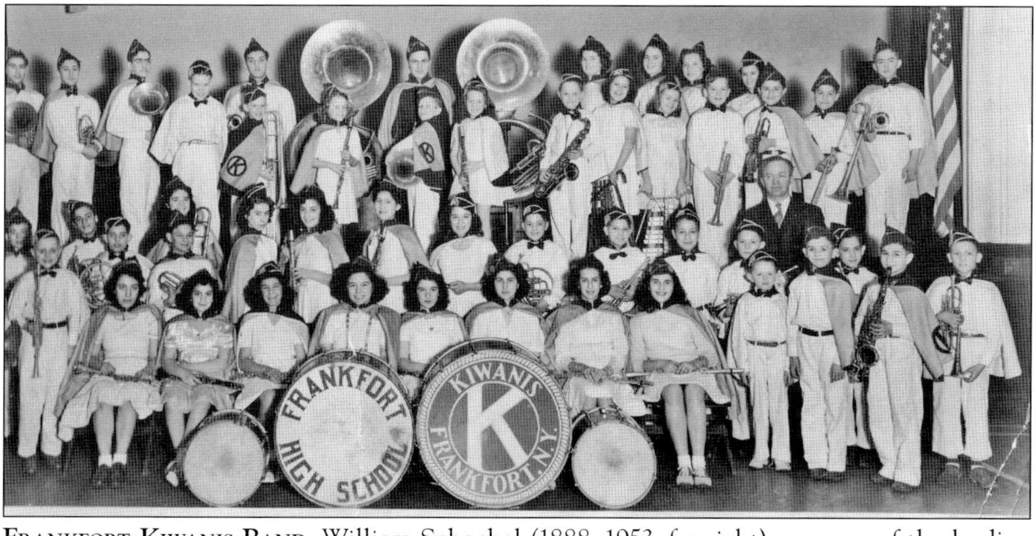


**Frankfort Kiwanis Band.** William Schachel (1888–1953, far right), was one of the leading promoters and the director of the Kiwanis Band, which gained statewide recognition and numbered over 100 members at one time. The band was made up of high school students and adults and played at community concerts and parades. Also identified is Joseph Thurston, in the back row, fifth from the left. (Courtesy of Angela Thurston.)

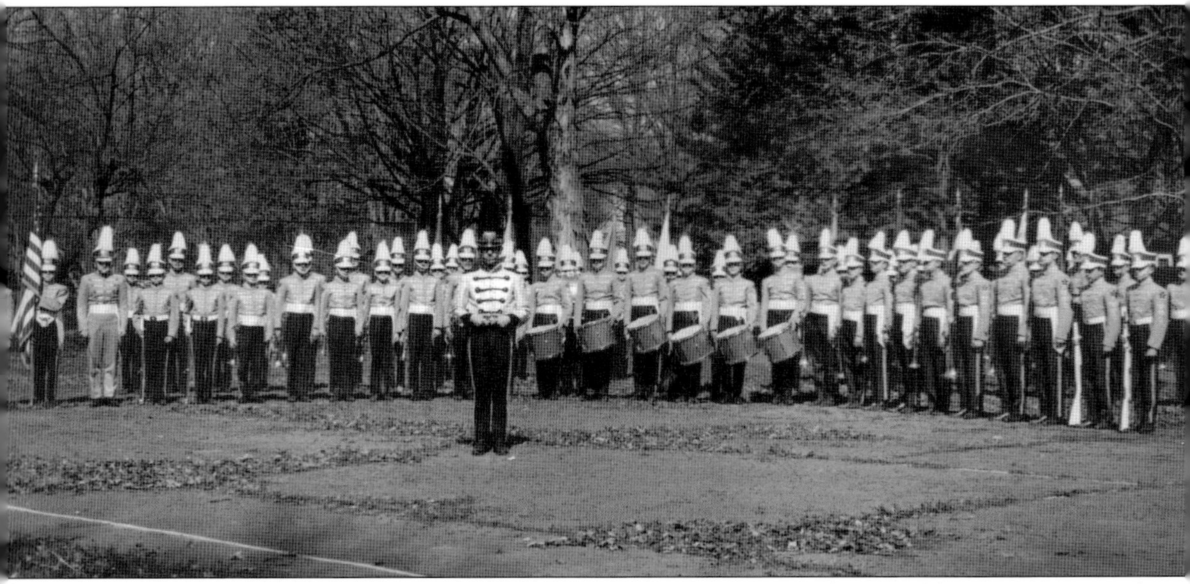

**Starlighters Drum and Bugle Corps.** Frankfort's first junior drum and bugle corps started in 1959, sponsored by American Legion Post 845 and led by director Joseph Thurston and drum instructor Jack Wedemeyer. They had a sterling career, winning the championships of the Central New York Junior Drum Corps Association and the Hudson-Berkshire Junior Drum Corps circuit, which was comprised of first-rate junior drum corps from New York and Massachusetts. After winning the Hudson-Berkshire competition in Pittsfield, Massachusetts, on a Saturday night in 1962, early Sunday morning as they came home, the corps was met by the local police at the Thruway in Herkimer, for a good reason. They were proudly escorted through the valley villages with people cheering them along the way and a hundred well-wishers waiting for them when they returned to the American Legion in Frankfort. It was a proud moment in Frankfort's history. (Courtesy of Angela Thurston.)

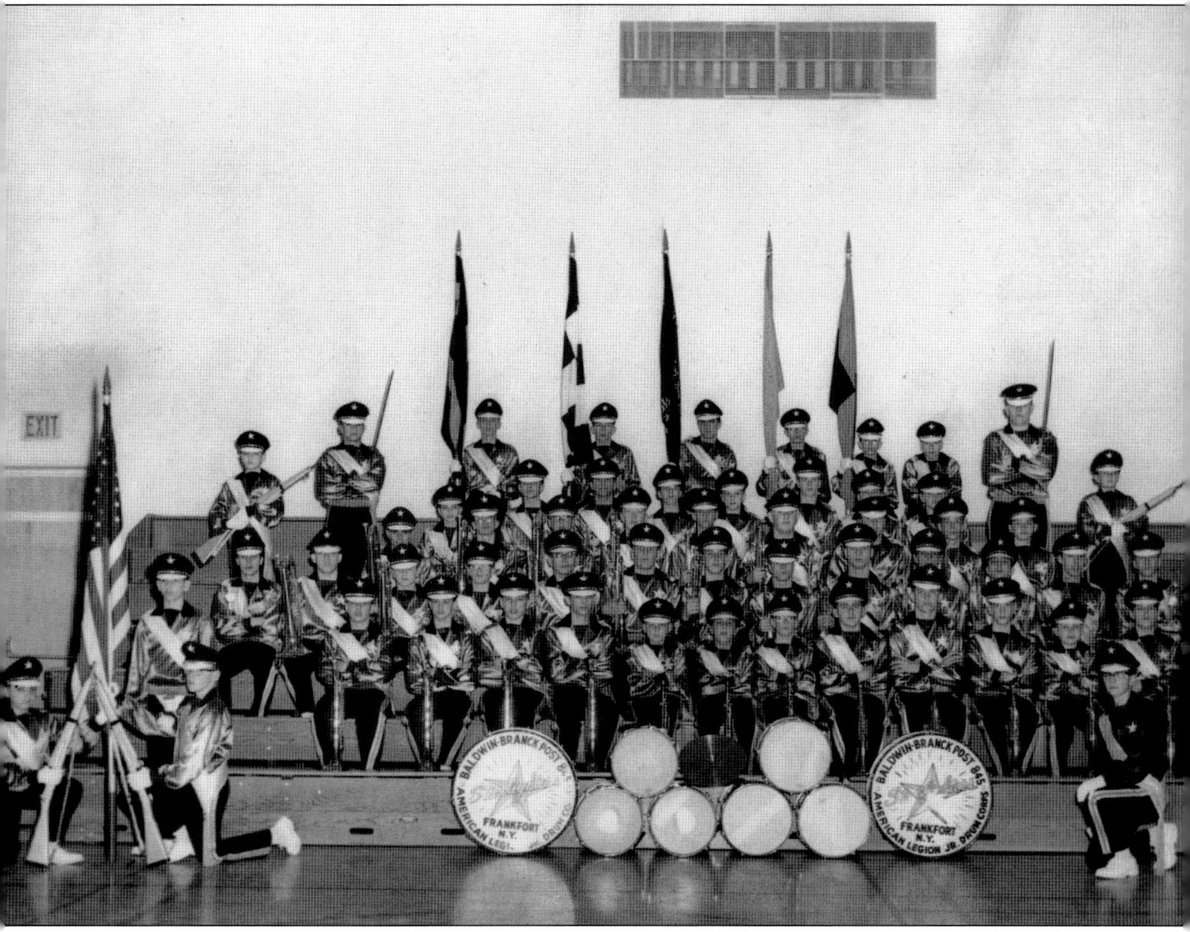

**FRANKFORT STARLIGHTERS, 1962.** Highlights of the Starlighters' career included leading the American Legion Convention parade down Fifth Avenue in New York City and playing during intermission at the exhibition game of the new American Football League between the Boston Patriots and the Buffalo Bills in 1960. The band included, from left to right, (first row) Jim Lille and Ron Vivacqua (rifles), Augie Maida (flag), and Pat Winkler (far right); (second row) Savey Lombardo, Joe Palumbo, Jim Tripple, Angelo Candella, unidentified, John Eramo, unidentified, Anthony Perritano, Francis Frank, Gary Miles, John Ackley, and unidentified; (third row) Don Davidson, Mario Gazzilli, Bob Sportello, unidentified, Ross Cushman, Pete Tamburro, unidentified, Ernie Sportello, Hank Bonn, unidentified, Joe Kinney, Steve Schorer, and John Mutchler; (fourth row) Joe Nardi, Dan Clayton, unidentified, Tom Flynn, Lance Nehr, John Keagel, Larry Hubbell, Bill Davis, and unidentified; (fifth row) Mario Pumilio, Dominick Lassarella, Paul Tucci, Jim Recchio, three unidentified, Jim Accatto, and Nick Paoni (rifle); (sixth row) George Winkler (rifle), Harold Gregory (sabre), Eugene Kipper, Jim Riente, Pete Caiola, George Amendolare, Anthony Barretta, Donnie Fiorentino, and Gary Conover (sabre).

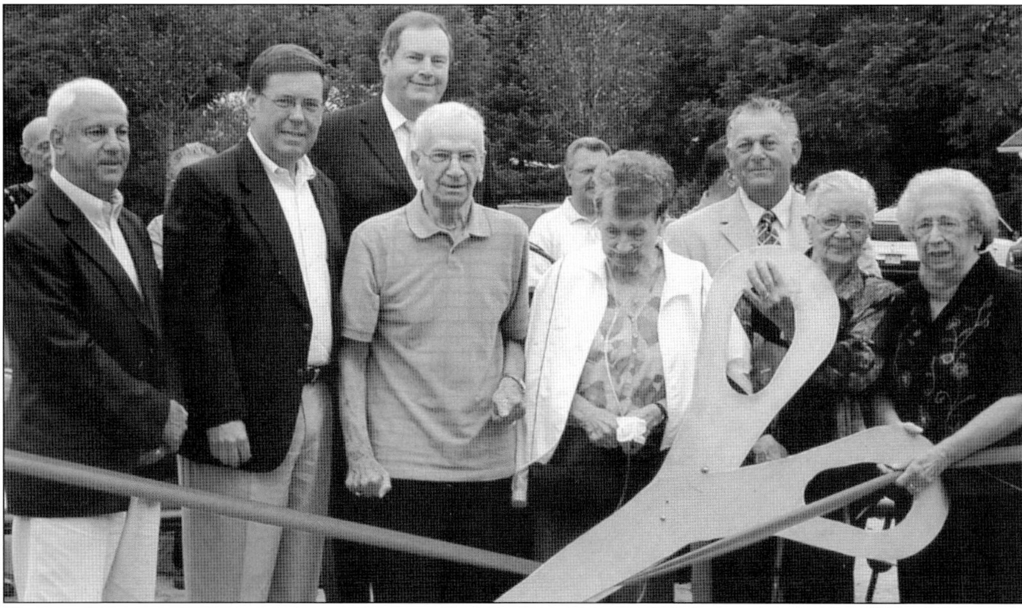

**Starlighters Park.** A park at the corner of Main and Litchfield Streets was dedicated in honor of the Starlighters Drum Corps on August 30, 2008. Special honor was given to departed band members Andy Jankowiak and Donnie Fiorentino. Seen cutting the ribbon are, from left to right, legislator Peter Manno, Sen. James Seward, Michael and Phyllis Fiorentino, Rose Jankowiak, and Angela Thurston; (second row) assemblyman Marc Butler and Mayor Frank Moracco. (Courtesy of Angela Thurston.)

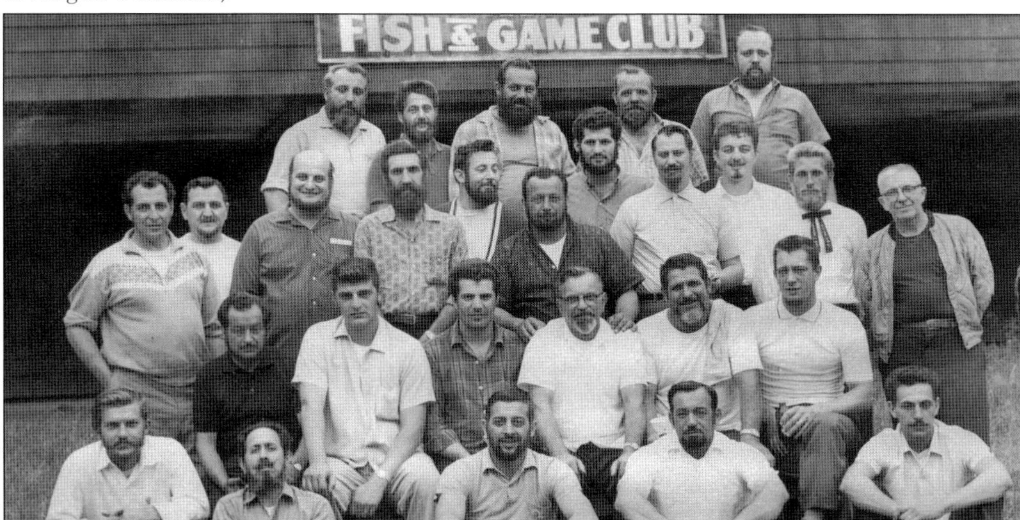


**1963 Centennial Celebration.** Many of these men grew facial hair to celebrate the town's centennial in 1963. They are, from left to right, (first row) unidentified, James Vivacqua, Sam Sgroi, Joe Sarmie, and Al Abdallah; (second row) Louis Urgo, Paul Puleo, Rich P., Frank Stolark, Thomas Cardinal, and Harold Kellogg; (third row) Charles Cesario, Fred Ruffalo, John Pizzo, Joe Russitano, Joe Potenza, Tony Potenza, Paul Loiacano, Ace Corwin, Richard Mussey, Bill Ferguson, and Nate Earl; (fourth row) John Puleo, Frank Moracco, Frank Potenza, Harold Gregory, and Walt Ward. (Courtesy of William Ferguson.)

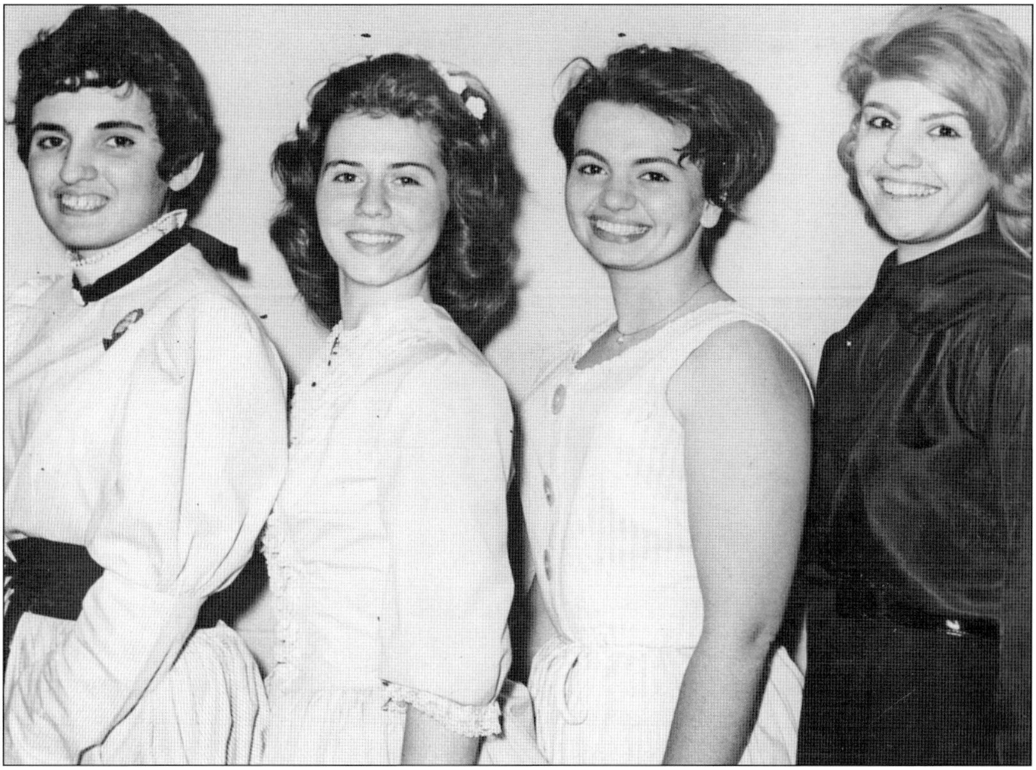

**Centennial Queen and Her Court.** Linda Short was crowned Miss Frankfort Centennial at a coronation ball at Frankfort Town Hall to kick off the centennial celebration events of June 30–July 4, 1963. Among her duties was to lead the parades at the beginning and end of the event. Shown are, from left to right, the queen and her court: Purdy Costanza, Linda Short, Rosalie Julian, and Rosemarie Cushman. (Courtesy of the Village of Frankfort.)

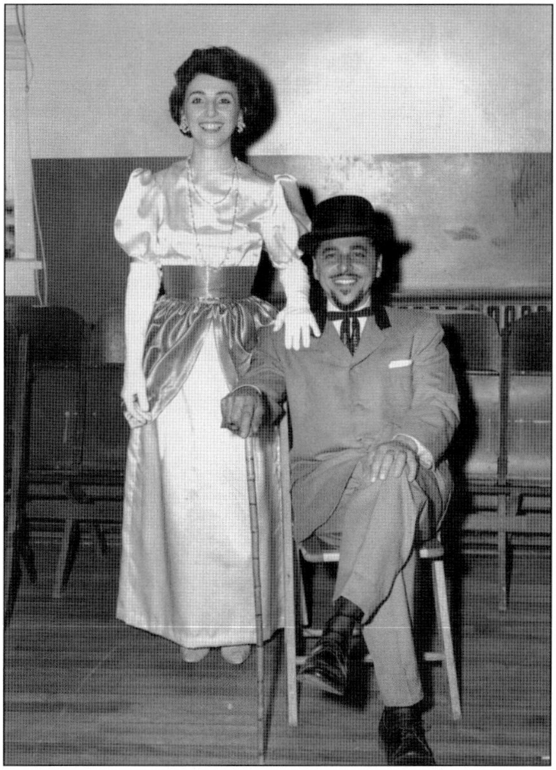

**Centennial Belle and Brother of the Brush.** Mary and Dominick Green are dressed in their centennial finery. Mary was a member of the Thurston Belles, and Dominick, a member of Hotel Thurston Chapter of Brothers of the Brush, was one of the Thurston Dudes. The centennial celebration included an "acqua-batic" water show, youth day activities, an Old Friends Day honoring the village's oldest residents, and a Brothers of the Brush beard judging. (Courtesy of Dominick and Mary Green.)

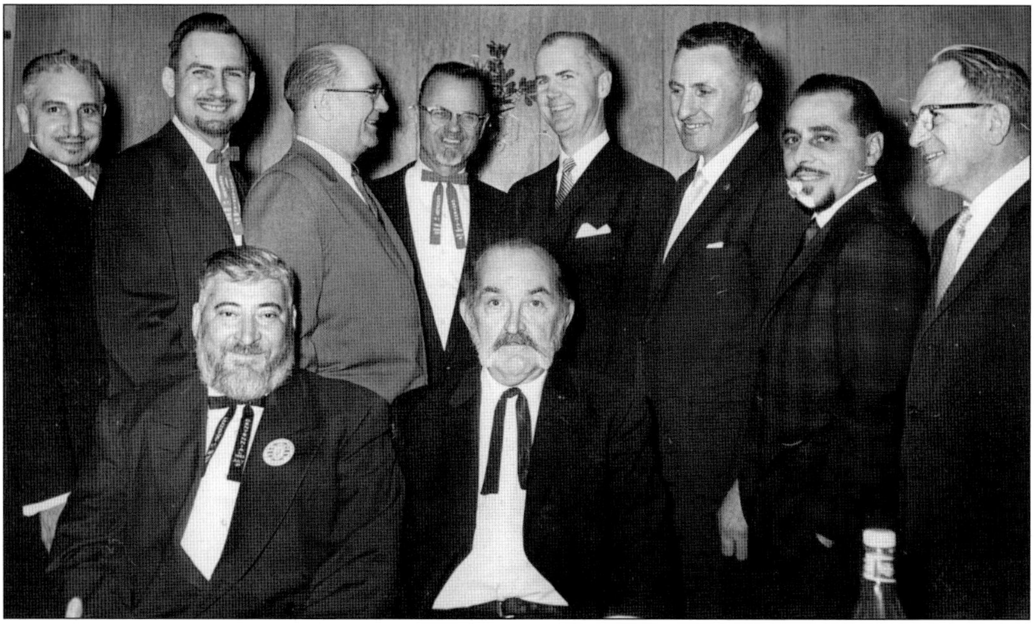

**POWER SUBSTATION DEDICATION.** During the centennial celebration, a dedication was held for the new power substation on Litchfield Street. Seen here are, from left to right, (sitting) Earl LaValla and John Tucker; (standing) village trustee John Favat, village trustee Frank Polizzi, unidentified, Frankfort mayor Stanley Stolark, New York State Power Authority chairman James Fitzpatrick, unidentified, village trustee Dominick Green, and school board member Frank Pontolillo.

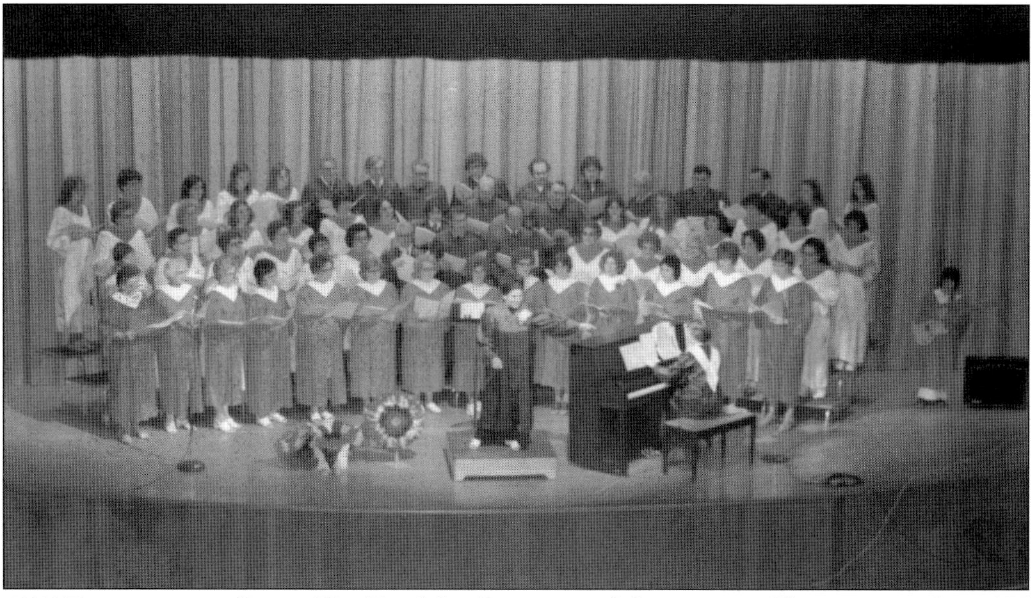

**1976 BICENTENNIAL CHOIR.** The Frankfort Bicentennial Community Choir organized in 1975 in honor of the country's upcoming 200th anniversary under codirectors Carole Crimmins and LaVergne McMurray. The Young at Heart Senior Citizens of Frankfort purchased red, white, and blue robes for the singers who performed throughout the area. On July 4, 1976, the choir presented a patriotic program for village family day and the dedication of Frankfort's "liberty bell." (Courtesy of Carole Crimmins.)

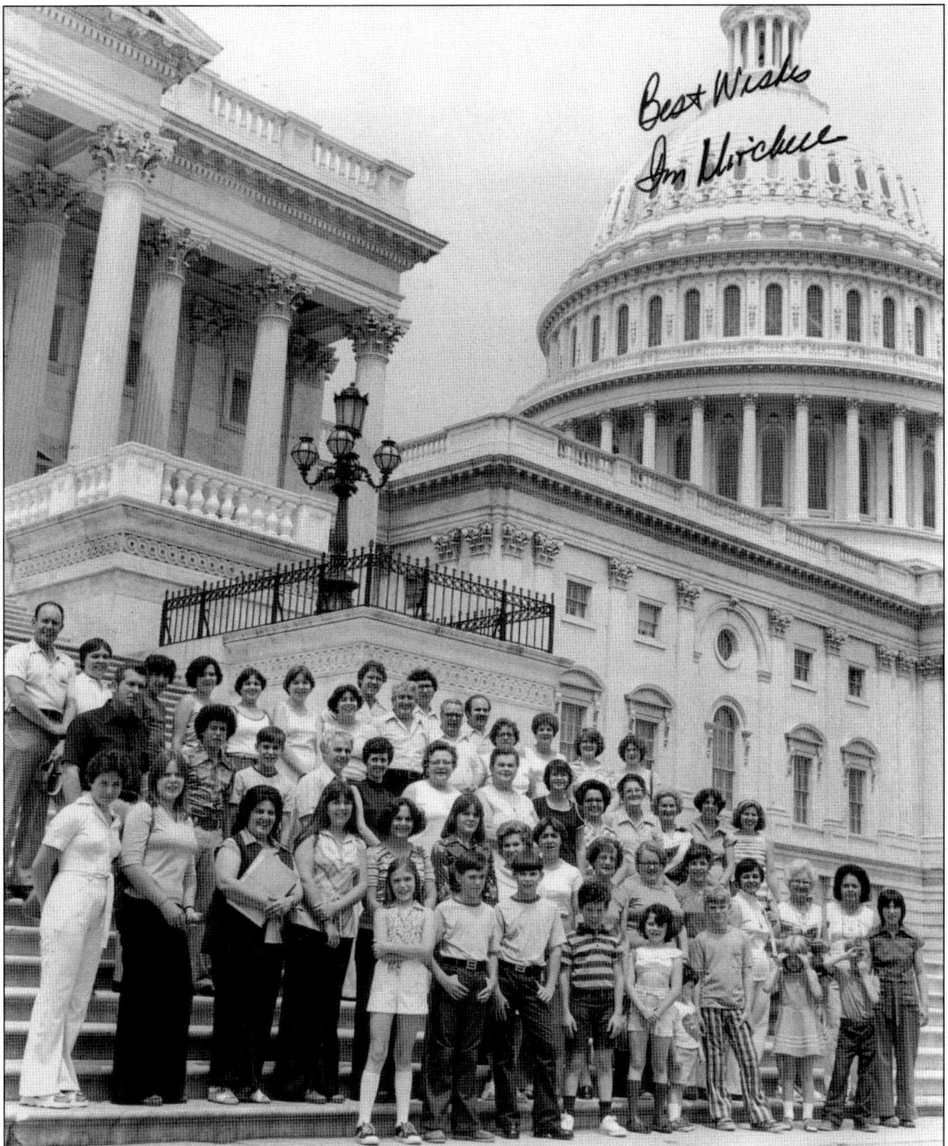


**Choir Performs in Washington, DC.** The next summer, the Bicentennial Community Choir visited Washington, DC, where it performed at an event near the White House on July 9, 1977, and met First Lady Rosalynn Carter. The band included, from left to right, (first row) Elaine Connors, Matthew Connors, Brian Connors, Mark Cook, Melinda McMurray, Steve McMurray, Paul Whitney, Anne Whitney, Scott Whitney, and Gina Crimmins; (second row) Sue Ortello, Michelle Connors, Carole Crimmins, Jackie Connors, Diana Forlenza, Maureen Collins, unidentified, Linda Vivacqua, Josephine Stolark, ? Bouck, Eileen Manno, Nancy Aversa, Jennie Lambert, and Mary Pearson; (third row) Jerry Crimmins Sr., Jerry Crimmins Jr., Bill Connors, LaVergne McMurray, Jane McMurray, Dorothy Fancher, Anna Schuster, Liz Farouche, Mamie Lille, Eva Valent, Helen Ketz, Patti McKevitt, and Barbara Whitney; (fourth row) Jim Connors, Rodhanna Connors, Jim Vivacqua, Sue McMurray, Roseann Unverdorben, Eileen Collins, Andrea Falzarano, Marty Bennett, Sal Talarico, David Loiacano, Ed Grainger, Bob Vore, Nancy Rowland, Lois Sciortino, Noreen Ketz, and Mary Beth Cobb. (Courtesy of Carole Crimmins.)

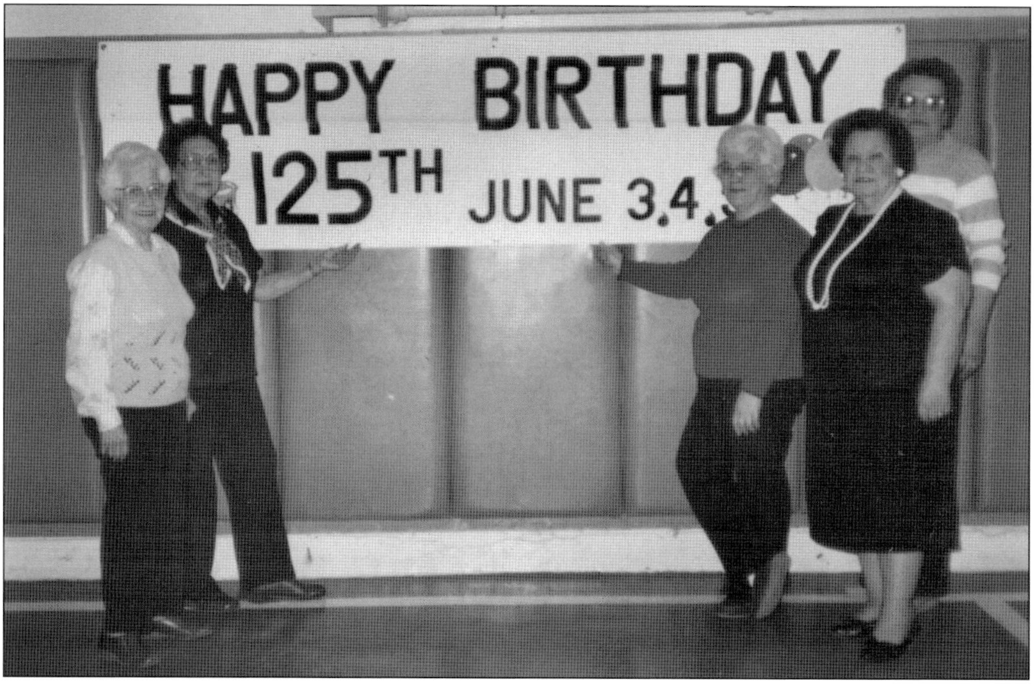


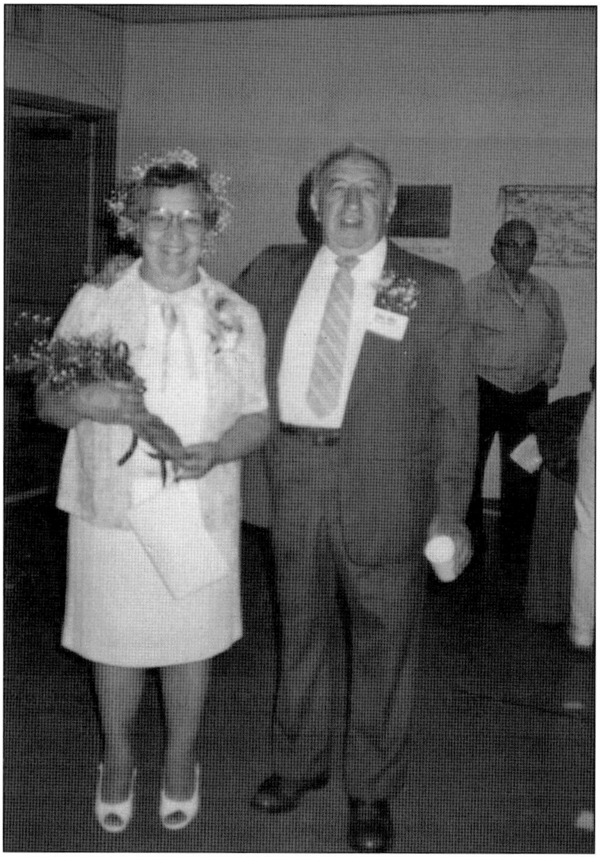

**VILLAGE'S 125TH ANNIVERSARY.** On June 3–5, 1988, the village of Frankfort celebrated its 125th anniversary. The three-day celebration included a tree planting in the village park with Frankfort mayor Francis Grates signing a proclamation, a tour of the new village hall, exhibits, youth games, and local business sales. Seen above are members of Frankfort's Young at Heart Senior Citizens, from left to right, Marie LaMonica, Mary Barbuto, Clara Potenza, Wanda Valent, and Rosi Rizzo. At left are anniversary king and queen Dominic "Smokey" Lille and his wife, Marie, both lifelong residents of Frankfort. Dominic (1921–2000) was the Frankfort town judge for over 20 years and a charter member of the Frankfort Youth Association and Frankfort American Legion Post 845. Marie (1924–2008) was the librarian at the Frankfort Free Library and worked in the cafeteria at Frankfort-Schuyler schools for many years. (Both, courtesy of the Village of Frankfort.)

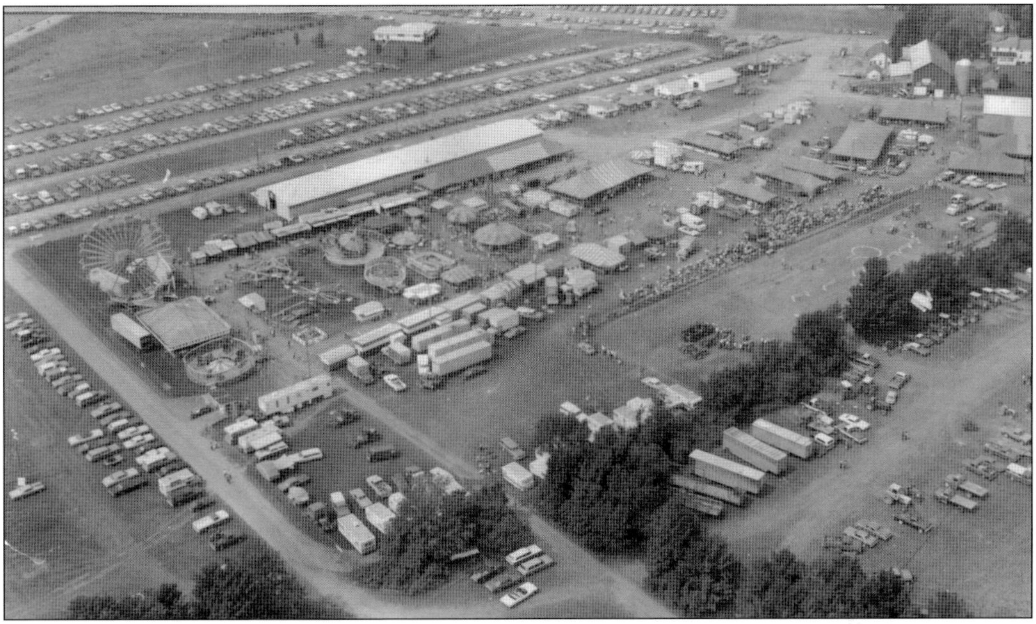

**Herkimer County Fair.** One of the area's biggest attractions, the Herkimer County Fair, was held in Herkimer from 1842 to 1917 and dissolved in 1918 because of World War I. It started up again in 1923, only to end again five years later. In 1948, a Frankfort community fair was held behind Frankfort Town Hall on West Main Street. The Frankfort Community Fair Committee incorporated as the Herkimer County Fair Association in 1950 and moved to Cemetery Street in 1958. The photograph above was taken in 1976, while the 2012 photograph below shows the fairgrounds with Route 5S in the background. A ribbon-cutting ceremony took place for the highway on August 28, 1968. The Herkimer County Fairgrounds host a number of events throughout the year, including the Great American Irish Fest, and the Herkimer County Fair is held in mid-August. (Both, courtesy of Herkimer County Fair.)

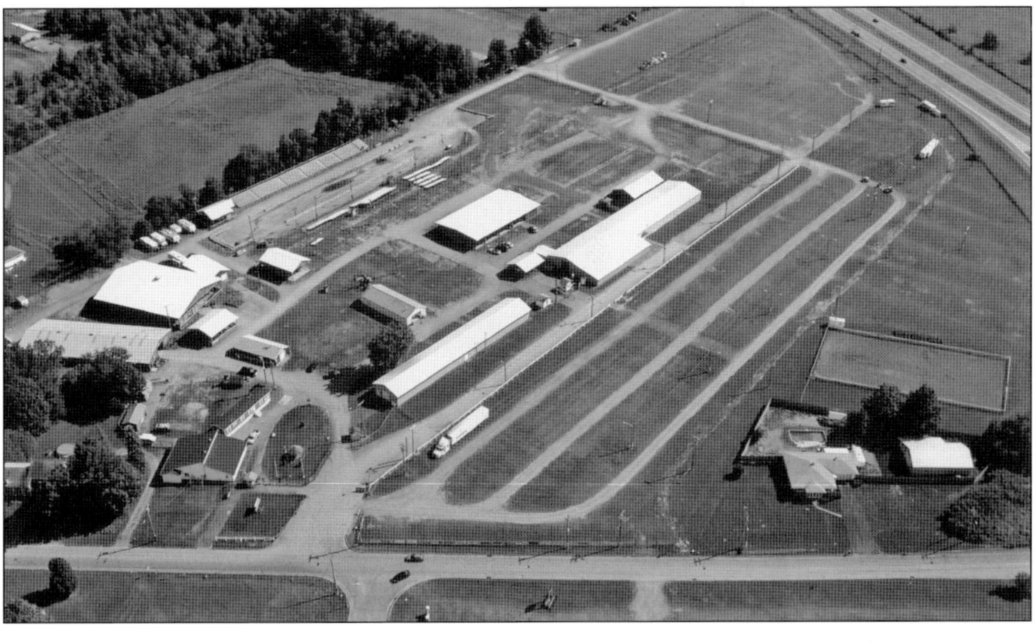

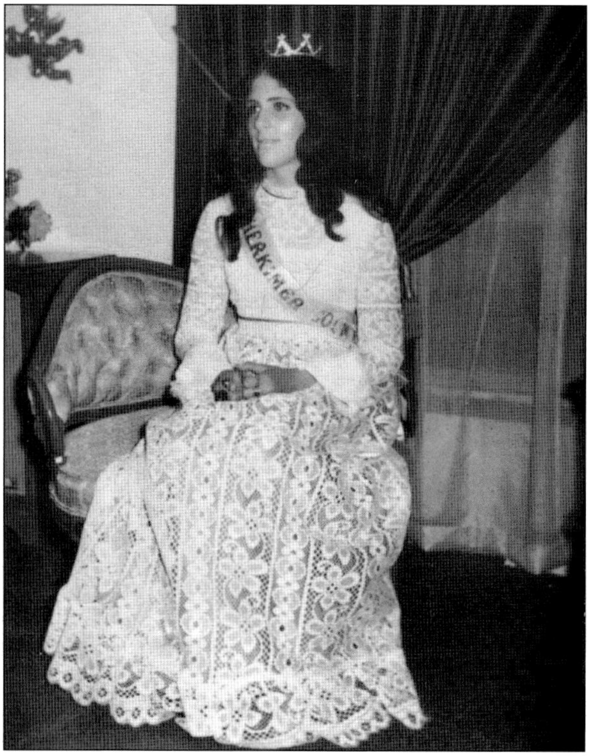


**HERKIMER COUNTY FAIR QUEENS.** It would not be a Herkimer County Fair without a queen. Mary Jean Button (left) of Frankfort was the queen in 1972 and was crowned on August 15 by the preceding year's queen, Carol Senif of West Winfield. The runners-up were Candy Denapole of Middleville and Cathy Ferdula of Ilion. Button went on to represent Herkimer County at the New York State Fair that year. She married Jody Grippe in September 1975. Wendy Grippe (below) of Frankfort was crowned queen on August 18, 1976. The first runner-up that year was Michele Dack of Ilion, followed by second runner-up Susan Mower of Jordanville, third runner-up JoAnne Rumrill of Frankfort, and fourth runner-up Debbie Young of Schuyler. Eleanor Crouch of Mohawk was the pageant chairwoman, and Gerald Quayle was the fair president. (Both, courtesy of Jody Grippe.)

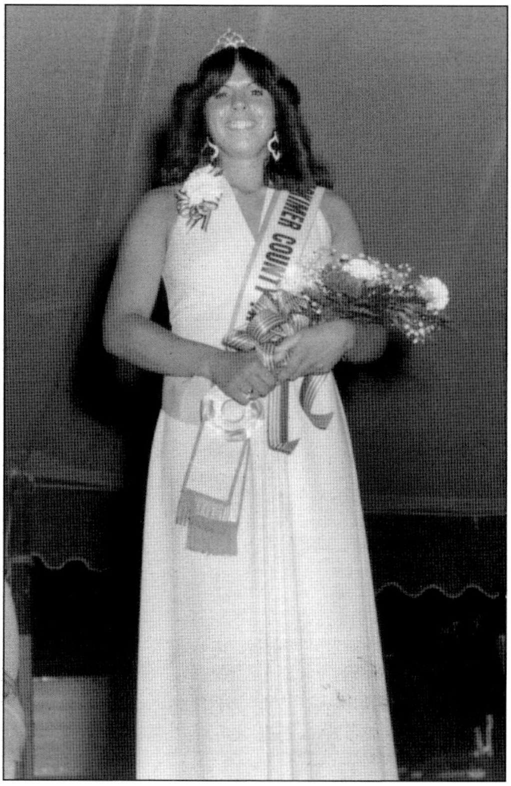

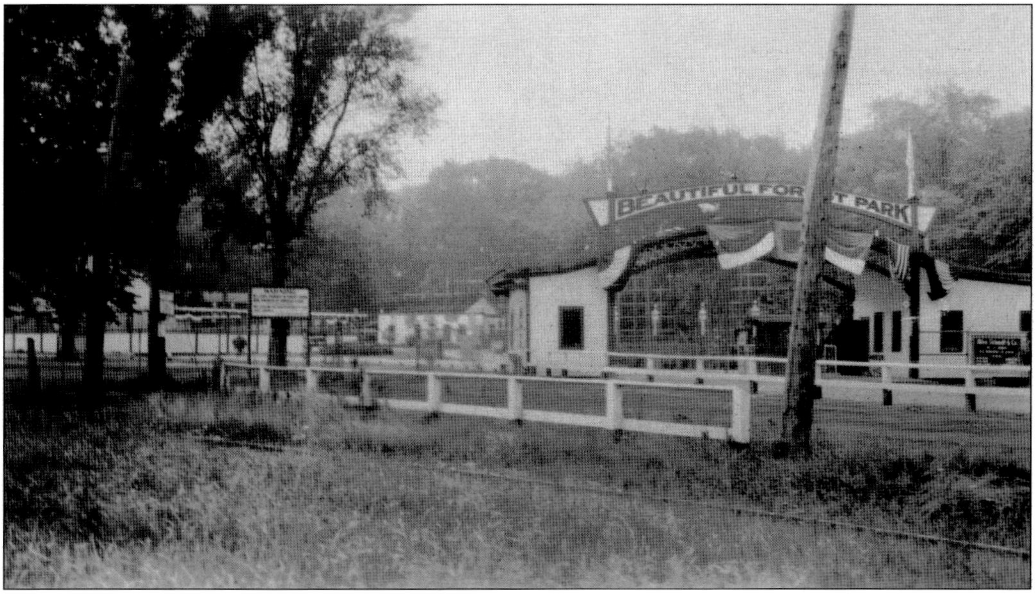


**Forest Park.** Called "Central New York's Playground," Forest Park, at the town's western edge near Utica, was a center of attraction until the 1930s and was later the site of Chicago Pneumatic. The Utica & Mohawk Railroad Company, which operated the area's trolley system, bought land east of the Masonic home and built what was then known as Utica Park in 1891 as a way to entice people to ride the trolleys. The park featured a dance pavilion that hosted band concerts, a baseball diamond, a bicycle racing track, a roller coaster and other amusement rides, and a restaurant. The park closed in the mid-1930s, after attendance declined and people were able to travel farther afield for recreation. (Both, courtesy of the Oneida County Historical Society.)

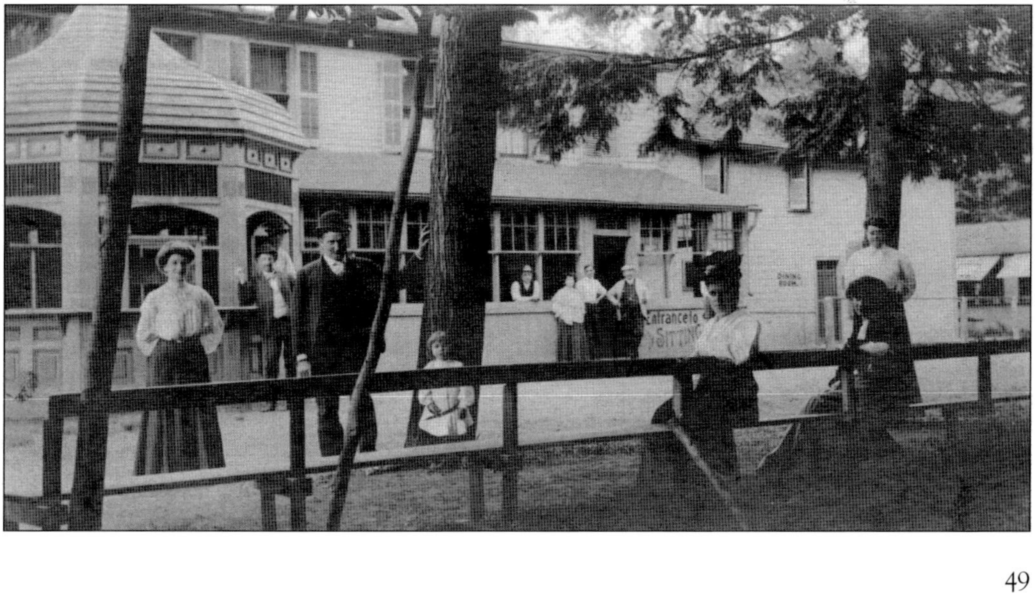

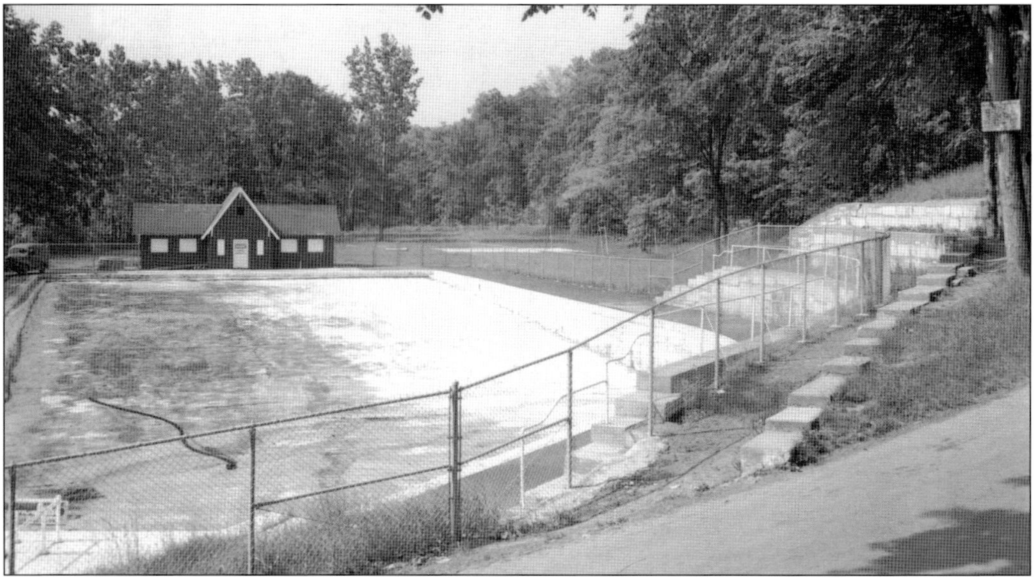

**FRANKFORT MUNICIPAL POOL.** Located at the entrance of Lehman Park, this pool was one of the finest and largest in the state. It was constructed as a Works Progress Administration (WPA) project under the supervision of Louis Clauser (1895–1975). Construction began in 1935 and was completed in the spring of 1937. The pool graduated from a depth of one foot to 10 feet and featured three diving springboards and a wading pool for children.

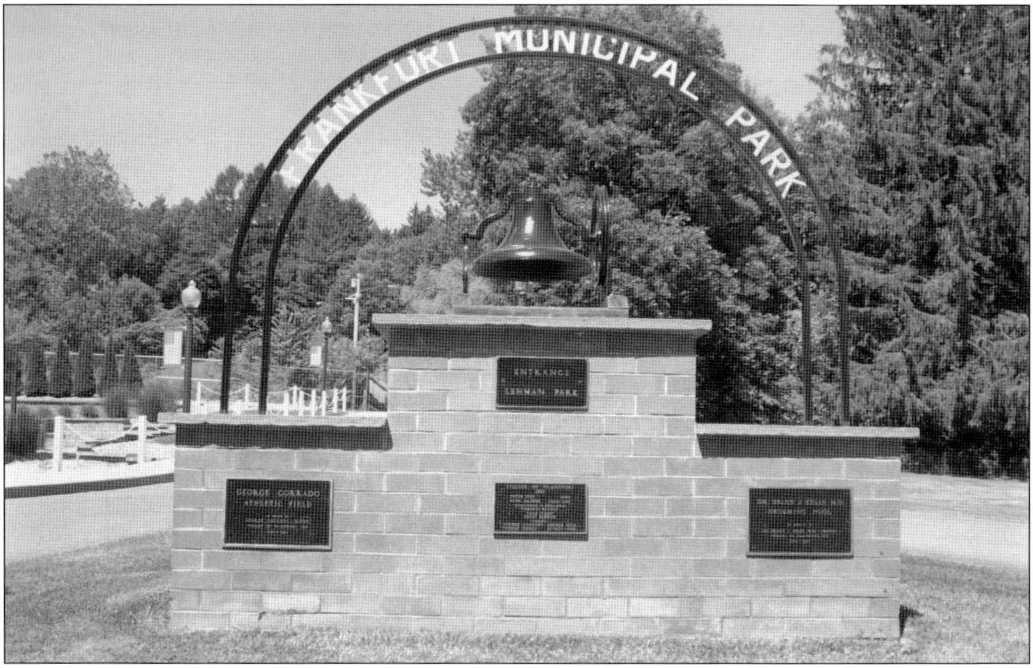


**LEHMAN PARK.** This iron arch, which includes the bell from Sarah M. Piper School, greets visitors at the entrance of Lehman Park on Litchfield Street. The memorial was erected in 1976, when Joseph Reina was mayor. The plaque on the bottom left reads "George Corrado Athletic Field," and the plaque on the right reads "Dr. Brian J. Kelly, M.D. Swimming Pool." The village used a legacy by H.A. Lehman to create the pool and park.

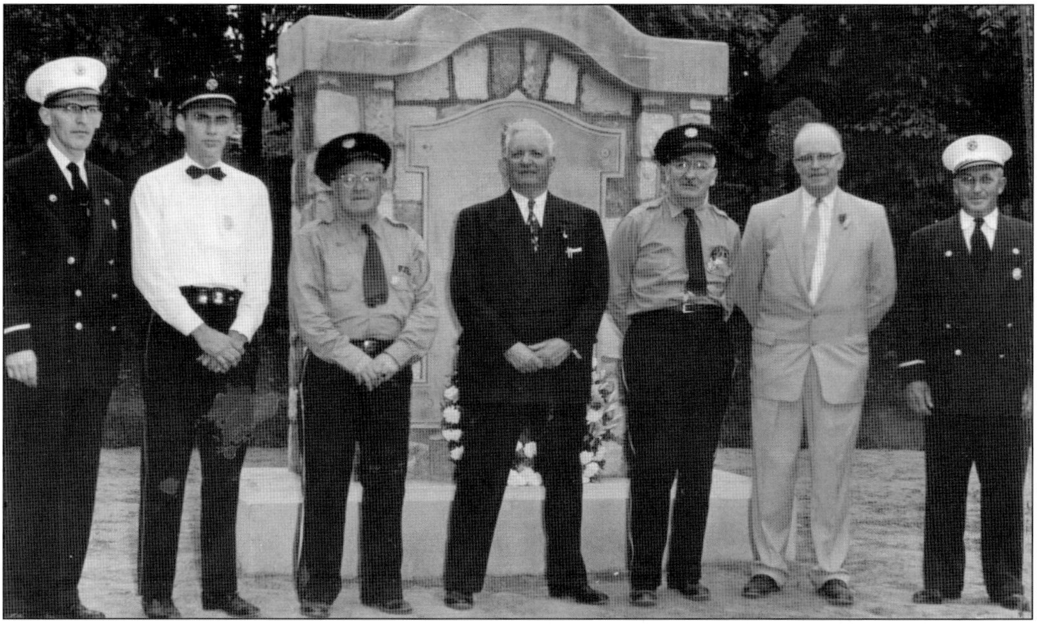

**FIREMEN'S MONUMENT.** The Firemen's Monument was dedicated on May 22, 1955, in Lehman Park. Seen here are, from left to right, Edward Corbett; John Shields, Mohawk Fire Department chief; Louis Clauser, Frankfort Fire Department treasurer; Frankfort mayor George Corrado; master of ceremonies James Walter Callahan; Britton Van Auken, president of the New York Firemen's Association; and Carl Dreizler, Frankfort Fire Department chief. (Courtesy of the Frankfort Fire Department.)

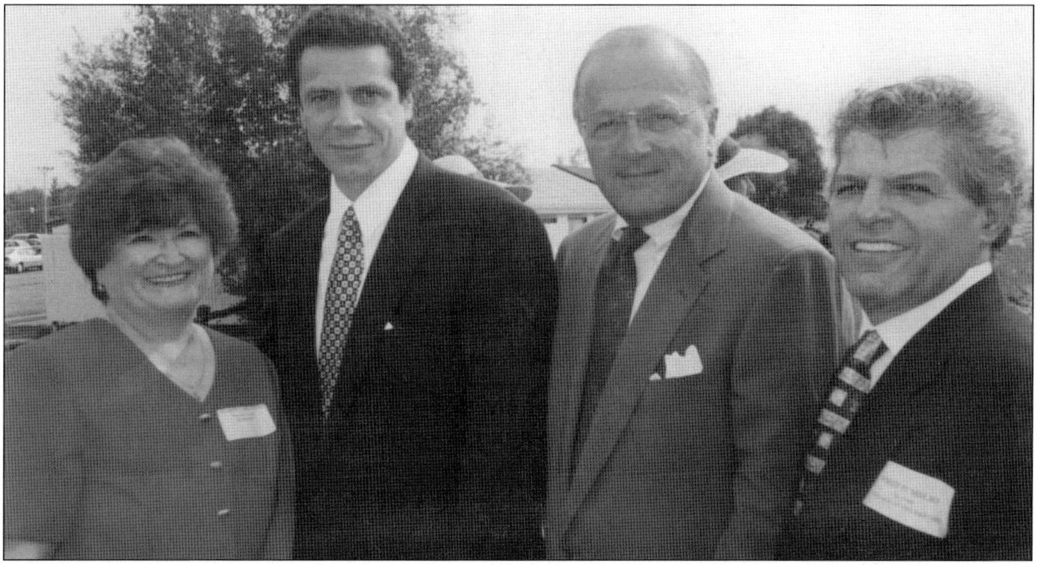

**FRANKFORT MARINA.** The customer service center of the Crown Blue Line, a major operator of self-skippered boats, was opened at the Frankfort Marina on July 3, 1997. Funding for the project was provided by the New York State Department of Housing and Urban Development (HUD). Seen here at its opening are, from left to right, Sharon Carlesimo, village clerk; Andrew Cuomo, HUD secretary; Congressman Sherwood Boehlert; and Frankfort mayor Fred Pumilio. (Courtesy of the Village of Frankfort.)

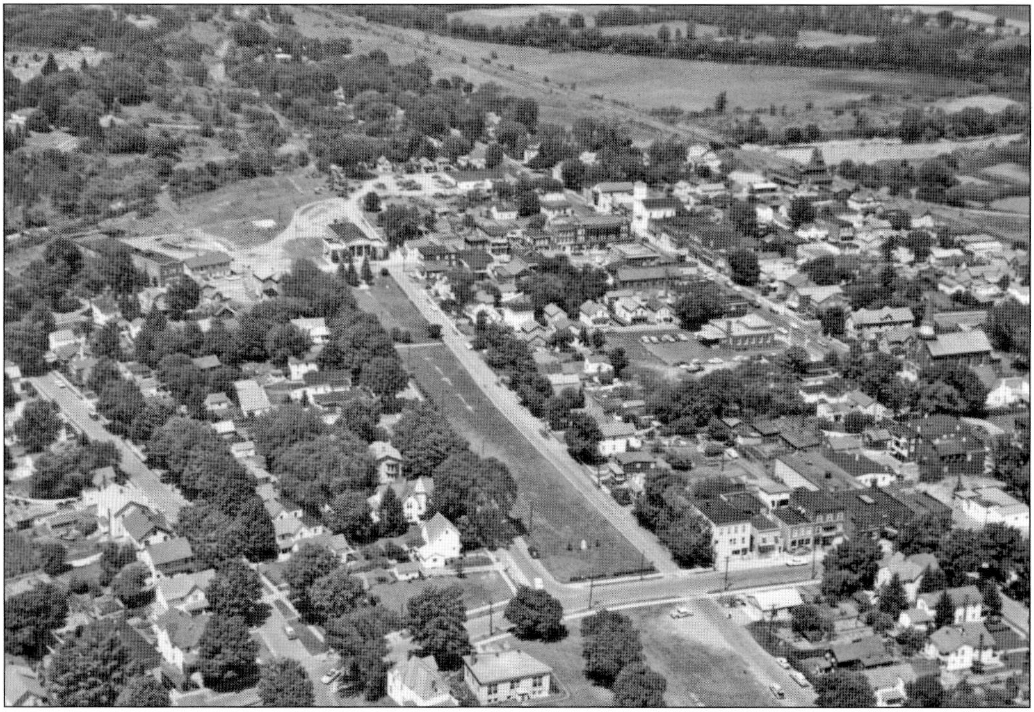

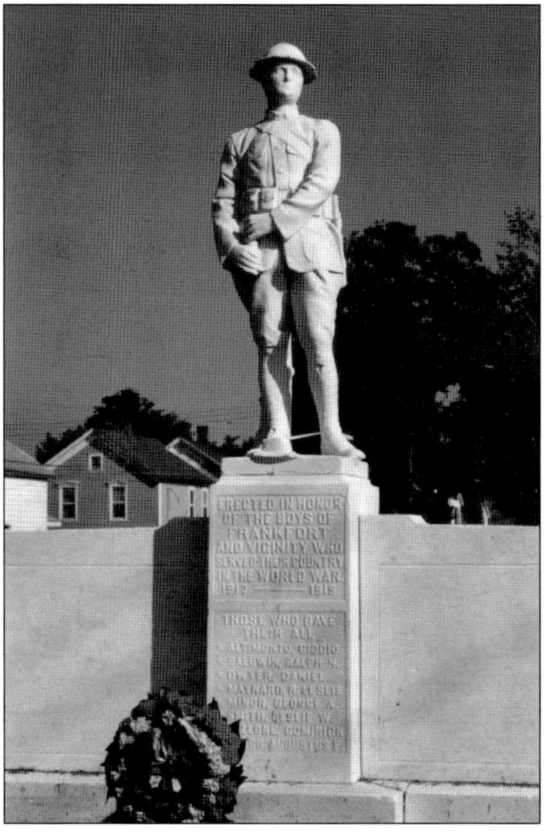


**FRANKFORT MEMORIAL PARK.** The aerial view above of Memorial Park (foreground) is reminiscent of the Lincoln Memorial Reflecting Pool in Washington, DC. The long shape of the park is unique in itself, however, as it clearly marks where the Erie Canal bed went through the village. The statue of the American Doughboy (left) sits in the park near the town hall. It was dedicated in 1929 in tribute to the Frankfort soldiers who died in World War I: Giddio Altimonto, Ralph Baldwin, Daniel Dwyer, R. Leslie Maynard, George Minor, Leslie Smith, Dominick Vallone, and Augustus Reach. At the ceremony, held on the 12th anniversary of the first contingent leaving Frankfort, Altimonto's young son unveiled the statue. Utica pilot Jack Wright flew low over the marker and dropped white carnations to the crowd of 1,500.

# *Three*

# CHURCHES

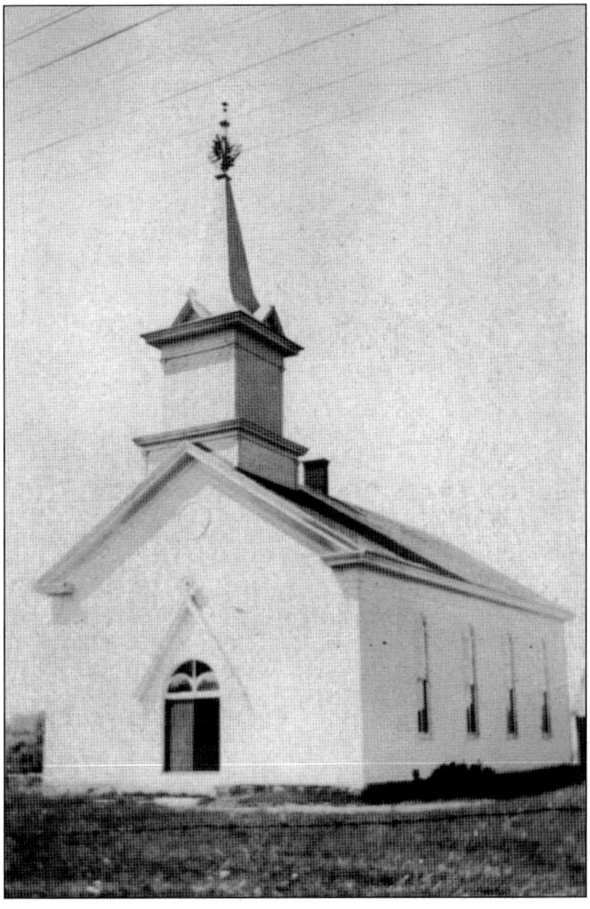

**FRANKFORT HILL METHODIST EPISCOPAL CHURCH.** This church was constructed in the 1880s near the intersection of Albany and Higby Roads. In 1944, the church's board of trustees took bids to tear down the structure. Its lumber was then sold and its altar and other furnishings were given to a New London church. (Courtesy of Keith McNally.)

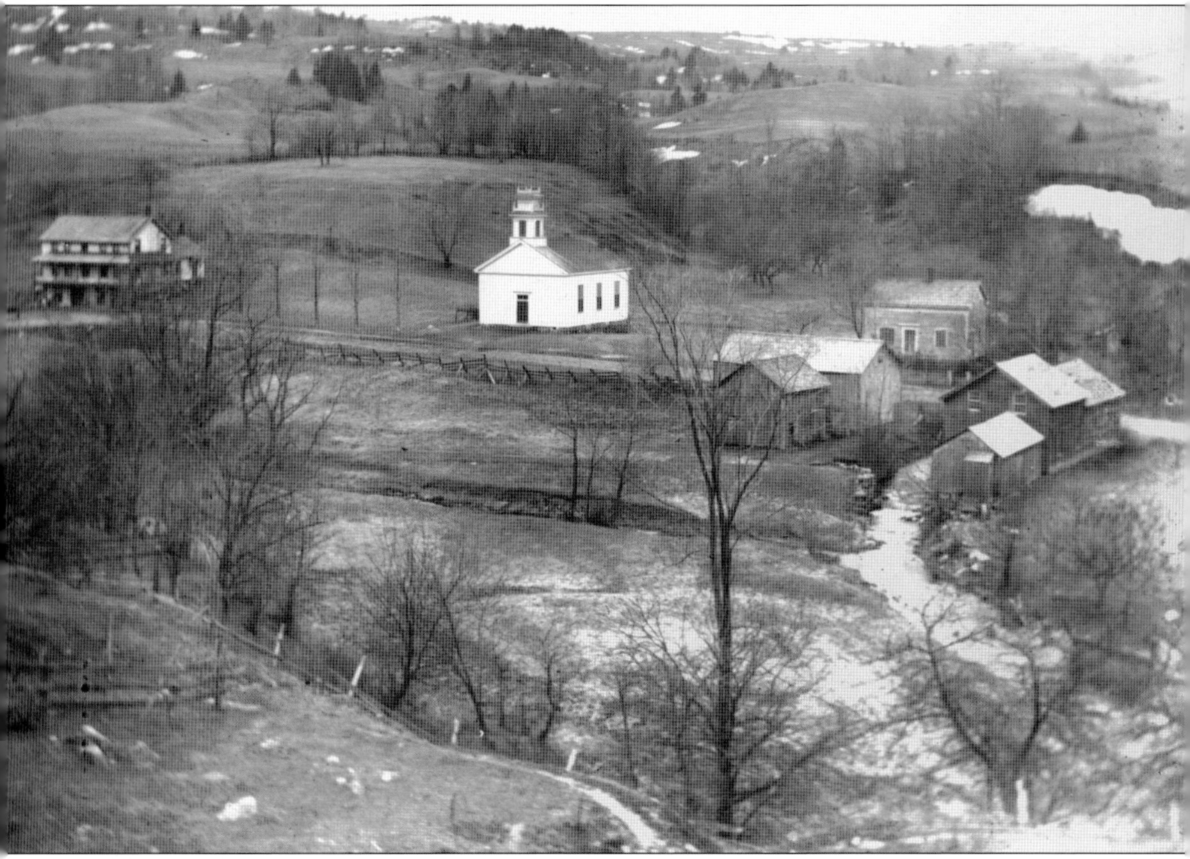

**Frankfort Center Union Church.** This wood-frame church on Center Road was built in 1861, replacing an earlier church that was built around 1838 by the Frankfort Hill Methodist Society to bring together a congregation. The new church had white clapboard siding and mullioned windows framed with green shutters. The interior had aisles down both sides and several wooden pews. A Packard pump organ was at the right of the altar. In the 1920s, attendance declined, although there were occasional revival meetings. By the mid-1930s, there was no longer a congregation, and the church fell into disrepair. The land was then sold to a neighboring landowner, and the building was razed. The Packard organ was donated to the West Frankfort Methodist Church by Edgar Dougherty after that church and organ were destroyed by a fire. (Courtesy of Eunice Hanson.)

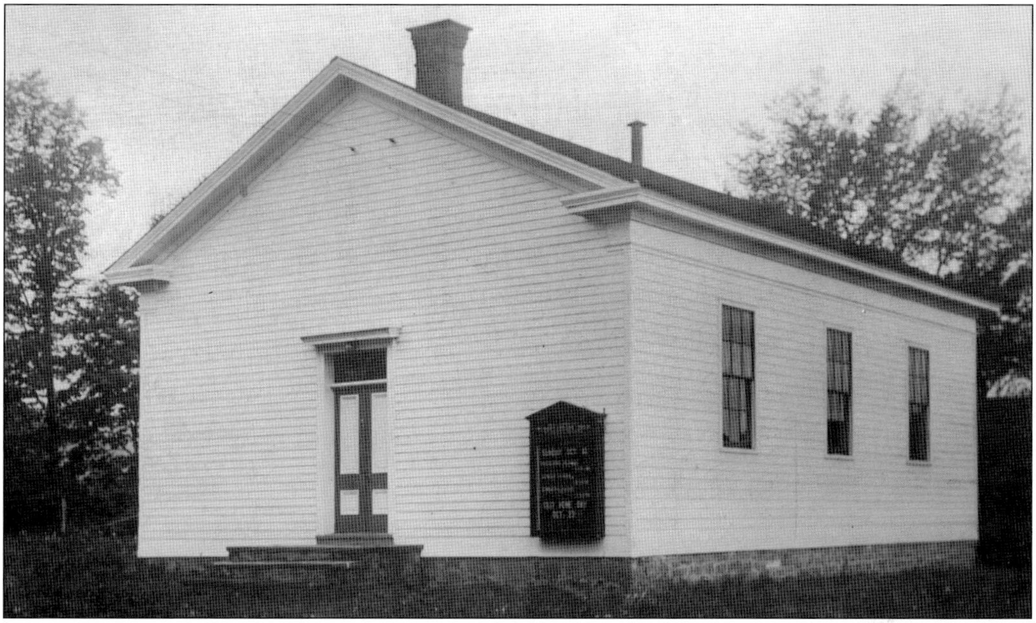

**West Frankfort Methodist Church.** This small, rural church was built on Frankfort Center Road in 1840 after Rev. Lyman Beach, a circuit-riding preacher, organized the Methodist Episcopal Society there in 1839. Some of the early families that attended the church were the Fergusons, Kingsleys, and Morrises. A fire consumed the church on March 11, 1964, burning its entire contents and destroying the building on the day before its 124th anniversary.

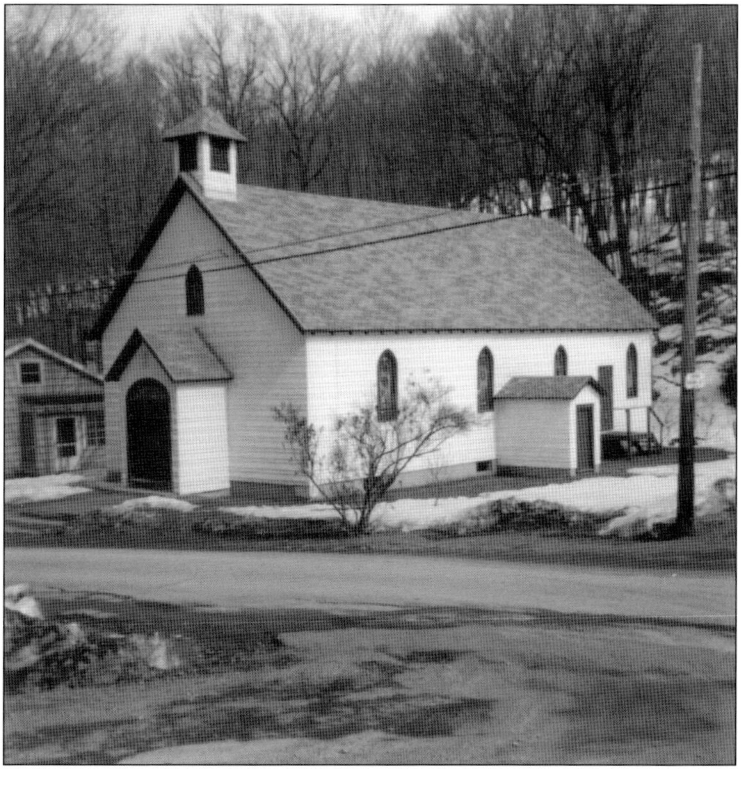

**St. Theresa's Church.** Rev. Patrick Wallace undertook a campaign to have a church built to meet the spiritual needs of Frankfort Center's Roman Catholic residents, and this chapel was built in 1927 as a mission of SS. Peter and Paul Catholic Church. A shrine and rose garden were later added. A shortage of new priests and a decline in its congregation eventually led to its closure. The last service was held on August 25, 1996.

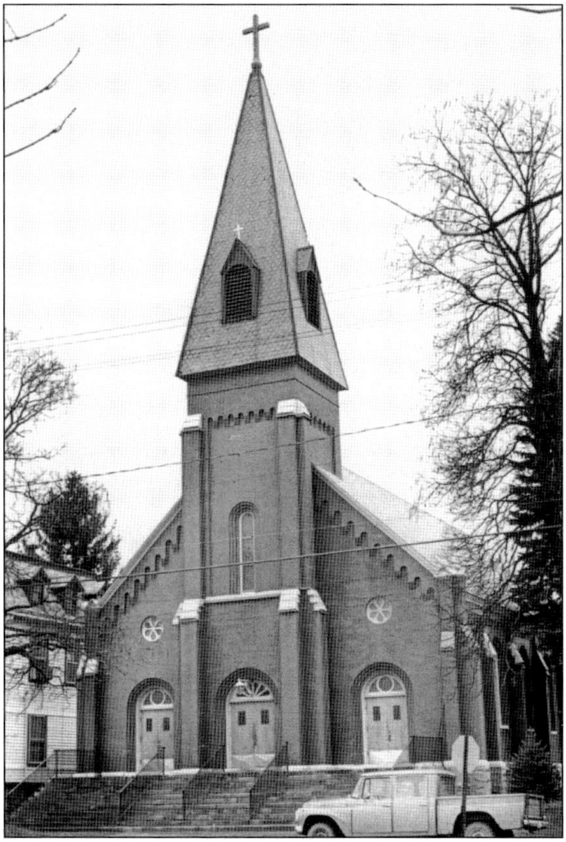

**SS. PETER AND PAUL CATHOLIC CHURCH.** Catholic worship began in Frankfort as early as 1845, mostly among Irish residents who held home masses with visiting priests. In 1867, the Annunciation Parish in Ilion made Frankfort an out-mission, and in 1885, supervision of the mission was transferred to St. Francis de Sales in Herkimer. After the Herkimer pastor, Rev. James Halpin, pushed for the construction of a church, a cornerstone was laid on June 26, 1887, and construction was completed in time for Christmas services that year. The church was located at 202 Second Avenue. Three entrances led into separate vestibules, and the church finish and pews were ash. Three aisles led up to the sanctuary with interior carpeting. Memorial windows were of cathedral stained glass, and the ceiling was decorated with pictures of the apostles. (Below, courtesy of Our Lady Queen of Apostles.)

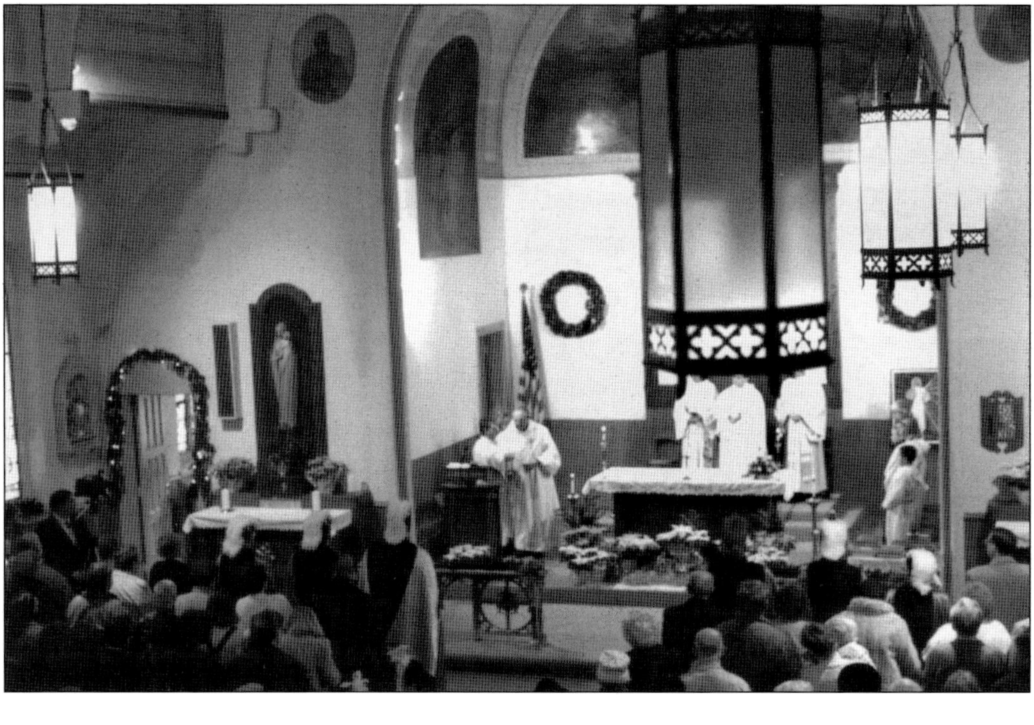

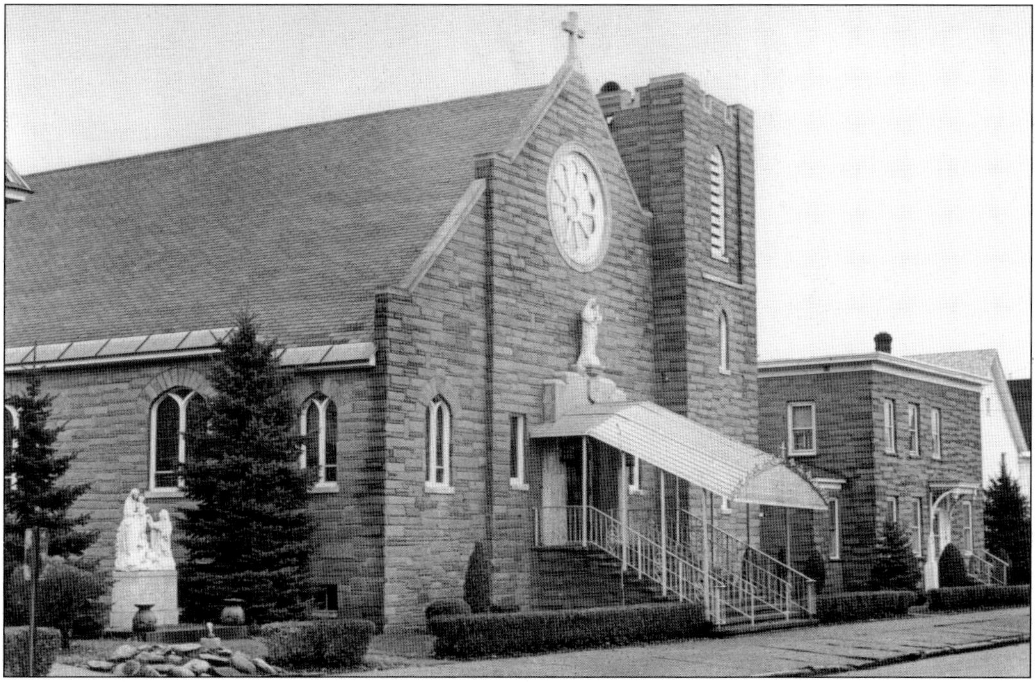

**St. Mary's Catholic Church.** Around 1900, Italian immigrants began settling in Frankfort and attending SS. Peter and Paul Catholic Church. In 1917, they were able to have their own congregation when they became a mission of St. Anthony's Church in Herkimer, and a small building behind SS. Peter and Paul was used as their place of worship. On September 7, 1927, St. Mary of Mount Carmel became a separate parish. They acquired land on Frankfort Street, and construction began in October 1937 for a church and rectory. The basement served as the church from 1938 until the stone church was finally completed and dedicated on May 30, 1952. The image below shows the interior of the basement during the wedding of Joseph and Angie Thurston on September 2, 1950, with Fr. Michael Fufferd officiating. (Below, courtesy of Angela Thurston.)

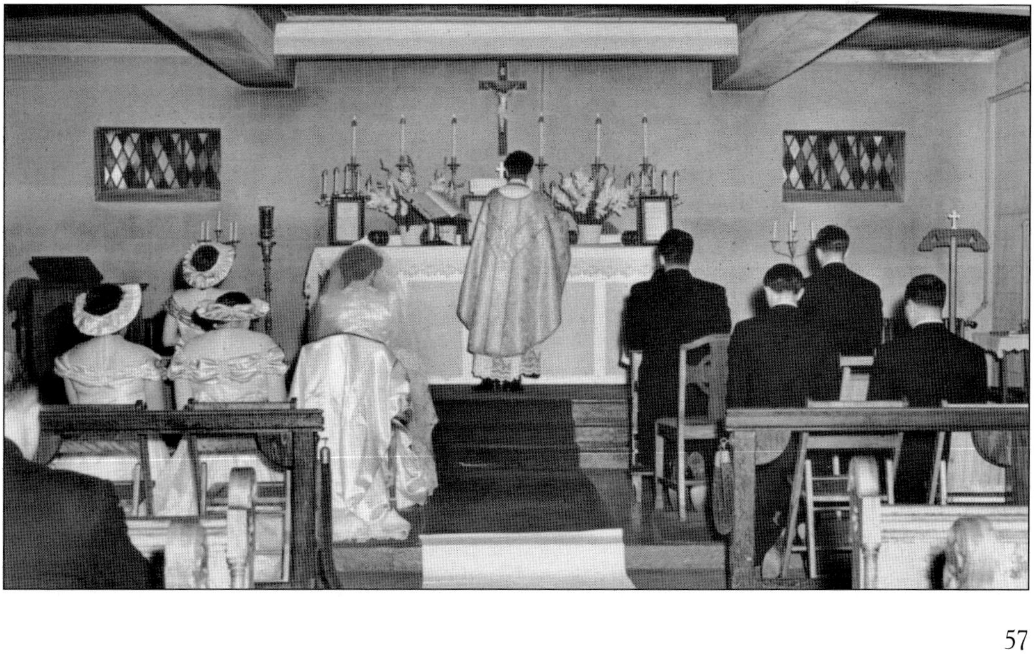

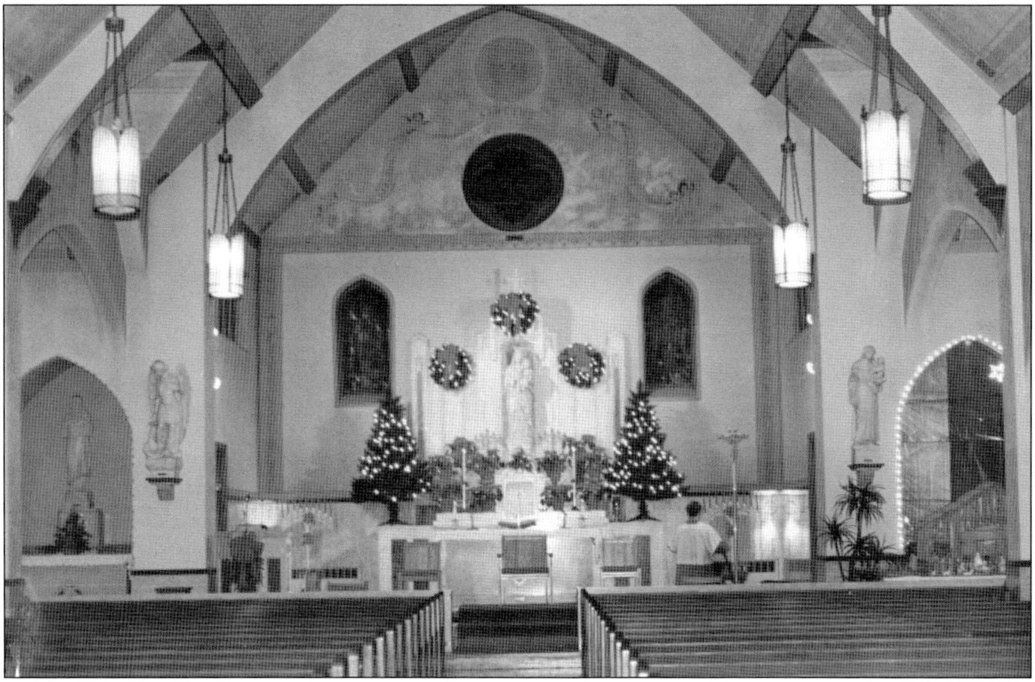

**St. Mary's Interior.** On May 30, 1952, the Gothic stone church of St. Mary's was completed and dedicated. On September 9, 1962, the cornerstone of St. Mary's Elementary School was laid, and the school opened in September 1963. The church interior features Italian marble for the altars, pulpit, statues, and stations of the cross. The seven sacraments are artistically represented on the ceiling of the church. (Courtesy of Our Lady Queen of Apostles.)

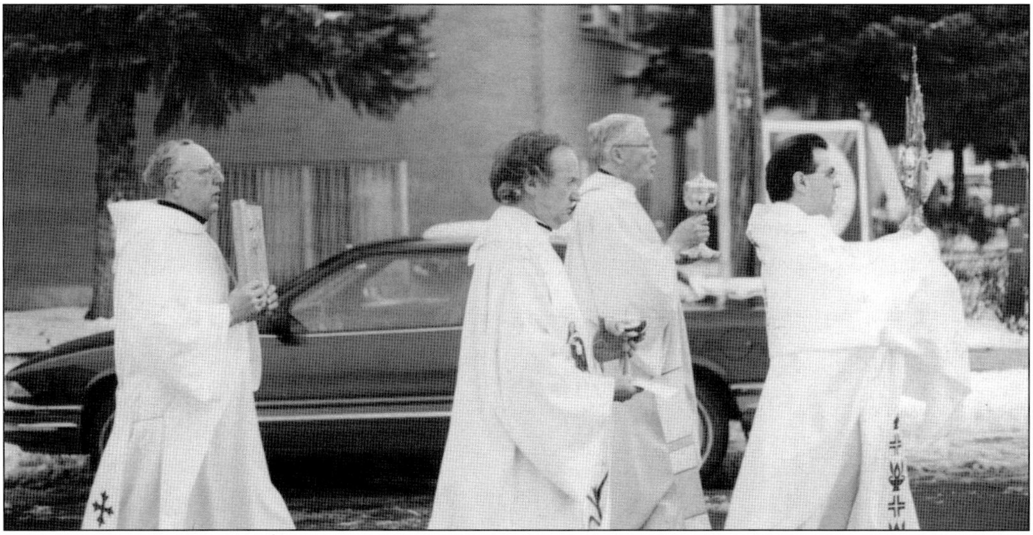

**Catholic Churches Merge, January 1995.** Frankfort's two catholic churches merged in 1995, with St. Mary's becoming home to both parishes. A mass of transition was co-celebrated by three priests associated with both churches. Shown carrying in procession from SS. Peter and Paul Catholic Church are, from left to right, deacon Sam Salamone with the lectionary; Rev. Anthony Curran with the chalice; Rev. John Waldron with the ciborium; and Rev. Robert DeMartinis with the monstrance. (Courtesy of Our Lady Queen of Apostles.)

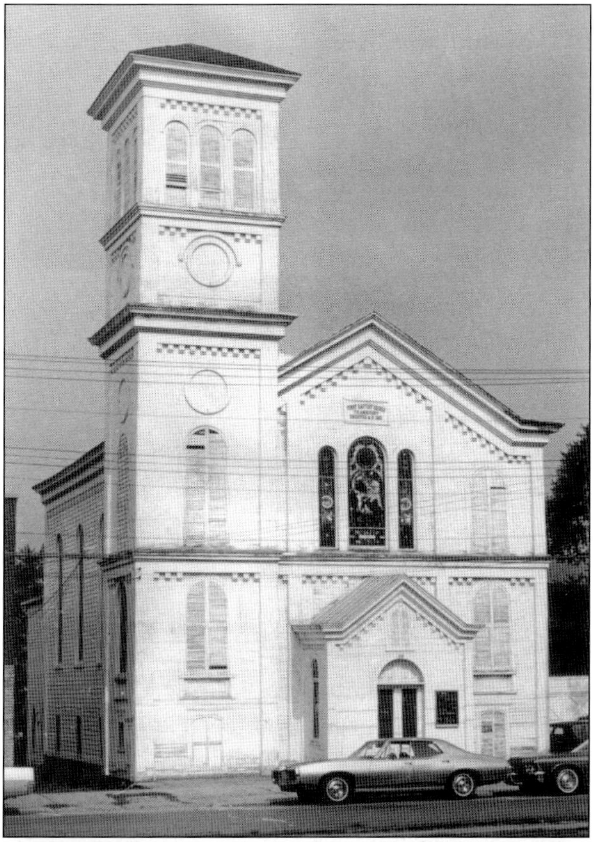

**First Baptist Church.** Baptists began meeting in the Masonic hall in 1829 before building their own church in 1836. Their first structure burned in 1861, and a new church (right) was promptly built and dedicated the following year. In 1886, the entire church structure was raised to make room for Sunday school rooms in the basement and the addition of a choir loft, a study, and a kitchen. In 1982, the steeple was cut away and capped. The church closed in the 1990s when the Ilion and Frankfort congregations merged. The bell that hung in the church tower was made in West Troy in 1862. In 2000, it was removed and given to Brunswick Baptist Church. The photograph below shows the interior of the church during the wedding of LaVergne McMurray and Eleanor Jane Knox on June 20, 1959. (Below, courtesy of LaVergne McMurray.)

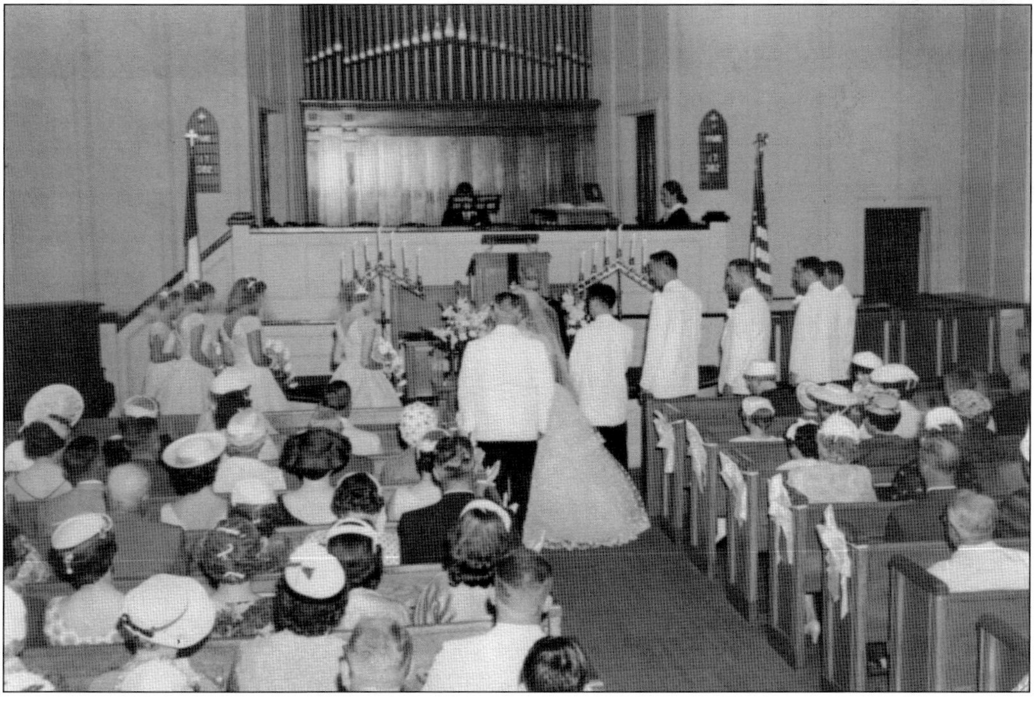

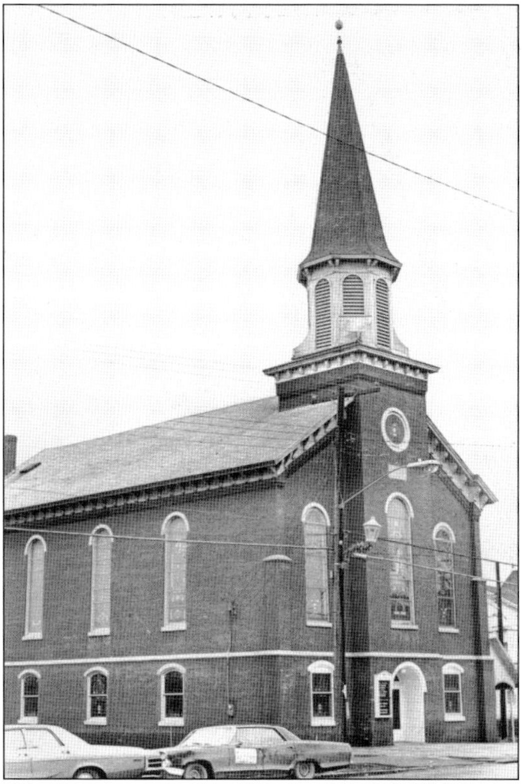

**Frankfort United Methodist Church.** A Methodist class was organized in Frankfort in 1832. In 1849, a pastor was named and a church was formally organized, meeting in a small building on Litchfield Street. In 1869, the church at left was built on the corner of Main and Church Streets and dedicated. The parsonage, at 135 East Main Street, was built during the pastorship of Rev. S.W. Brown (1891–1895), and Rev. M.G. Seymour (1899–1900) put stained glass windows in the church. The interior was remodeled under Rev. F.B. Severance (1904–1907) and an addition was built to the rear of the church in 1926 under Rev. W.K. Bradshaw (1922–1931). The photograph below shows the interior of the church during the wedding of Sue McMurray and Daniel Quackenbush on October 20, 1984. (Below, courtesy of LaVergne McMurray.)

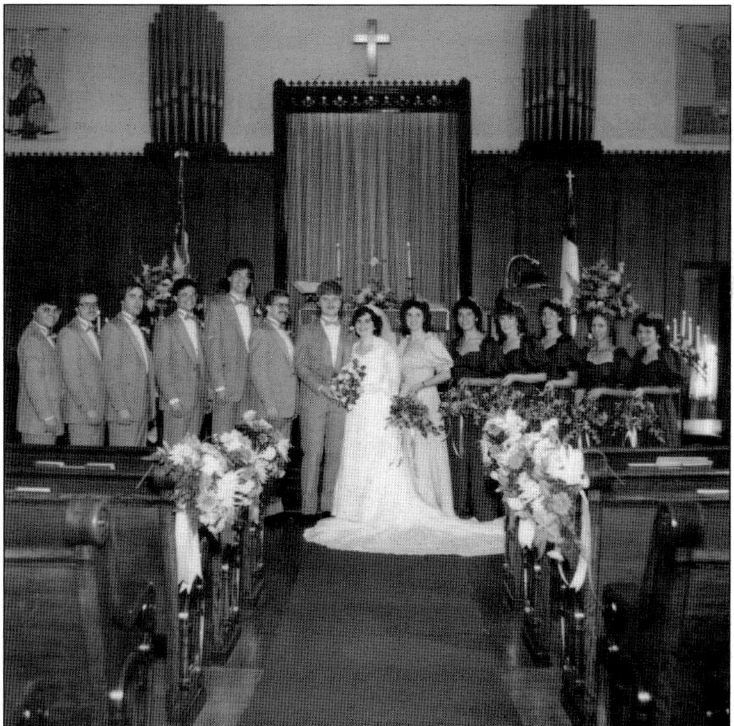

**NEW CHURCH BUILT.** Construction of a new Methodist church began in May 1991 on the old Route 5S. In addition to the sanctuary, it included classrooms, a fellowship hall, and a kitchen. The first service was held in November of that year. The stained glass windows and pews from the old church were moved to the new church. This photograph shows the old church being razed. It is now the site of a Rite-Aid. (Courtesy of Village of Frankfort.)

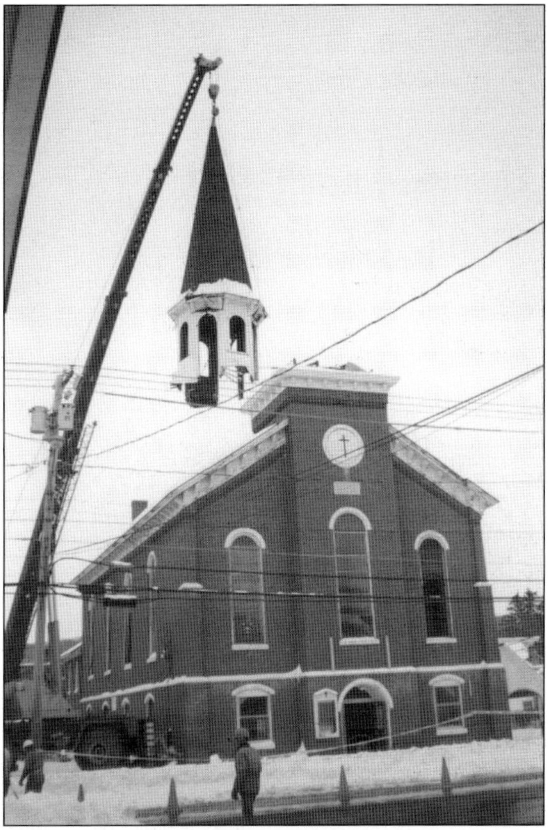

**ITALIAN METHODIST CHURCH.** The church below, on West Main Street, was originally built as a Universalist church in 1844. Rev. William Caldwell of the Frankfort Methodist Church founded the Italian Methodist Mission in 1910, and five years later, this building was purchased to be the place of worship. It was the last mission church in the Methodist Church Northern New York Conference when it closed in 1956. Today, it is a private residence.

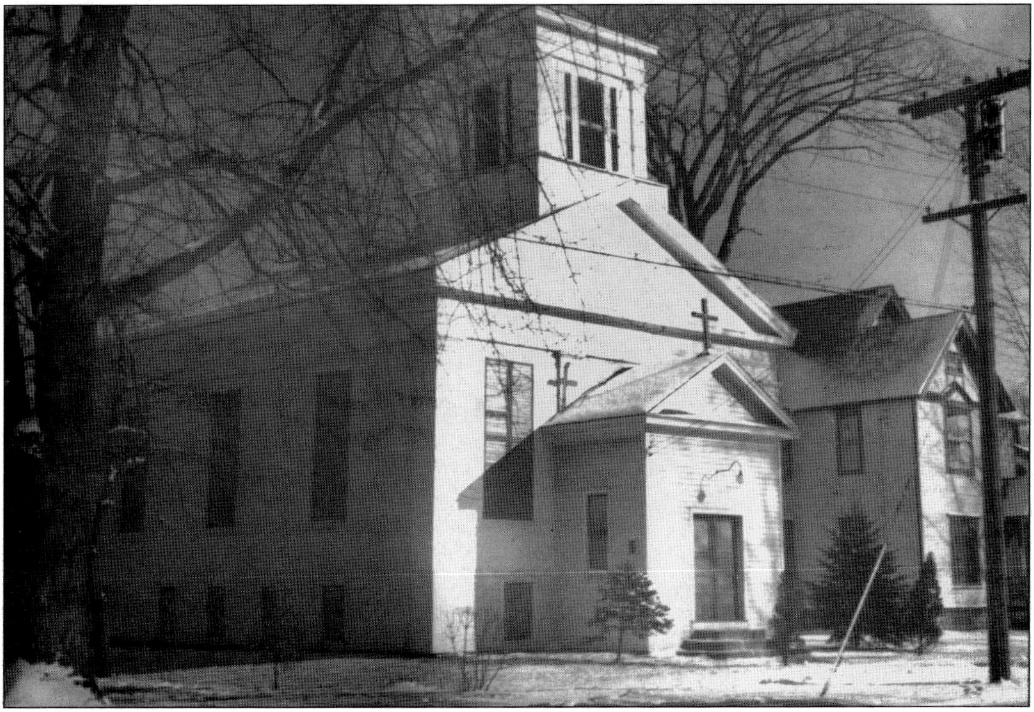

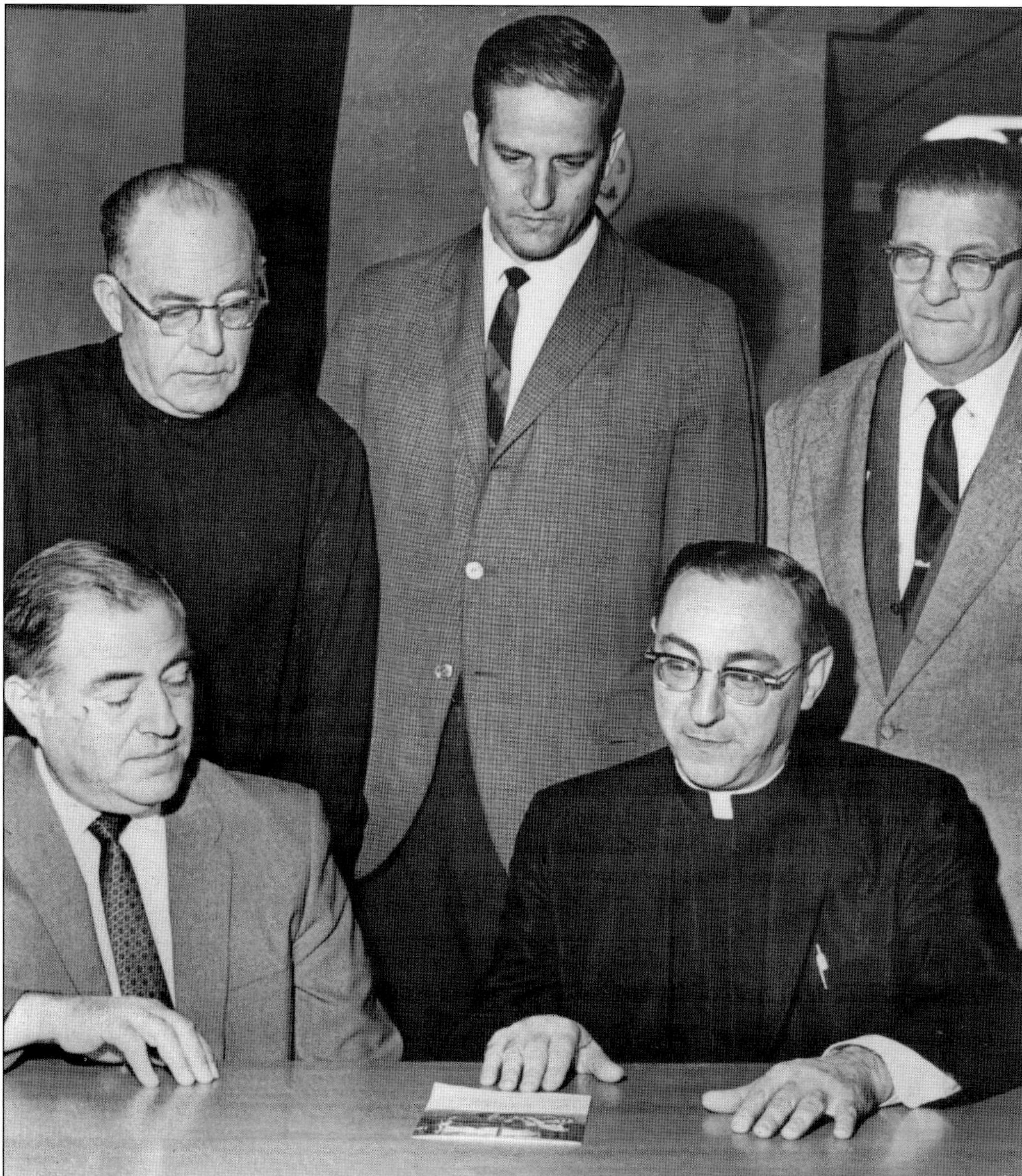

**Ecumenical Service.** This photograph shows the clergymen of the Frankfort churches in November 1969 at a meeting to plan for the United Community Thanksgiving Service on November 26 in St. Mary's Church. The clergymen are, from left to right, (seated) Nicholas Kinney, chairman of the Ecumenical Council at St. Mary's; and Rev. Alfred Lamanna, pastor of St. Mary's; (standing) Rev. Edward J. Taney, pastor of SS. Peter and Paul; Rev. Raymond F. Linza, pastor of the Methodist church; and Rev. Raymond F. MacCumber, pastor of First Baptist Church. (Courtesy of Our Lady Queen of Apostles.)

# *Four*

# Schools

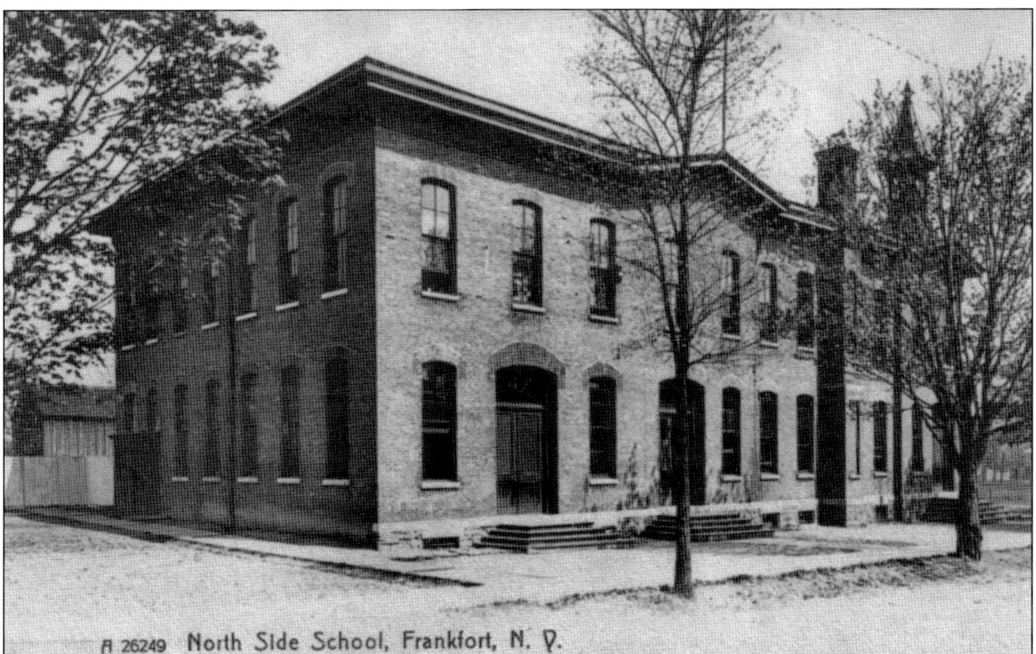


**Church Street School.** The original red schoolhouse on Church Street, built as early as 1859, was replaced with this two-story brick school known as Church Street Elementary School and North Side School on the corner of Church and Orchard Streets. In 1928, a severe explosion in a neighboring home damaged the school, and it was replaced by a new school. Today, it is occupied by the village offices. (Courtesy of Chad Wohler.)

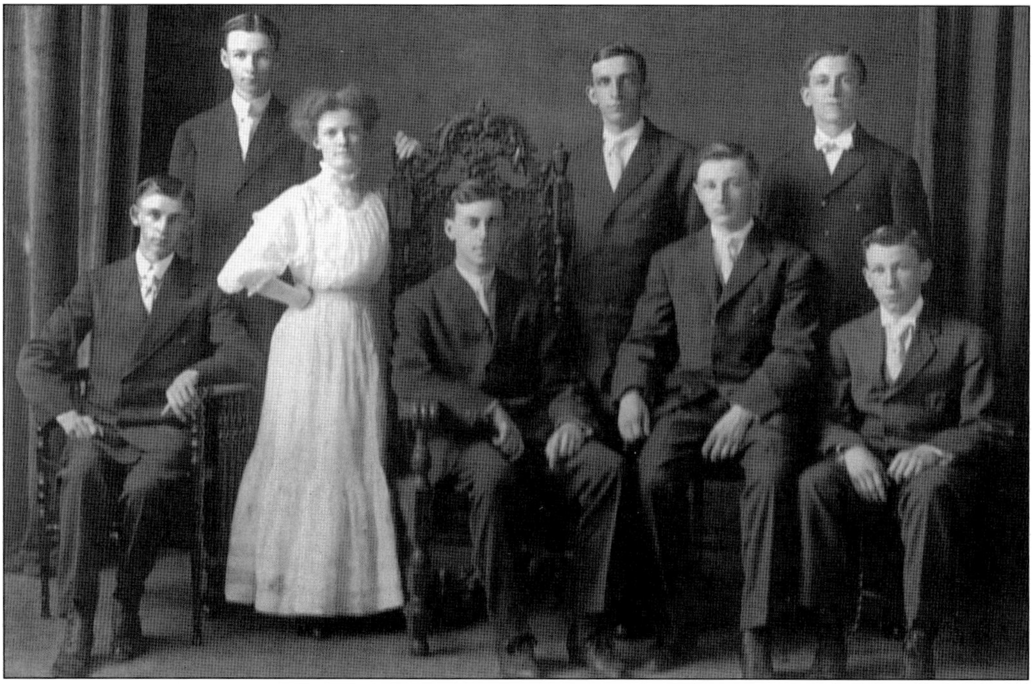

**FRANKFORT HIGH SCHOOL CLASS OF 1908.** Frankfort High School was built in 1897 on the corner of Frankfort Street and Third Avenue. The graduating class of 1908 included, from left to right, Frederick Steiger (1890–1953), Hugh Mixer (1890–1957), Mabel Griffin, George Thurston (1890–1952), Frank Vidulich (1890–1959), Reuben Brockway (1890–1987), Roger Weeden (1891–1961), and Justin List (1891–1954). The school was later renamed Sarah M. Piper School. (Courtesy of the Frankfort Free Library.)

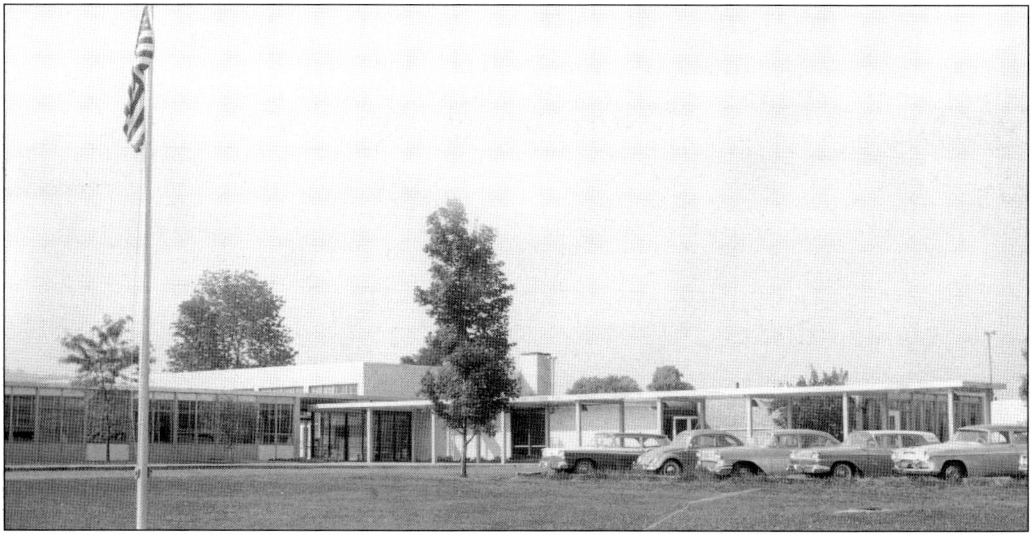

**REESE ROAD ELEMENTARY.** Designed by Urbahn, Brayton & Burrows, this was an ultra-modern building when it opened in 1957. Before the school was built, students had attended Sarah M. Piper School, on the corner of Frankfort Street and Third Avenue. When West Frankfort Elementary School closed in 2011, the students were transferred here. It is now known as Frankfort-Schuyler Elementary School.

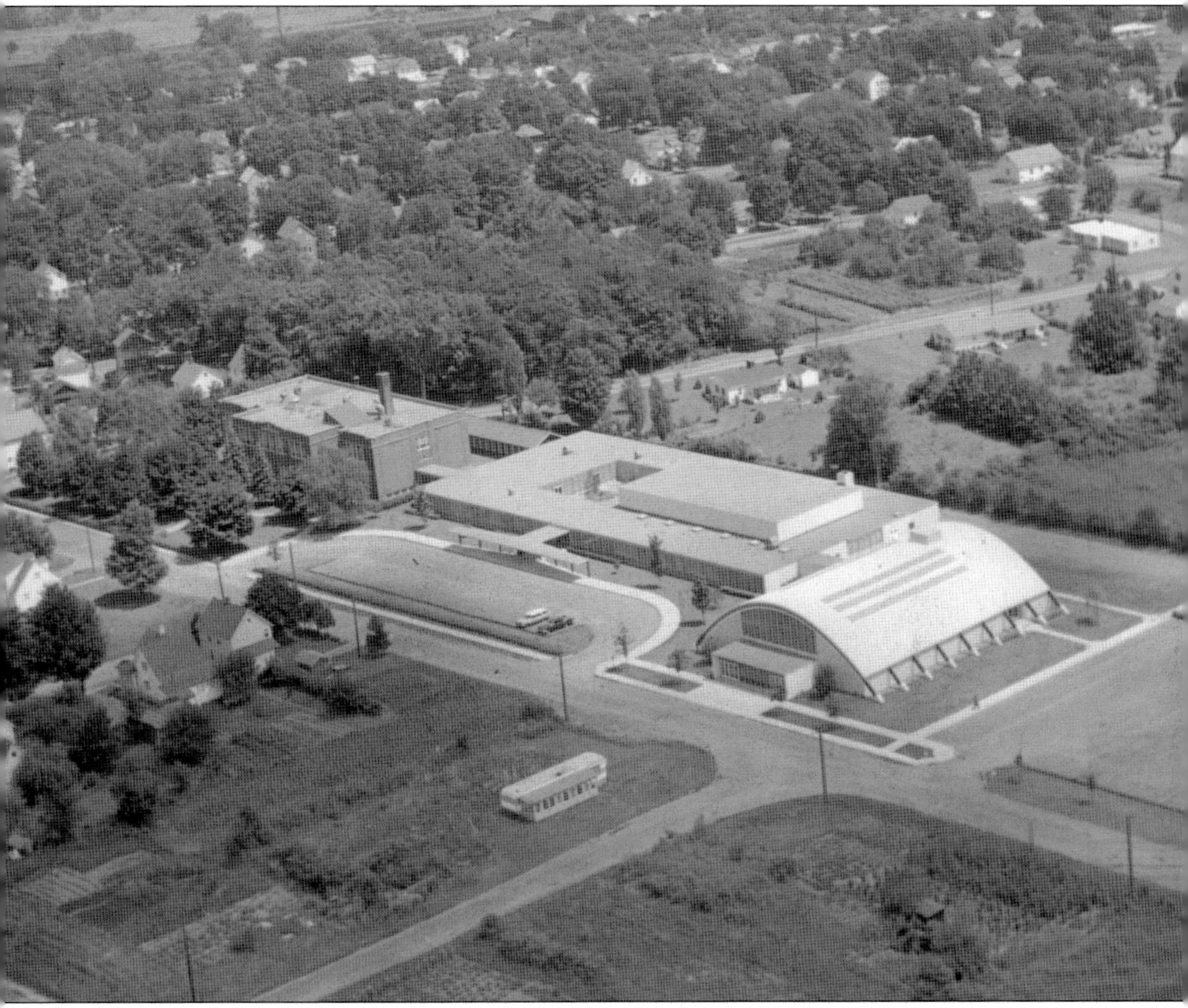

**Frankfort-Schuyler High School.** This aerial view shows the Frankfort-Schuyler Central School District, located on Palmer Avenue and established on July 1, 1954. In addition to the village schools, the district also comprised the former Union Free School District of the village and part of the former Union Free District No. 1 (East Frankfort), along with 11 common school districts. Two additional common school districts were annexed later. By 1960, the facilities included the high school, for grades 8–12; Northside Elementary School, for kindergarten through fifth grade; Reese Road Elementary School, for kindergarten through seventh grade; and West Frankfort Elementary School, for kindergarten through sixth grade. The original Frankfort High School, built in 1926, is on the left. In November 1954, taxpayers approved a $2.1-million bond issue for the building of an addition, a gymnasium, and Reese Road Elementary School.

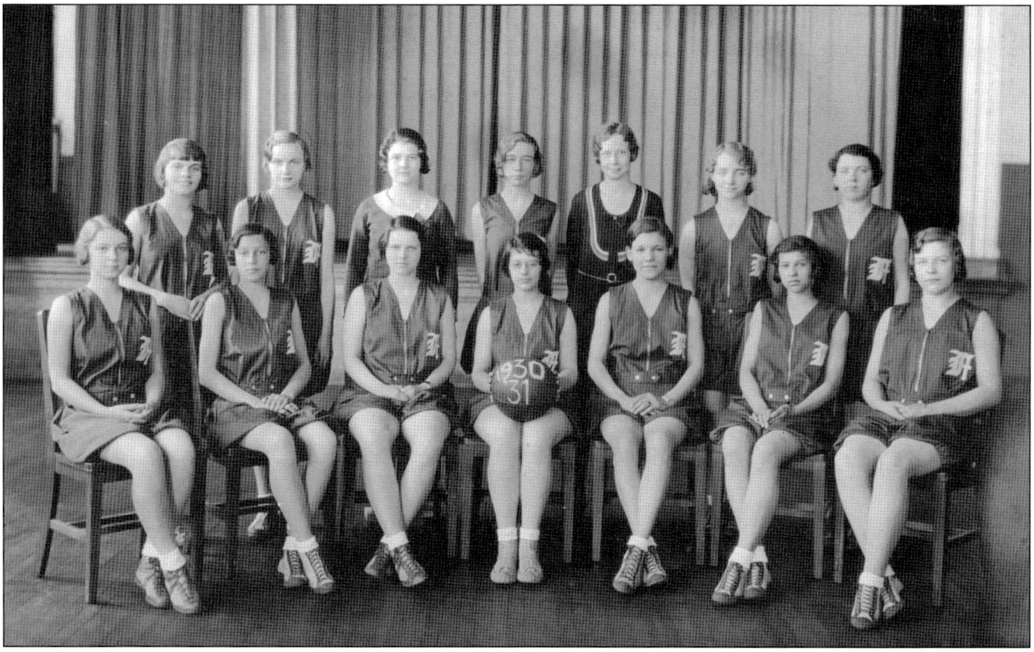


**FRANKFORT HIGH SCHOOL WOMEN'S BASKETBALL TEAM, 1930–1931.** This team included, from left to right, (first row) Ruth Rich, Marjorie Hollenbeck, Thelma Torbitt, Ruth Winckle, Grace Iocovozzi, Sadie Pasek, and Mildred Fischer; (second row) Alice Hyde, Helen Horton, Blanche Baker, Isabelle Lake, teacher Mildred Toulson, Dorothy Schachel, and Helen Murray. (Courtesy of Frankfort Free Library.)

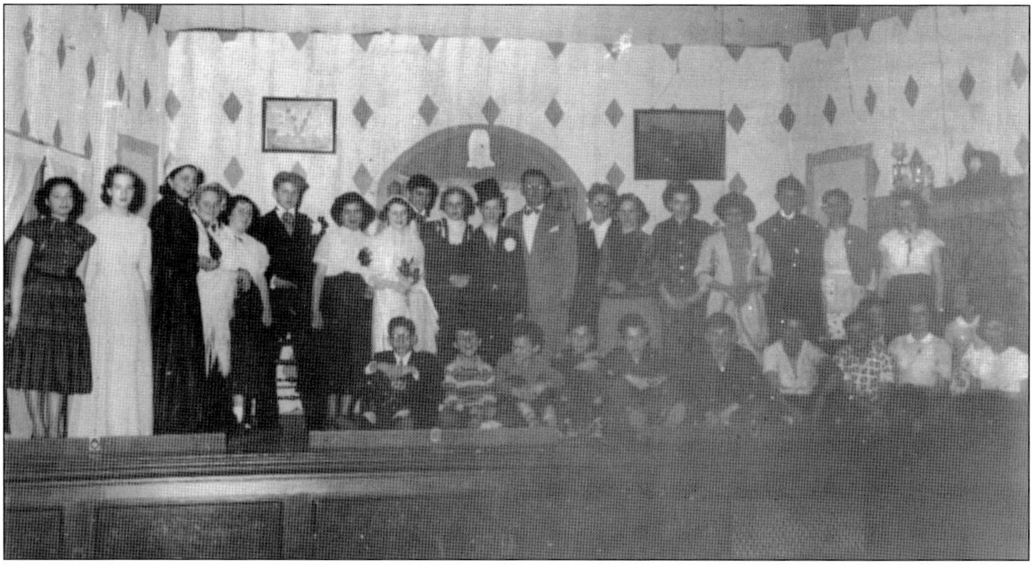

***LITTLE WOMEN* EIGHTH-GRADE CAST, 1952.** The cast of this play included, from left to right, (sitting) Joseph Spatola, Joe Fresco, Joe Gillette, Joe Rocco, Richard ?, Jim Filingeri, three unidentified, Helene Sharo, and two unidentified; (standing) Marion Onafaro, June Matteson, Saundra DiMaggio, Joan Matheson, Mary Jane Nicastro, unidentified, Matia Puzzilla, Rosemarie Cushman, Joe Minosh, Rosemarie Chuff, two unidentified, Willard Dougherty, Nancy Jackson, Joan Ryde, unidentified, Charles Murzin, and two unidentified. (Courtesy of Dorine Jenkins.)

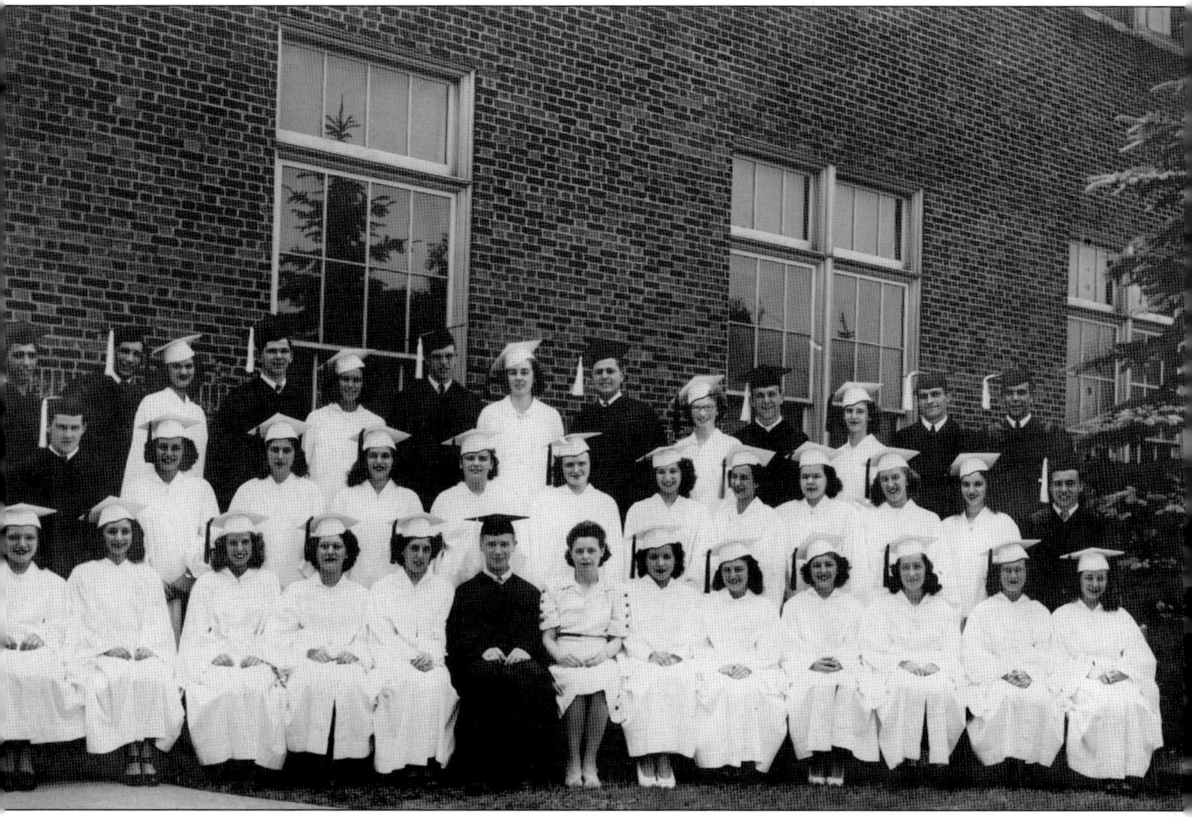

**Frankfort High School Class of 1946.** This class included, from left to right, (first row) Jane Caiola, Florence Tocco, Florence DiGristina, Phyllis Papa, Rosemarie Seppi, Richard Soukas, teacher Theresa Graves, Josephine Leto, Carolyn Romeo, Sadie Castardi, Marian Wiltse, Molly DePalma, and Janet Hollister; (second row) Robert Conley, Estelle Kipper, Phyllis Chard, Frances Varlaro, Alice Smith, Shirley Windecker, Anna Minosh, Virginia Lambert, Joan Wilkinson, Catherine Christian, Ida Cataline, and Dominick Vore; (third row) Anthony Feliciano, Frank Plano, Fena Zito, Stanley Ray, Joyce Lints, Robert Torbitt, Margaret Sterling, Joseph Frank, Jewel Dreizler, Joseph DiMaggio, Winifred Hight, Samuel Gerdano, and Samuel Caruso. (Courtesy of Frankfort Free Library.)

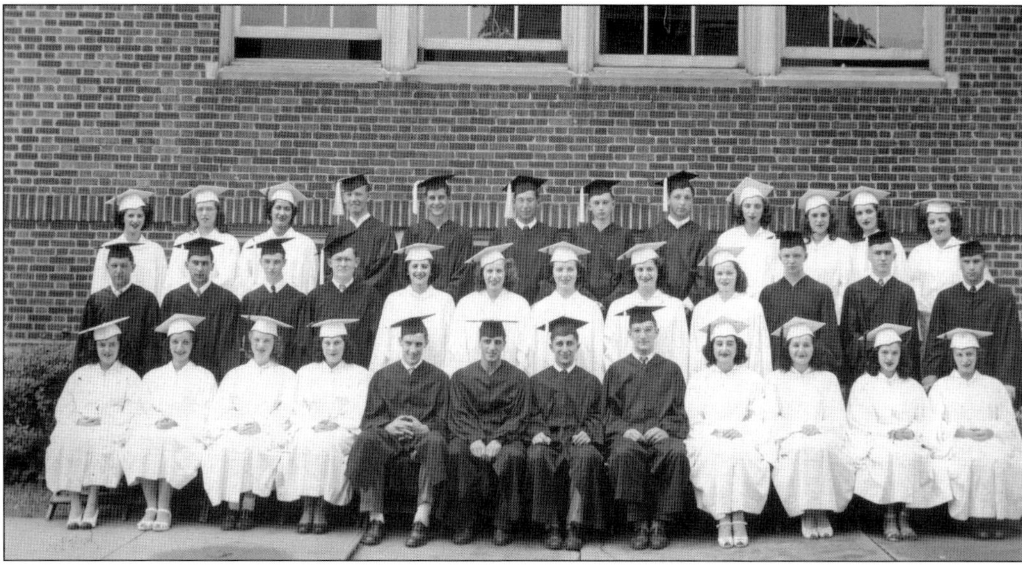

**Frankfort High School Class of 1948.** Seen above in front of the high school is the class of 1948, which included, from left to right, (first row) Mary Pepitone, Rose Librera, Margaret Knoblock, Carmela Puleo, Joseph Bono, Frank Reina, Francis Blanco, James Case, Marie Maida, Mary Gelose, Virginia Serway, and Carmela Filingeri; (second row) Paul Maphia, Salvatore Nicolette, Joseph Terras, Edson Beckwith, Dolores Gorea, Muriel Krick, Mary Ann Collins, Marie Plano, Ann Waldron, Francis Sharmack, John Steinhilber, and Alex Chard; (third row) Frances Durse, Marilyn Wilson, Catherine Latella, John Murray, Dominick Merle, James Case, Thomas Nedzynski, Robert VanDusen, Florence DiMaggio, Nina Zito, Josephine Cataline, and Dolores Thomas. The photograph below shows the 1948 Frankfort cheerleaders. They are, from left to right, Mary Ann Collins, Dolores Gorea, Marie Maida, Elvira Gatto, Ann Waldron, Frances Durse, and Muriel Krick. (Both, courtesy of Marilyn Hughes.)

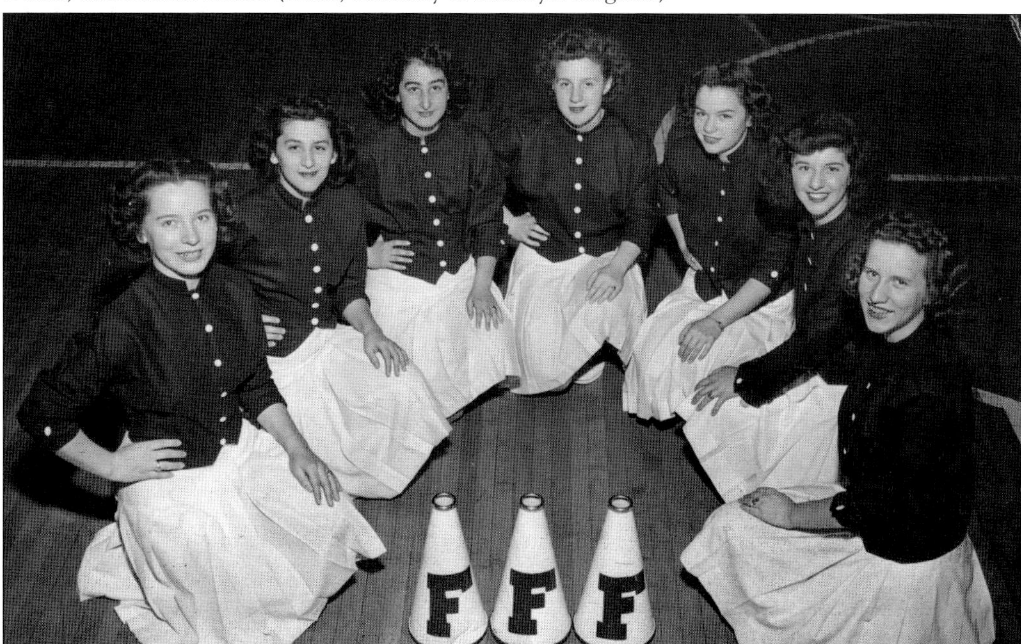

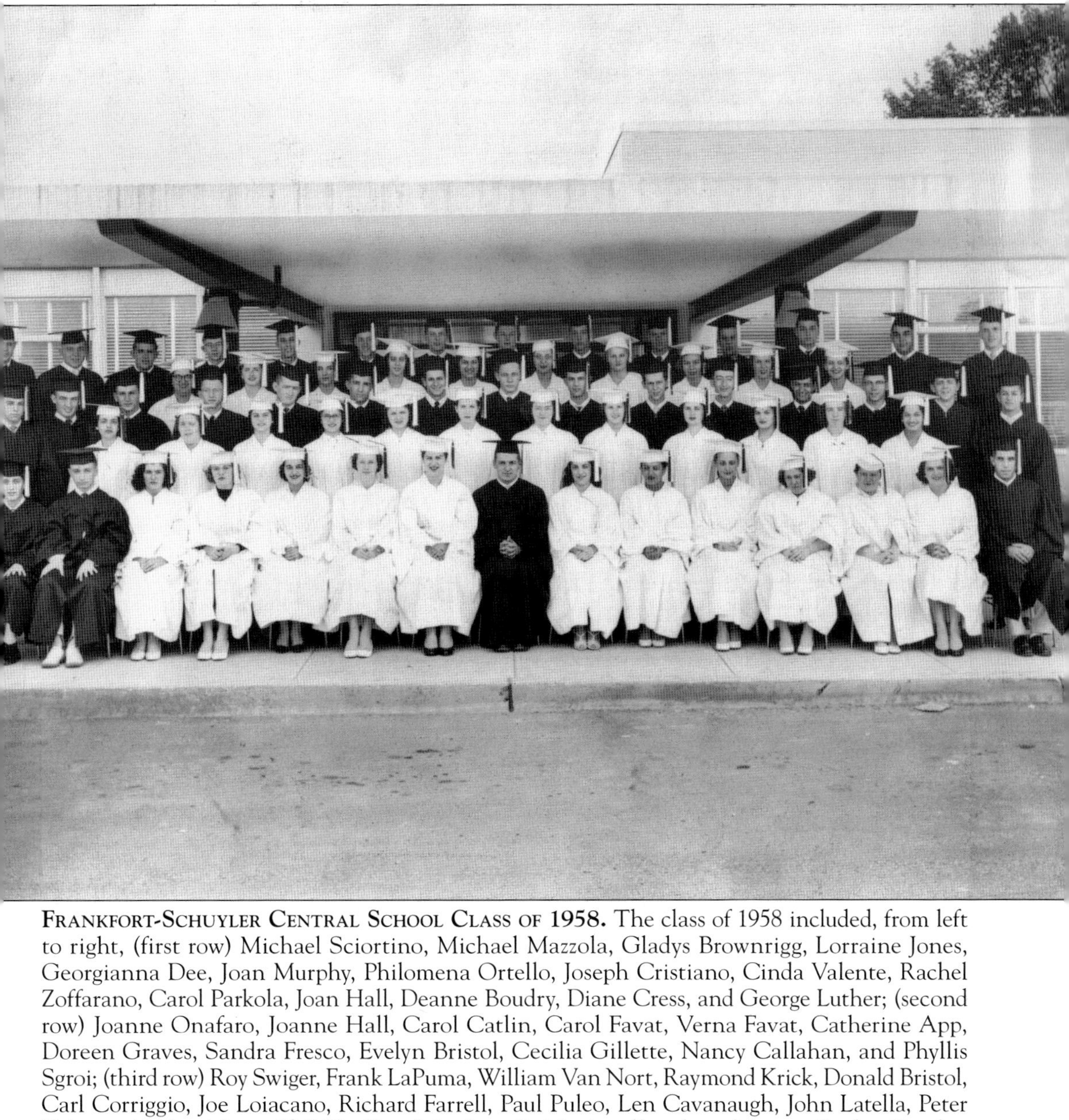

**FRANKFORT-SCHUYLER CENTRAL SCHOOL CLASS OF 1958.** The class of 1958 included, from left to right, (first row) Michael Sciortino, Michael Mazzola, Gladys Brownrigg, Lorraine Jones, Georgianna Dee, Joan Murphy, Philomena Ortello, Joseph Cristiano, Cinda Valente, Rachel Zoffarano, Carol Parkola, Joan Hall, Deanne Boudry, Diane Cress, and George Luther; (second row) Joanne Onafaro, Joanne Hall, Carol Catlin, Carol Favat, Verna Favat, Catherine App, Doreen Graves, Sandra Fresco, Evelyn Bristol, Cecilia Gillette, Nancy Callahan, and Phyllis Sgroi; (third row) Roy Swiger, Frank LaPuma, William Van Nort, Raymond Krick, Donald Bristol, Carl Corriggio, Joe Loiacano, Richard Farrell, Paul Puleo, Len Cavanaugh, John Latella, Peter Volente, Al Henrickson, Phil Chuff, and Anthony LaMonica; (fourth row) Joanne Spohn, Carolyn Baldwin, Joanne Henrickson, Margaret Hatton, Rita Castellano, Jeanette Rappa, Lannell Hakes, Margaret Mack, Mary Dempsey, and Rita Juteau; (fifth row) Jim Barnett, Howard Charbonneau, George Sylvester, Stan Wolanski, Tom Maneen, Joe DeGristina, Dave Russell, Henry Sharo, Wayne Kusinski, Jim Cristensen, Henry Kinney, Brian Bunce, George Feduccia, and Jim Hocking. (Courtesy of Rita Yashinski.)

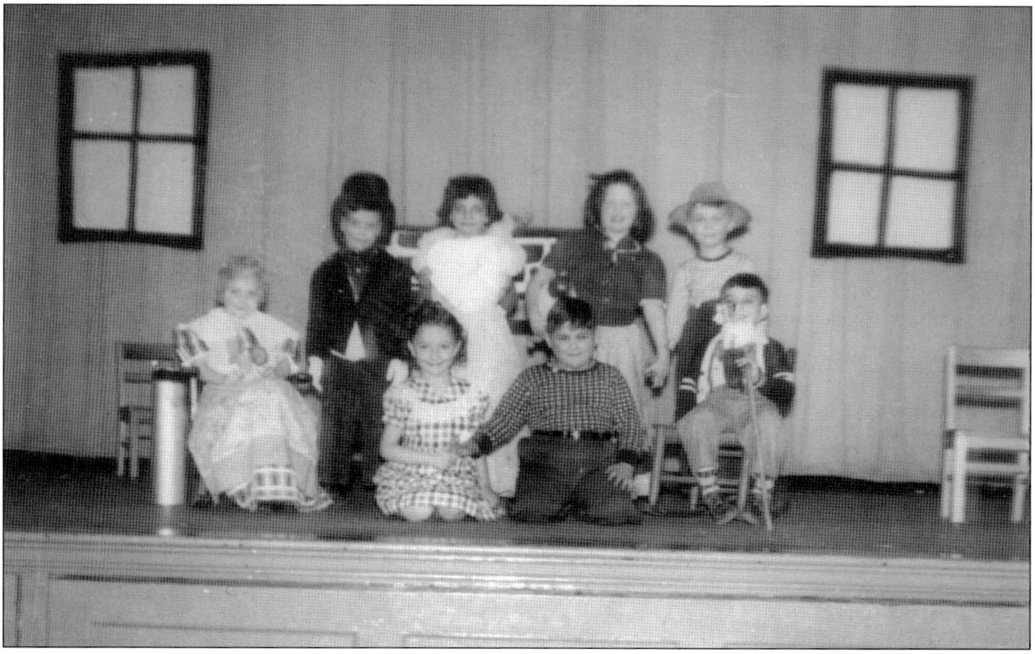

**North Side School Play.** This elementary school on the corner of Church and Orchard Streets was the site of many childhood memories, including this school play put on by the second and third grades around 1953. The actors included, from left to right, (first row) Kay Kilgress and George Bianchi; (second row) Evelyn Bunce, Joseph Frank, Carol Kipper, Pamela Walsh, Eugene Kipper, and Robert Manno. (Courtesy of Eugene and Eileen Kipper.)

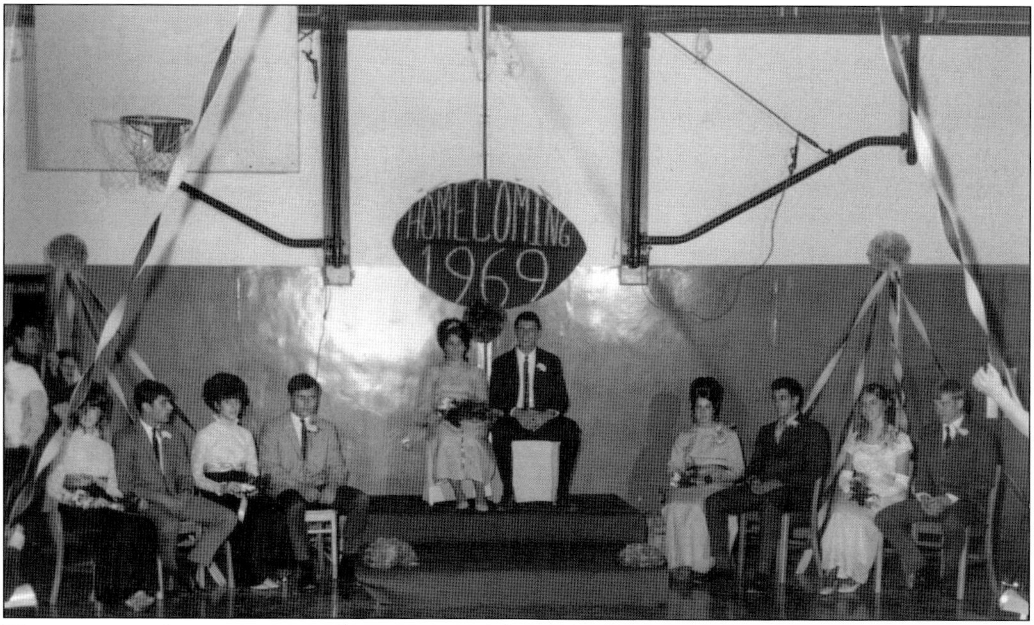


**Homecoming Court, 1969.** The 1969 Frankfort-Schuyler Central School homecoming court included, from left to right, Roseann Nicastro, Rick Plano, Marjo Brooks, Ken Brown, Mary Lille (queen), Mike Scalise (king), Jo Jo Bianchi, Jody Grippe, Miriam Carlson, and Dennis Tarnacki. (Courtesy of Jody Grippe.)

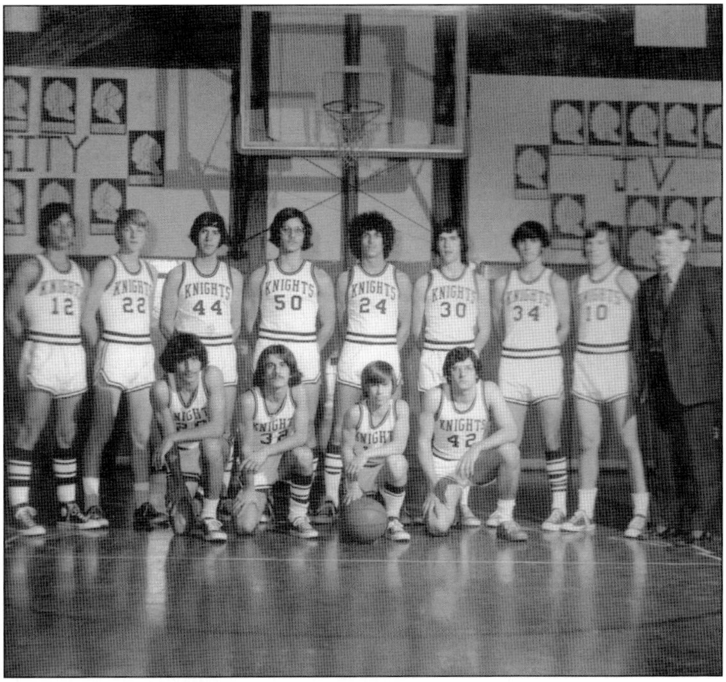


**FRANKFORT-SCHUYLER HIGH SCHOOL BASKETBALL TEAM, 1973–1974.** This team had a successful season, beating Beaver River 65-60 in the Section III finals and going on to play West Side in the finals, where it lost 77-62. The team included, from left to right, (kneeling) Joe Bellino, George Frank, Rich Murphy, and Andy Barberio; (standing) Mike Iagnocco, Peter Thomas, Rich Zabinski, Jim Nasto, Fred Pumilio, John Button, Joe Sullivan, James Wallace, and coach Tom Bracken. (Courtesy of Tom Bracken.)

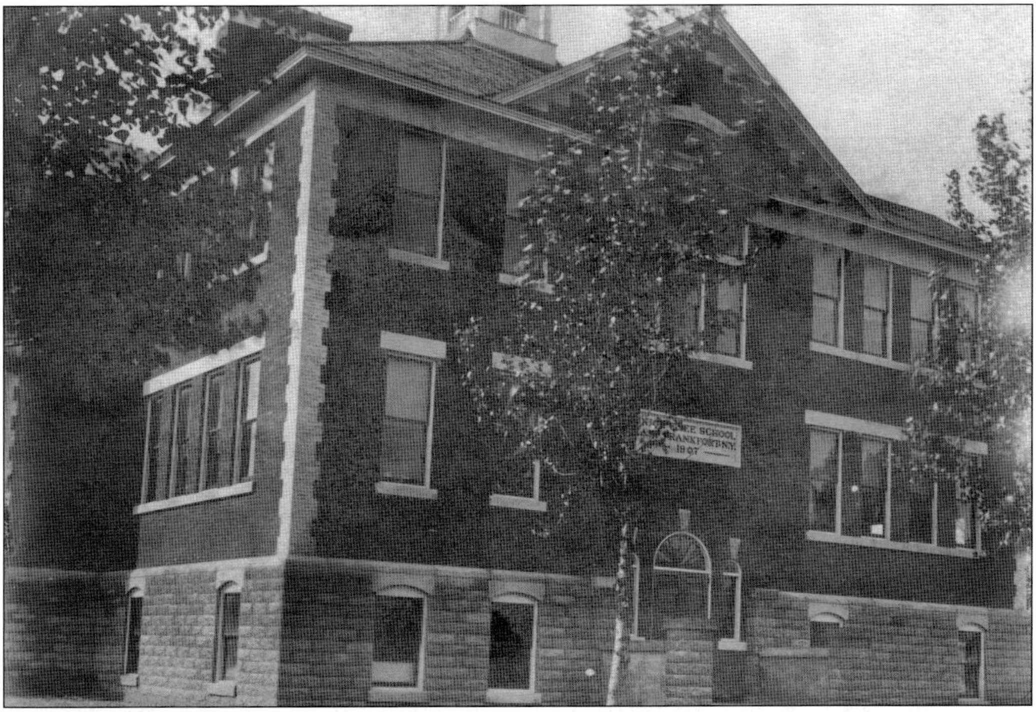

**EAST FRANKFORT SCHOOL.** Union Free School No. 1 was also known as East Frankfort School. In 1907, land was acquired for it on Bargy Road (now McGowan Road), and the school opened on March 24, 1908. In 1928, the school was annexed to the Ilion School District. In 1954, a gymnasium and auditorium were added. The school closed in 1973 and is now an apartment building. (Courtesy of Lillian Gaherty.)

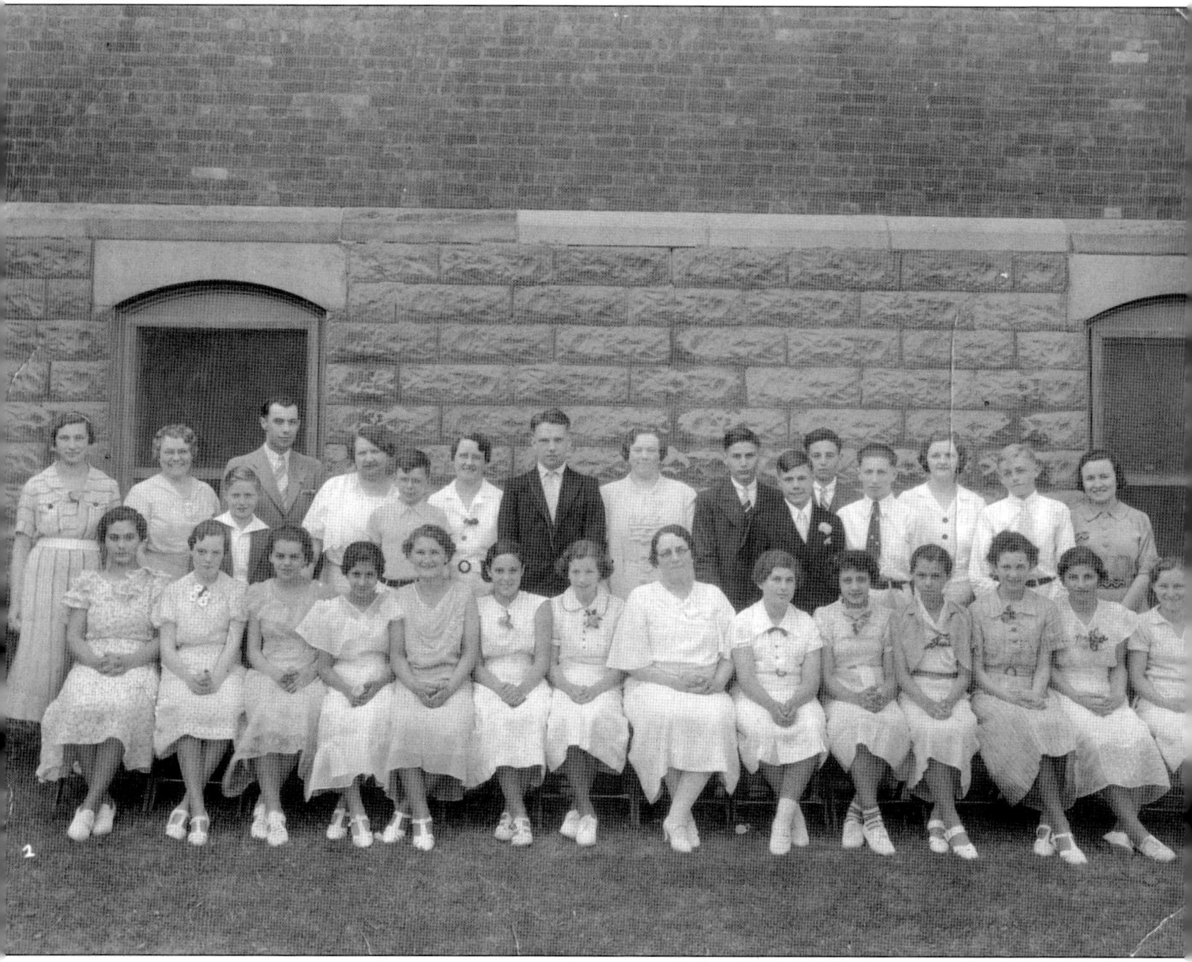

**East Frankfort Eighth-Grade Graduating Class, 1936.** The 22 graduates of East Frankfort School, accompanied by their principal, Mabel Petrie, and members of the faculty, visited the state office buildings at Albany, a custom in lieu of holding graduation exercises. The class had a luncheon at the Wellington Hotel, and, on its return, a banquet was held at the Carlton Restaurant in Herkimer. Seen here are, from left to right, (first row) Alma Kinney, Katherine Kast, Alice Van Alstine, Rose Nicolette, Virginia Sinardo, Eva Leonis, Mary O'Dell, Verna Casullo, Josephine Rich, Principal Petrie, Lula Van Dusen (class secretary), Joan Hoffman (class president), Anna Catlin, and Dorothy Farley; (second row) Grace Maneen, Grace Steele (fourth-grade teacher), William Van Vechten (sixth-grade teacher), Marjorie Shaul (third-grade teacher), Donald Osterhout, Catherine Meurant (fifth-grade teacher), Albert Greshle, Leona Whiter (second-grade teacher), Richard St. John, Anthony Dunadee (class treasurer), Salvatore Nicolette, Romeo Patrei, Leland Markley (class vice president), Virginia Mentz (seventh-grade teacher), Joseph Morgenson, and Margaret Harris (first-grade teacher). (Courtesy of Eva Tripple.)

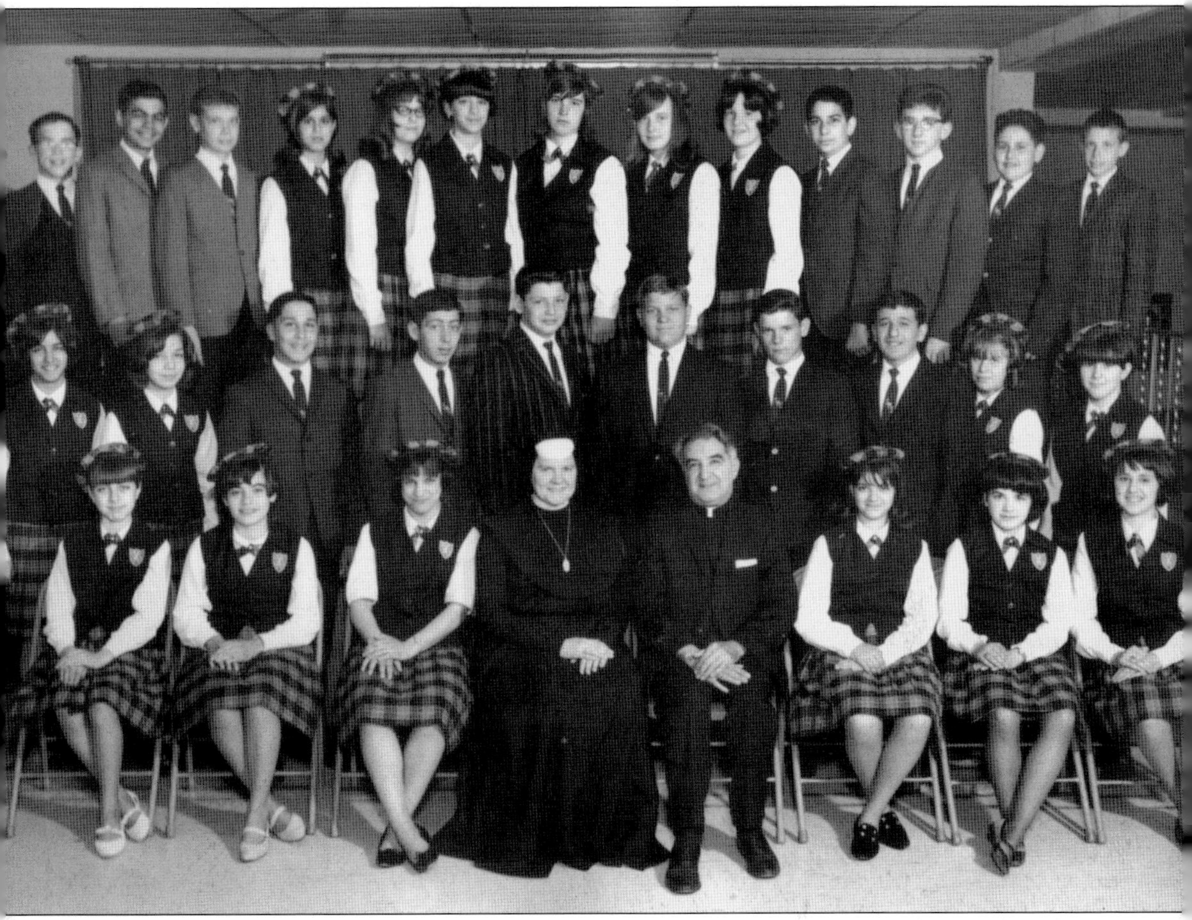

**St. Mary's School.** St. Mary's School opened in September 1962 with four grades. Staffing the school for its first two years were the Capauchin Sisters of Ringwood, New Jersey. From 1964 to 1981, the school was staffed by the Sisters of the Presentation and offered kindergarten through eighth grade. Construction on the school was completed in 1962 on the site of the former Sarah M. Piper School on the corner of Frankfort Street and Third Avenue. It was closed in 1981 when it merged with Annunciation School in Ilion. Seen here is the first graduating class, of 1966–1967, which included, from left to right, (first row) Geraldine Kattato, Mary Ahern, Gwendolyn Ganci, Sister Mary Dorothea, Rev. Michael Fufferd, Susan Leogrande, Francesca Recchio, and Mary Iocovozzi; (second row) Rosemary Chard, Mary Petrilli, John Girolamo, Thomas Vallone, Larry Tripoli, Anthony Tarnacki, John Tubia, James Thurston, unidentified, and Nora Riente; (third row) Salvatore Castardi, Craig Marrone, Andrew Zaffarano, Michael Fiorentino, Patricia Rosemyer, unidentified, Barbara Caruso, Sue Marcoline, Clare Thomas, Rose Farwege, Carmen Cross, Frank Vivacqua, Salvatore Vivacqua, and Michael Worlock. (Courtesy of Angela Thurston.)

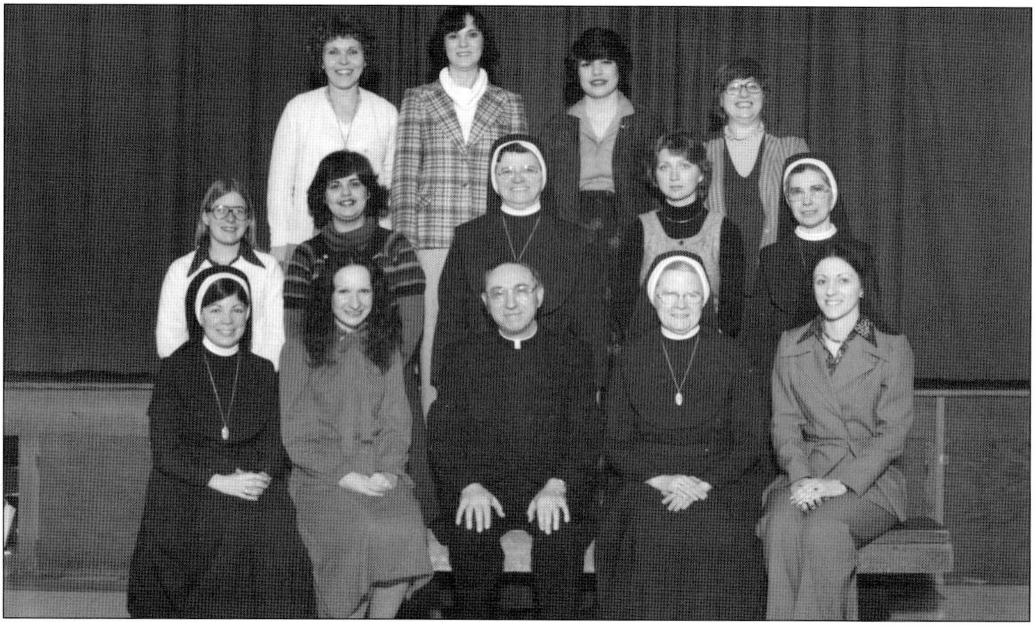

**St. Mary's Faculty, 1979–1980.** Seen here are, from left to right, (first row) Sister Maureen, Sue Holden, Fr. Alfred Lamanna, Sister Dorothea, and Marilyn Salvaggio; (second row) Kathy DeGarmo, Mary Ann Cirillo, Sister Mary Eucharia, unidentified, and Sister Mary Aidan; (third row) Leslie Favro, Regina Winkler, Cindy Magro, and unidentified. (Courtesy of Our Lady Queen of Apostles.)

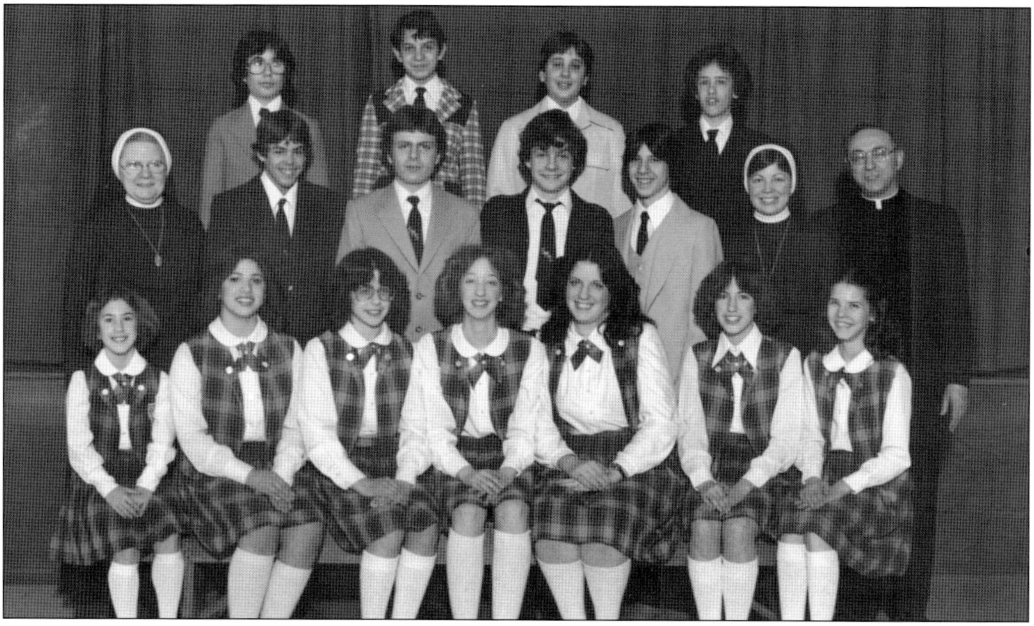

**St. Mary's Eighth Grade, 1979–1980.** Seen here are, from left to right, (first row) Tanya Bentz, Agatha Lombardo, Diane Parlagreco, Chris Belmont, Dresden Engle, Linda Spina, and Mary Niznik; (second row) Sister Mary Dorothea, Frank Gonyea, Frank Mirabile, Jim Martin, Louis Vulcano, Sister Maureen, and Fr. Alfred Lamanna; (third row) Mike Laura, John Javitz, Mike Wilk, and Tom Maneen. (Courtesy of Our Lady Queen of Apostles.)

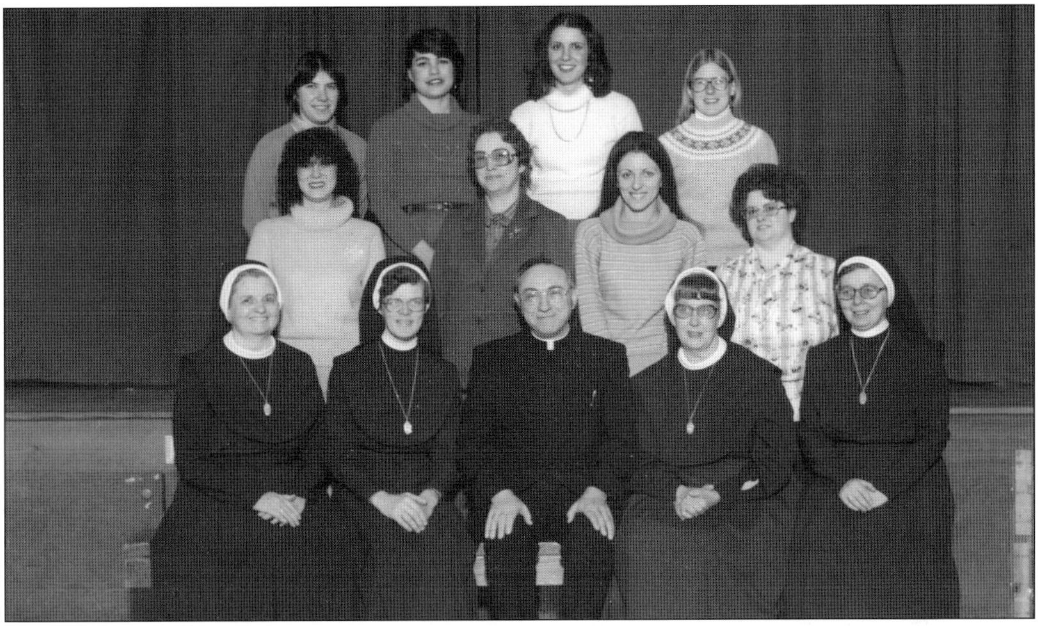

**St. Mary's Faculty, 1980–1981.** The last faculty at St. Mary's School included, from left to right, (first row) Sister Mary Xavier, Sister Mary Dominica, Fr. Alfred Lamanna, Sister Mary Angela, and Sister Jean Marie; (second row) Regina Winkler, Virginia Hunt, Marilyn Salvaggio, and Diana Sadlon; (third row) Jackie Zaffarano, Cindy Magro, Geri Perritano, and Cathy DeGarmo. (Courtesy of Marilyn Salvaggio.)

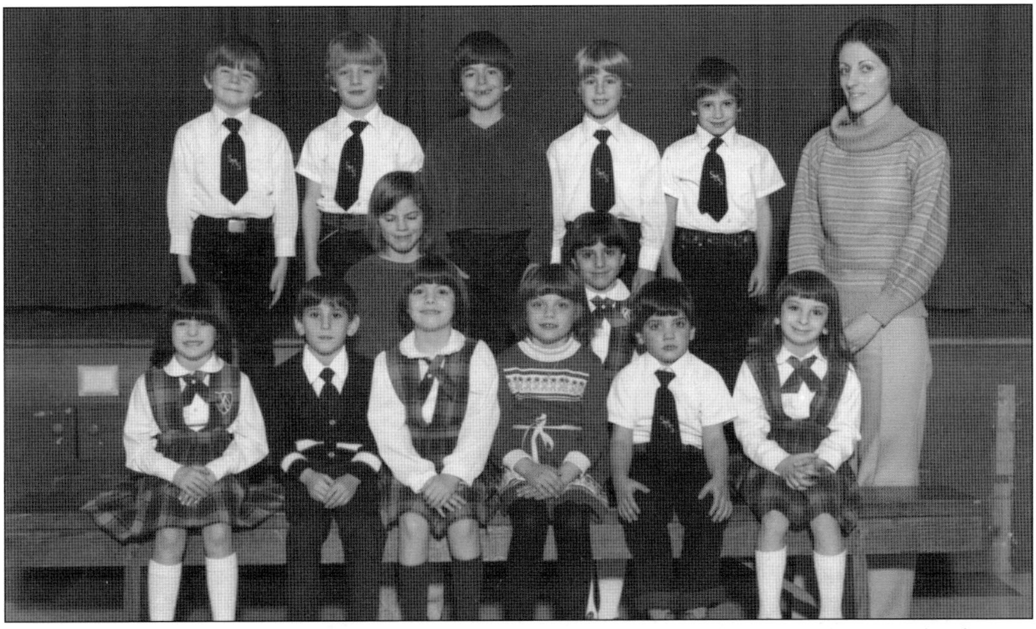

**St. Mary's First Grade, 1981.** This class included, from left to right, (first row) Christie Rutigliano, Bobby Scalise, Anna Maria Lombardo, Leslie Billman, Michael Giambrone, and Angeline McCumber; (second row) Tina Molling and Kim Cross; (third row) Robbie Martin, Jon Bryant, Scott Mathews, Frank Spina, Justin Palumbo, and teacher Marilyn Salvaggio. (Courtesy of Marilyn Salvaggio.)

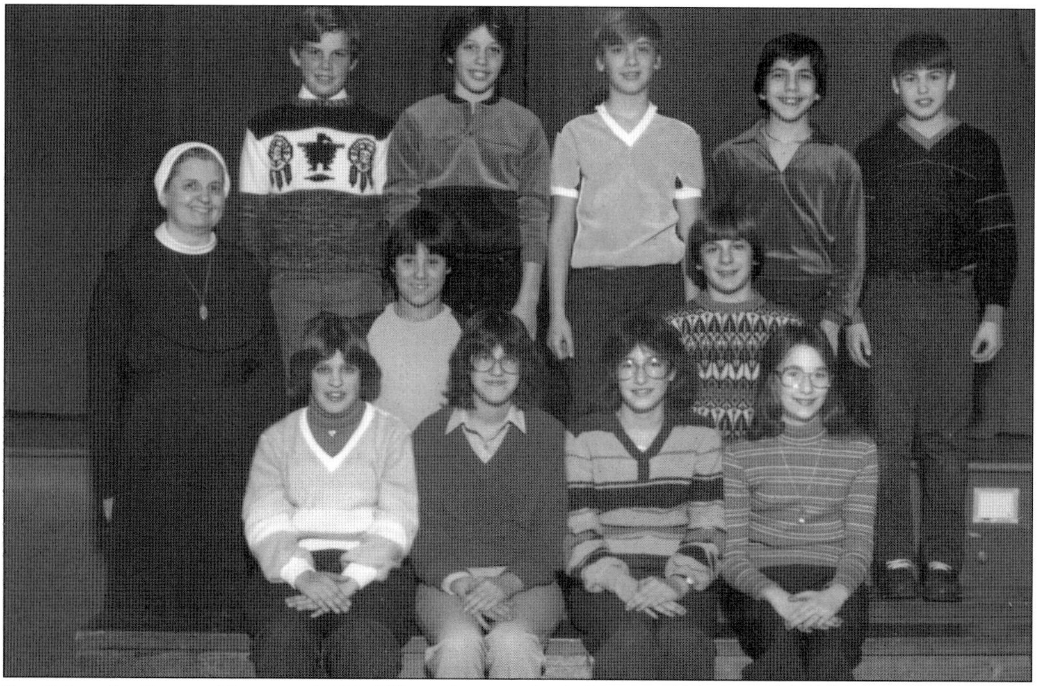

**St. Mary's Sixth Grade, 1981.** This class included, from left to right, (first row) Veronica Lombardo, Jane Spina, Lisa Yule, and Debbie Belmont; (second row) Sister Mary Xavier, John Randazzo, and Chuck Durse; (third row) Dan Bushey, Joe Cassella, Rod Usher, Mike Vulcano, and Tim Gonyea. (Courtesy of Our Lady Queen of Apostles.)

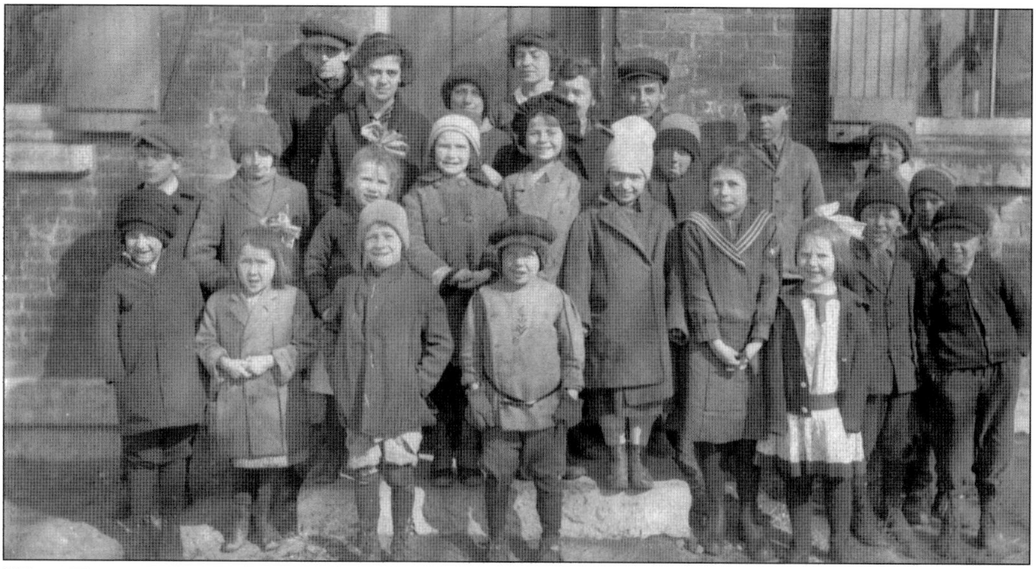

**West Frankfort School District No. 5.** This brick schoolhouse was built in 1853 at the end of Ferguson Road on old Route 5S. School records show that it had three rows of seats through the center and one on each side. Arthur Fenton (1874–1957) was a schoolteacher there in 1910. He received his teacher's certificate from West Winfield Academy and taught in the district schools in Richfield, Brighton, and West Frankfort. The boy standing to the left of the right window is James D. Ferguson III. (Courtesy of William Ferguson.)

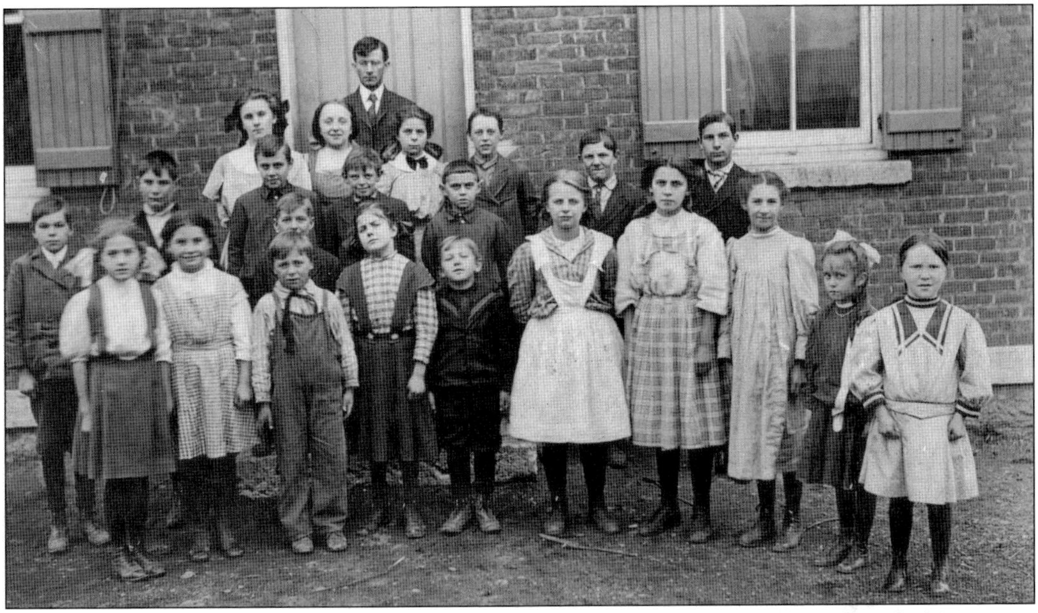

**DISTRICT NO. 5 STUDENTS, 1910.** Seen here are, from left to right, (first row) unidentified, Margaret Augar, James D. Ferguson with an unidentified boy behind him, Loretta Burke, unidentified, Marjorie Ferguson, Ruth Hughes, Jennie Blatt, Addie Faber, and Marjorie Morris; (second row) Bill Markle, unidentified, Bill Hughes, James C. Ferguson, and Edwin Hughes; (third row) Gertrude Hughes, Mary Ferguson, Ella Stevens, Frank Ferguson, Edward Burke, and Oscar Markle. Teacher Arthur Fenton is standing in the back. (Courtesy of William Ferguson.)

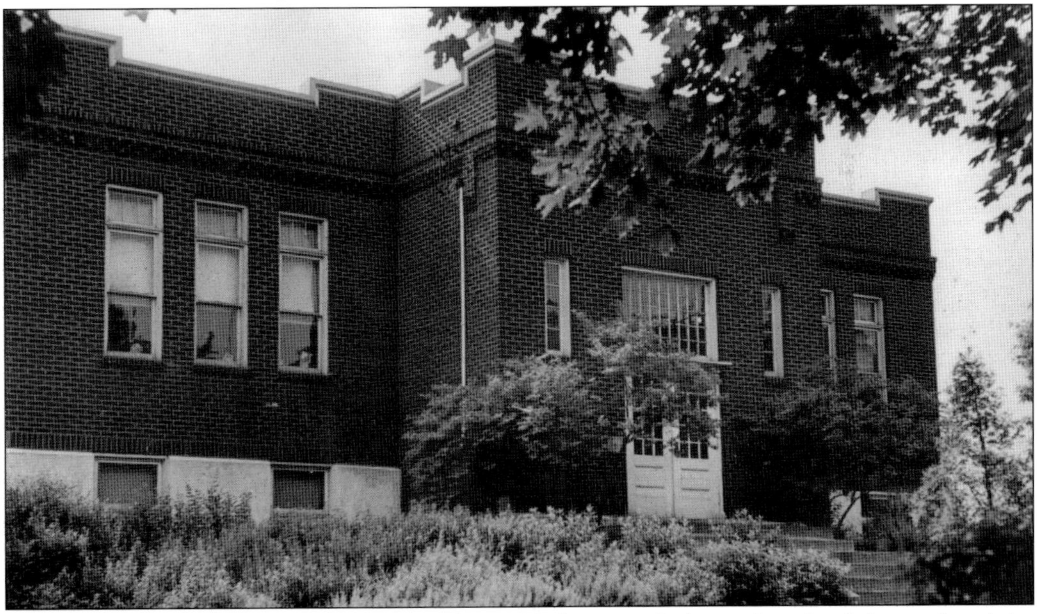

**WEST FRANKFORT ELEMENTARY SCHOOL.** This 1948 photograph shows the school that replaced the small brick district school. It was relocated across the street to the beginning of Ferguson Road, between the railroad tracks and the Erie Canal bed. It was a four-room school that taught grades one through eight, with two grades in each room. This building was replaced with a modern structure farther up Ferguson Road in 1962.

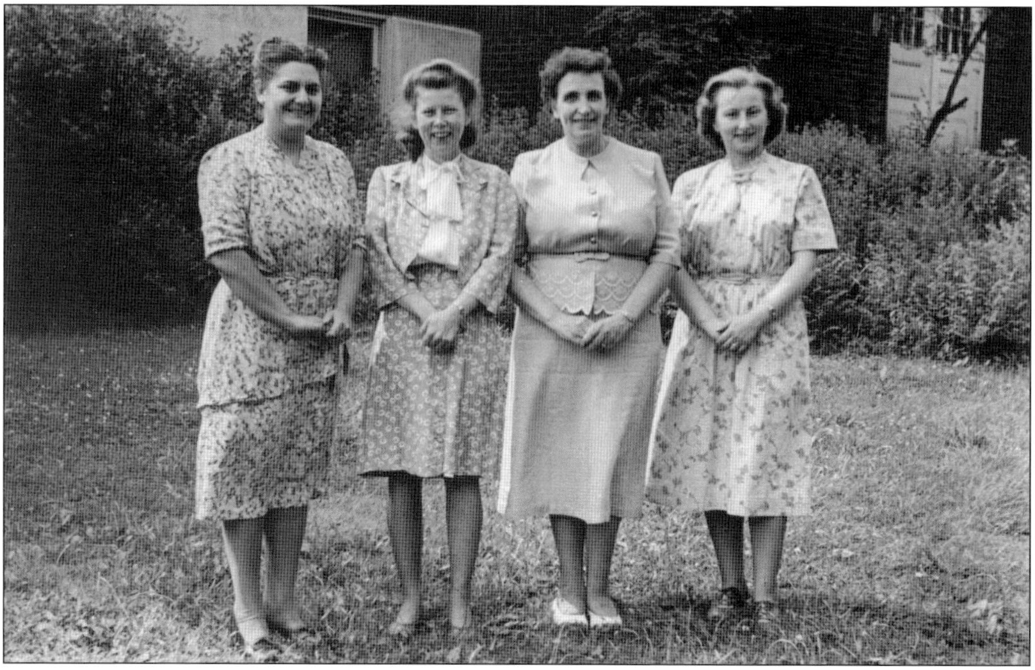

**West Frankfort Schoolteachers.** These four women were the teachers at West Frankfort Elementary School in 1948. They are, from left to right, Anne C. Marks (1913–2005), principal and seventh- and eighth-grade teacher; Mary (Neale) Maine (1915–2009), fifth- and sixth-grade teacher; Edna Stewart (1897–1975), third- and fourth-grade teacher; and Mildred (Darling) Ackley (1916–), first- and second-grade teacher.

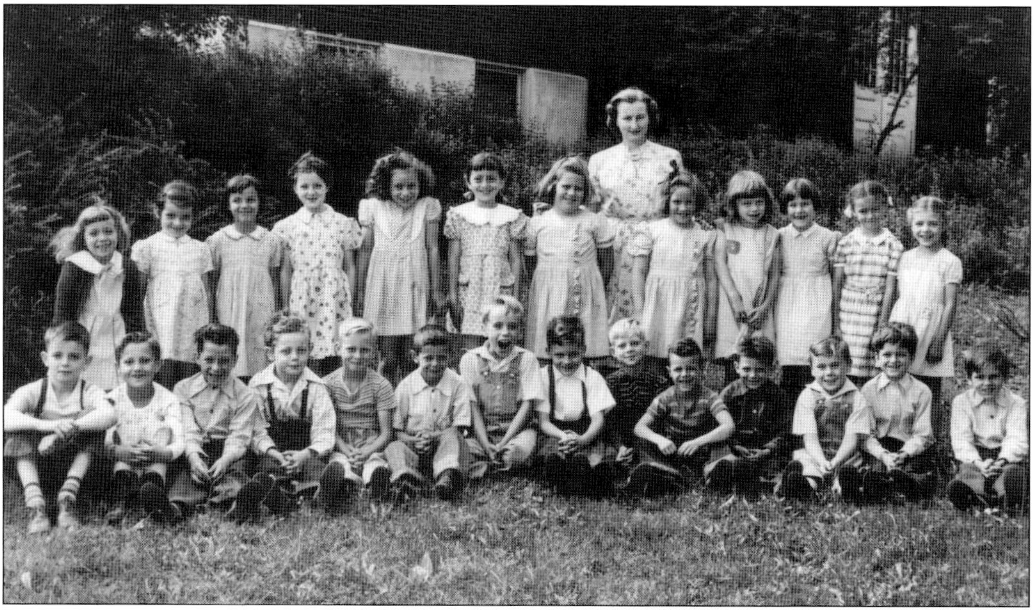

**First and Second Grade, West Frankfort School, 1948.** These students are, from left to right, (first row) Tom Williams, unidentified, Anthony Ruggerio, Dick Farrell, unidentified, Leonard Cavanaugh, Dewey Van Nort, four unidentified, David Van Nort, and two unidentified. The girls in the second row are unidentified. Teacher Mildred Ackley is standing in the back.

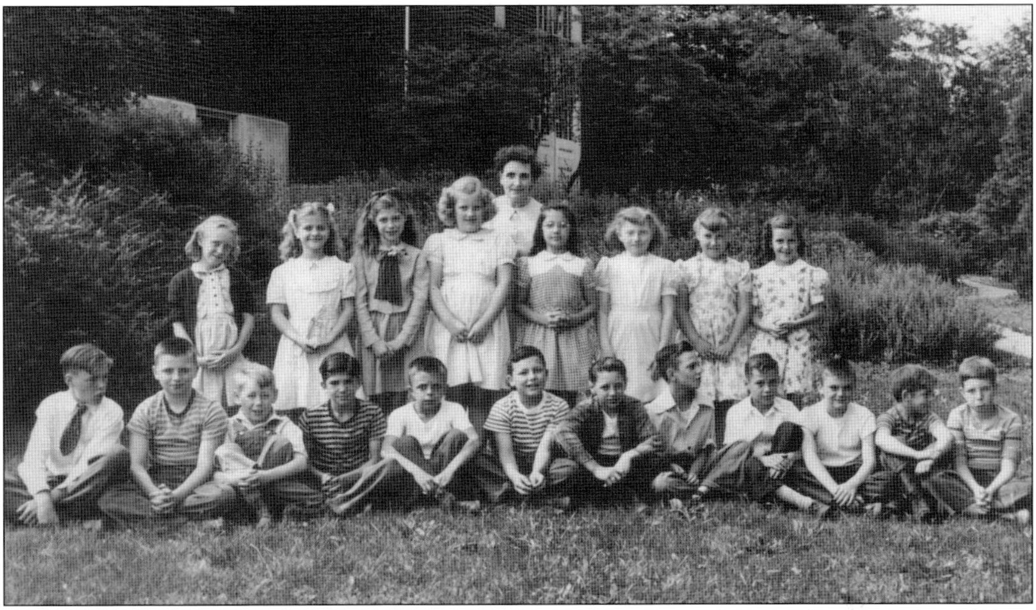

**Third and Fourth Grade, West Frankfort School, 1948.** These students are, from left to right, (first row) Willard Schuyler, Barry Franz, David Van Nort, Ronald Riehl, Charles Forbes, Salvatore LaBarbera, Robert Knapp, Richard Zakarewski, Paul Lewandowski, Dean Borden, Paul Riehl, and unidentified; (second row) Sharon Lee, Beverly Bernard, Pauline Schuyler, Eileen Volz, Harriet Amarosa, Elizabeth Ferguson, Beverly Ferguson, and Nancy Wendall. Teacher Edna Stewart is standing in the back.

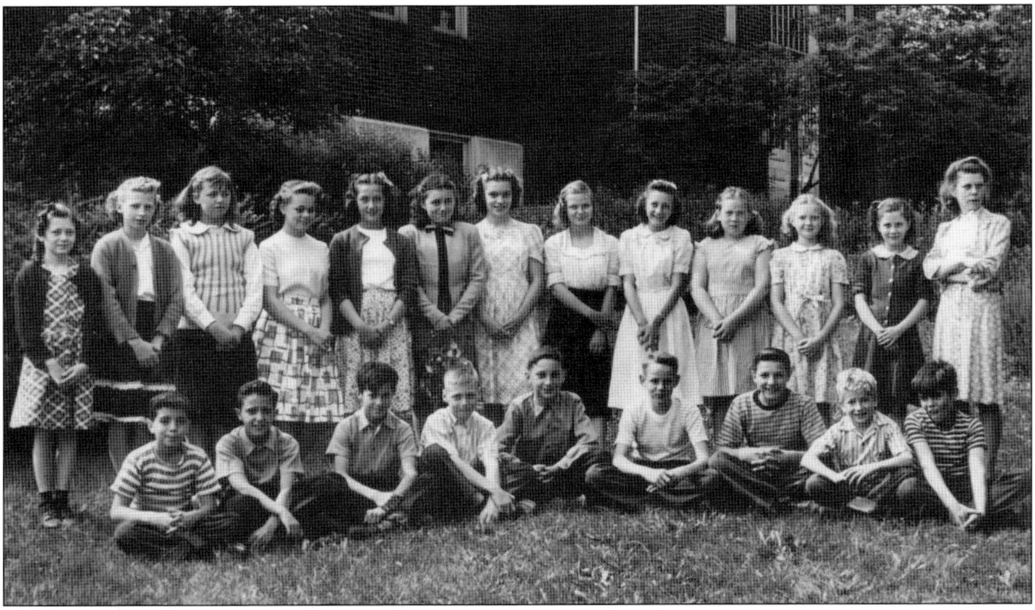

**Fifth and Sixth Grade, West Frankfort School, 1948.** These students are, from left to right, (first row) Johnny Balio, two unidentified, John Remington, Fred Lewandowski, Richard Stilwell, Frank LaBarbera, and two unidentified; (second row) Dawn Lee, Jean Homer, two unidentified, Connie Wildrick, unidentified, Martha Remington, Alice Stothers, Anna Rose Tomaino, Rosemary Van Nort, Patty Kusienski, unidentified, and teacher Mary Maine.

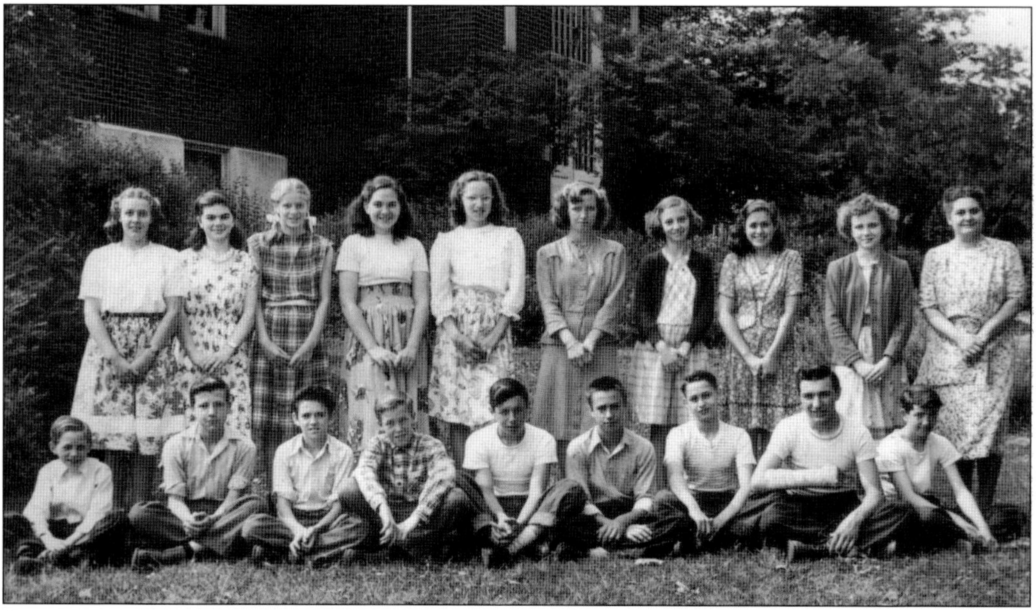

**Seventh and Eighth Grade, West Frankfort School, 1948.** These students are, from left to right, (first row) William Ferguson, Richard Wasyleski, Irvin Peters, Ronald Rehm, unidentified, Ronald Wendell, Kenneth Stilwell, Joseph LaBarbera, and unidentified; (second row) Iona Rieck, Noreen Williams, Betty Varney, Virginia Fox, Frances Czycon, Jean Homer, Dorothy Stothers, Irma Ryan, Marion Williams, and teacher Anne Marks.

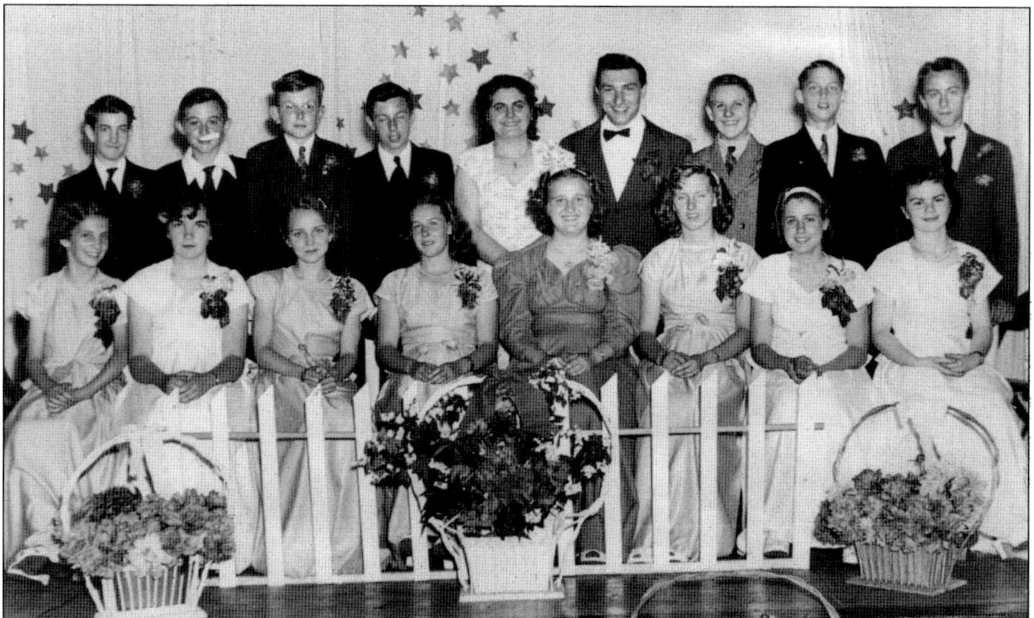

**Eighth-Grade Graduates, 1948.** Seen here are the graduates of the three schools of Dutch Hill, Brockway Road, and West Frankfort. They are, from left to right, (first row) Irma Ryan, Virginia Fox, Margaret Young, Iona Rieck, unidentified, Dorothy Stothers, Marion Williams, and Noreen Williams; (second row) unidentified, Jack McNally, Art Merry, unidentified, West Frankfort School principal Anne Marks, Joe LaBarbera, James Boden, Kenny Stilwell, and Ronnie Wendell.

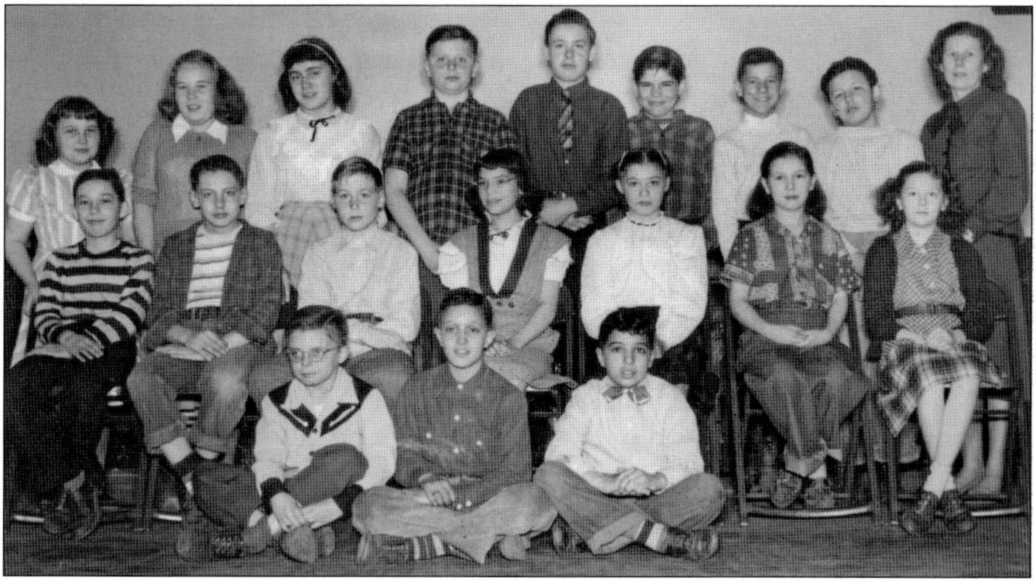

**Fifth and Sixth Grade, West Frankfort School, 1949.** Seen here are, from left to right, (first row) Charles Forbes, Louie Gigliotti, and John Balio; (second row) Paul Lewandowski, Bob Knapp, John Remington, Carolyn Meade, Pauline Schuyler, June Wildrick, and Dawn Lee; (third row) Bev Ferguson, Rosemary Van Nort, Betty Forbes, Barry Franz, Willard Schuyler, Donald Riele, Bob Wasyleski, Sal LaBarbera, and teacher Mary Maine. (Courtesy of Beverly Ferguson Gado.)

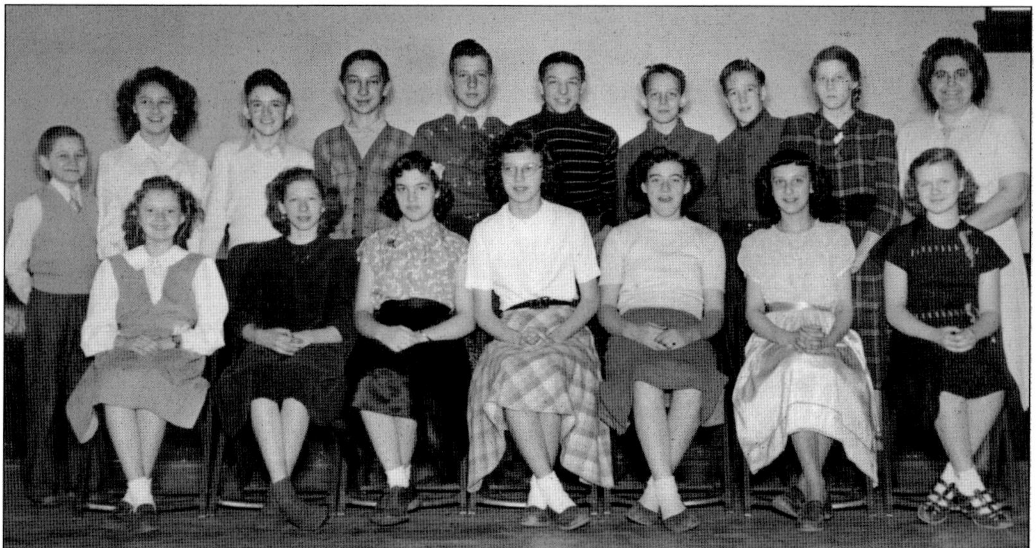

**Seventh and Eighth Grade, West Frankfort School, 1949.** Seen here are, from left to right, (first row) Patty Kusienski, Jean Homer, Martha Remington, Frances Czyczon, Georgianna Barnes, Anna Rose Tomaino, and Alice Stothers; (second row) Bill Ferguson, Connie Wildrick, Irvin Peters, Fred Lewandowski, Richard Wasyleski, Frank LaBarbera, Richard Stilwell, Ronnie Rehm, Betty Varney, and principal Anne Marks. (Courtesy of William Ferguson.)

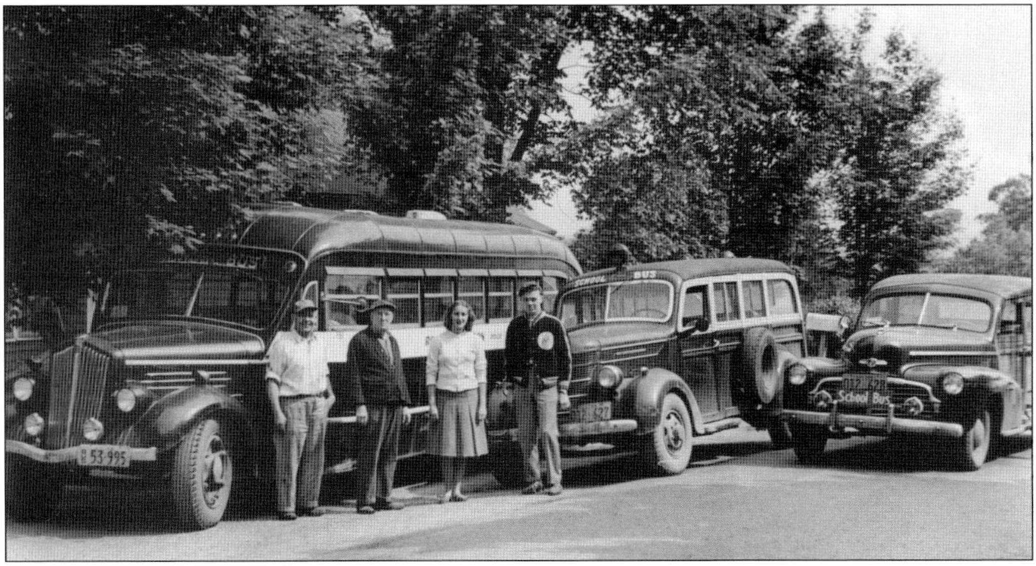


**ROY KULL BUS SERVICE.** Across Ferguson Road from West Frankfort School was the home of Roy Kull (1894–1985, far left), who operated a bus service for the school. Kull's son Harold (1925–2000, far right) and Harold's wife, Jean (1928–), both helped drive the buses. Maintenance man Joe Borden (1878–1955) is second from the left. The Kulls donated the land for the "new" West Frankfort School on the east side of Ferguson Road.

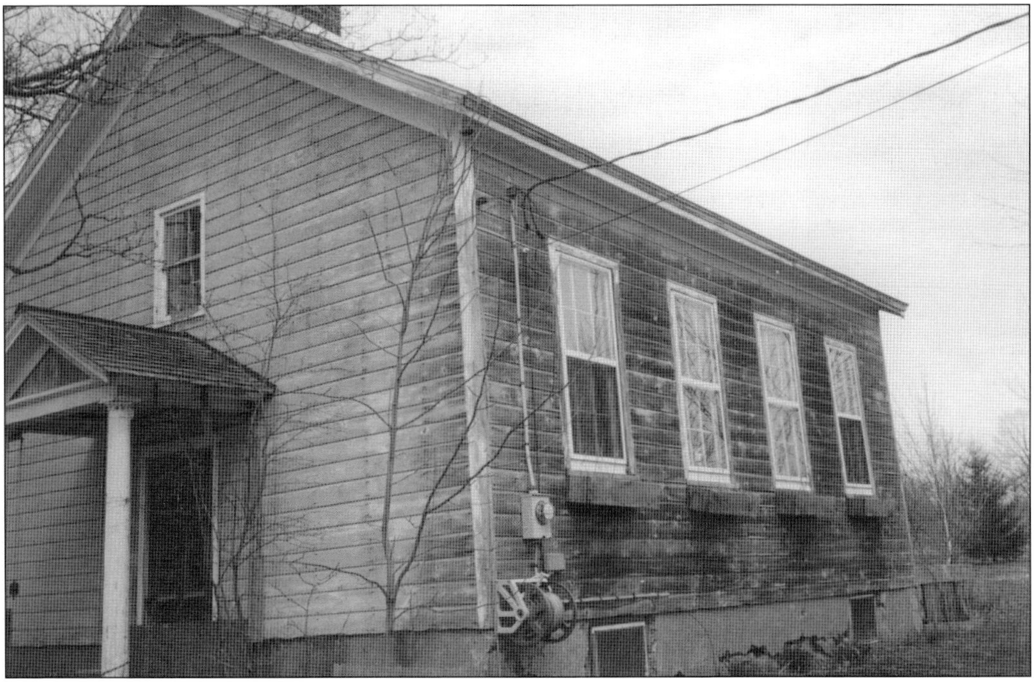

**SCHOOL DISTRICT NO. 4.** This schoolhouse on the corner of Graffenburg and Wilson Roads was originally built of stone in 1850 and was then made into a frame structure in 1888. The students eventually began attending New Hartford schools and then the district centralized with them in 1956, when one-room schools became a thing of the past. This building still exists today as a private residence. (Courtesy of Keith McNally.)

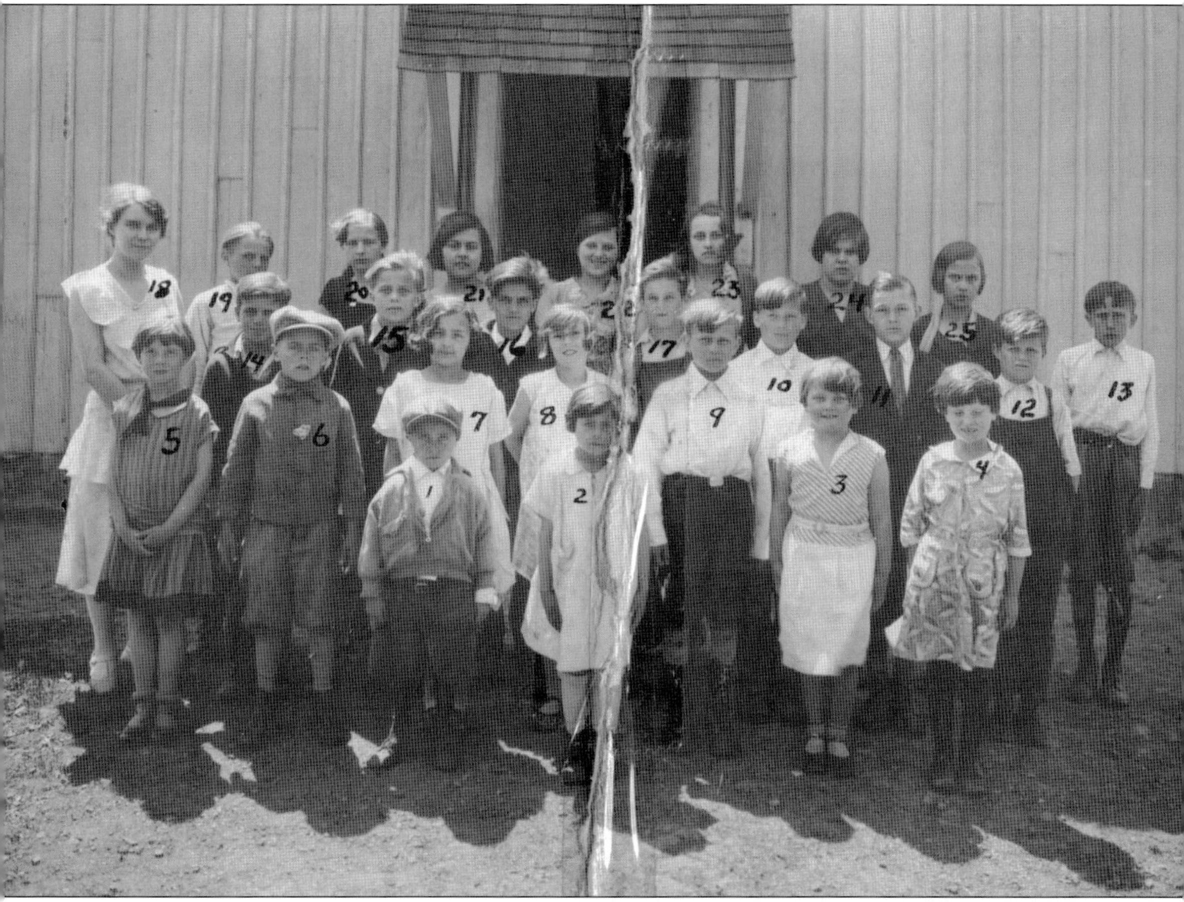

**FRANKFORT CENTER DISTRICT SCHOOL NO. 12.** Built around 1878 on Center Road near Frankfort Center, this school was used until 1954, when it was closed and deeded to the ladies auxiliary of the Frankfort Center Fire Department. In 1958, the property was deeded to the fire department, which sold it to James Ferguson, who then refurbished it into a private residence. A fire destroyed the building in 1983. This photograph was taken on June 13, 1932. Numbers were written on each student in the photograph for identification. They are (1) Lawrence Polisse, (2) Mary Polisse, (3) Jean Dresser, (4) Mary Stephenson, (5) Eunice Dougherty, (6) George Polisse, (7) Helen Dellinger, (8) Vera Jones, (9) Joseph Szczygiel, (10) Stanley Szczygiel, (11) Arthur Dellinger, (12) John Stephenson, (13) Stanley Cichol, (14) Savey Talarico, (15) John Cichon, (16) Thomas Talarico, (17) Thomas Stephenson, (18) teacher Madeline Varley (1910–1995), (19) Michael Pierhal, (20) Anna Szczygiel, (21) Thelma Dellinger, (22) Minnie Stephenson, (23) Anna Cichon, (24) Anna Carey, and (25) Gladys Carey. (Courtesy of Eunice Hanson.)

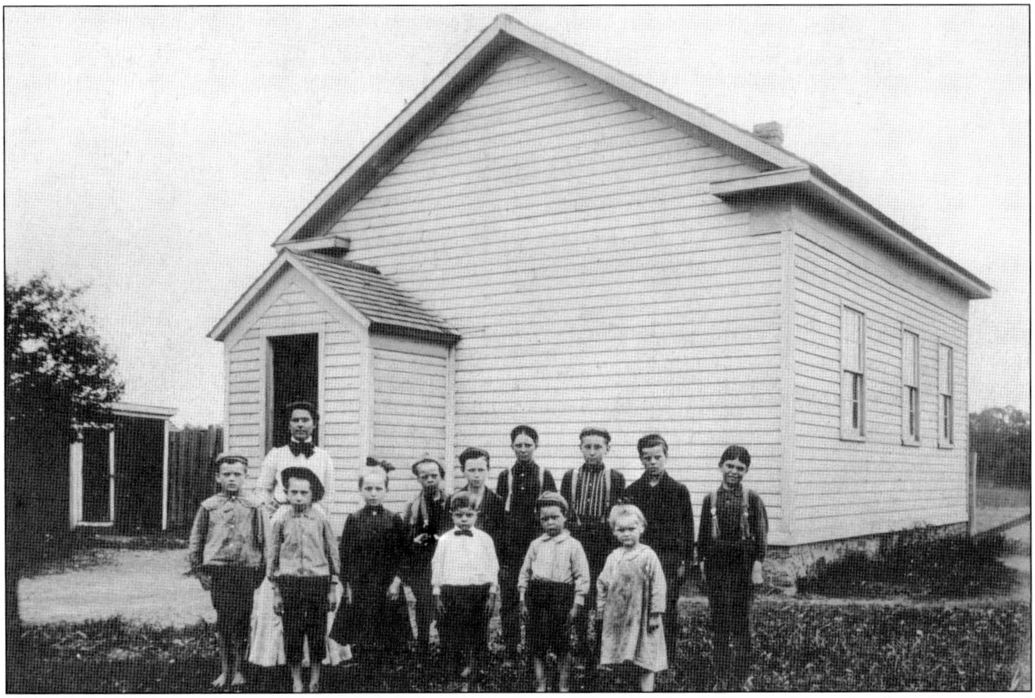

**Dutch Hill District School No. 6.** This frame school on Daley Road was built in 1855 and served local students until 1954, when the property was razed and sold to Nicholas and Martha Harmatiuk. Seen here around 1902 are, from left to right, (first row) James Bohling, Harry Markle, Jessie Bohling, Fred Dougherty, Henry Parker, and Agnes Bohling; (second row) teacher Malina Salladin Dougherty (1869–1968), David Evans, Leo Bohling, Homer Miller, Arthur Tucker, Robert Evans, and James Miller. (Courtesy of Eunice Hanson.)

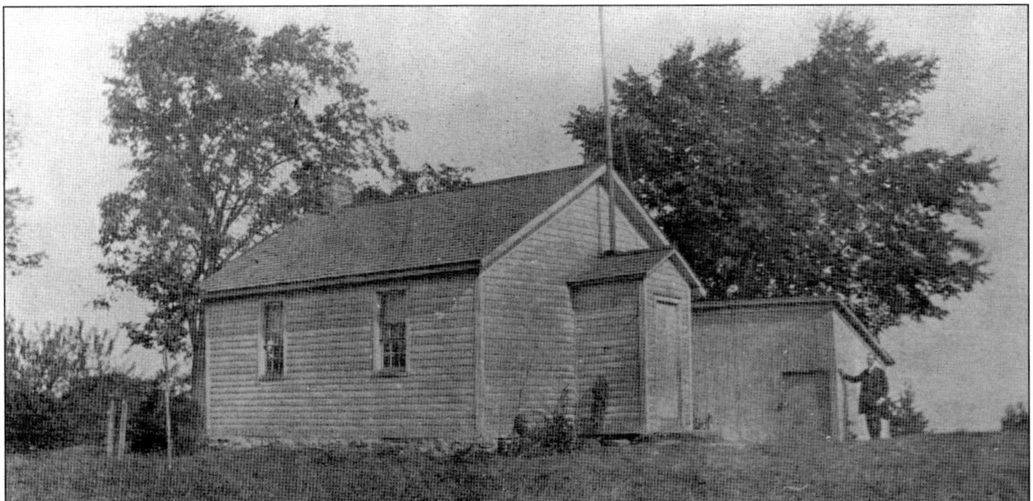

**Joslin Hill District School No. 7.** This wood-frame schoolhouse was originally built in 1822, according to school records. It was on Joslin Hill Road in the southeastern section of Frankfort. On July 1, 1954, the Frankfort-Schuyler Central School District was established, consolidating the Union Free School District in the village, a part of the East Frankfort School District, and 11 common school districts, including Joslin Hill.

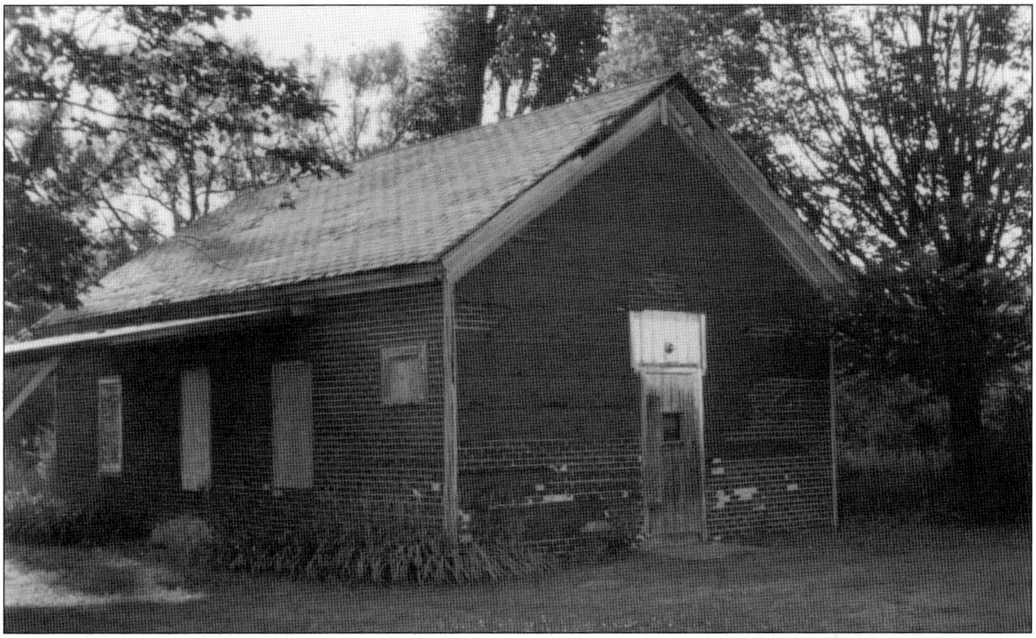

**Frankfort Hill District School No. 10.** This schoolhouse, on Albany Road near the intersection with Higby Hill Road, was built in 1841 and had board-and-batten siding. A faux-brick artificial siding was put on later. In 1956, the school district was annexed by the Sauquoit Valley Central School. Below, standing in front of the school in 1940, are, from left to right, (first row) Catherine DiNardo, Peter Weiss, Mary Demkowitch, Elizabeth Bardo, Donald Alukonis, Irene Tolpa, and Richard Wisniewicz; (second row) Leroy Bardo, Carmine DiNardo, teacher Lydia Fonda Bennett (1886–1952), Edward Dobrodziej, John Trietiak, and Paul Trietiak. Bennett taught in the rural schools of the Frankfort area for 26 years, retiring in 1942. (Both, courtesy of Keith McNally.)

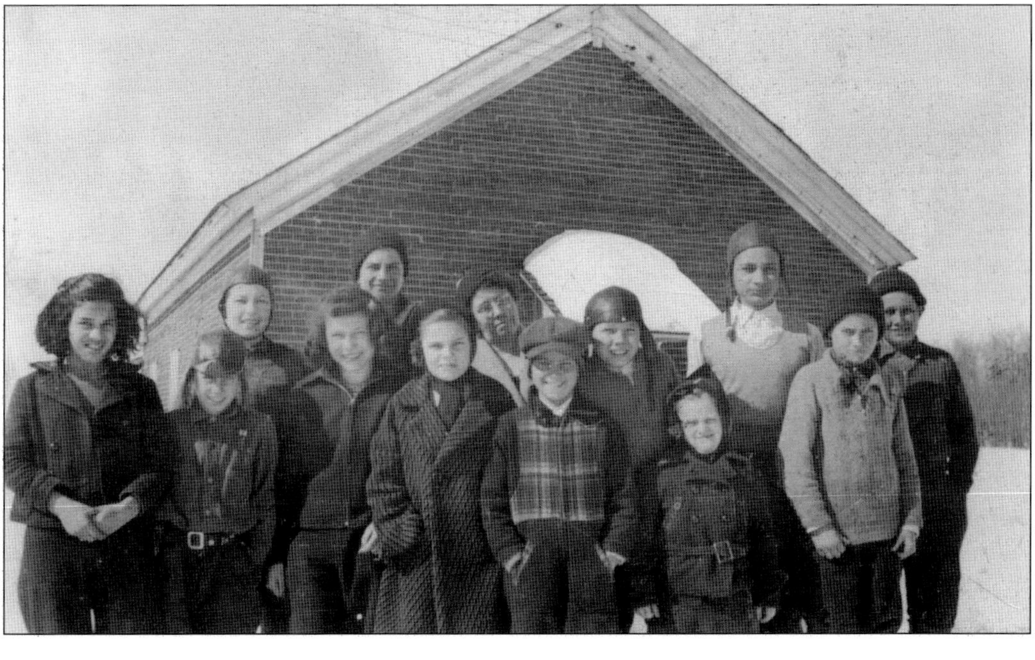

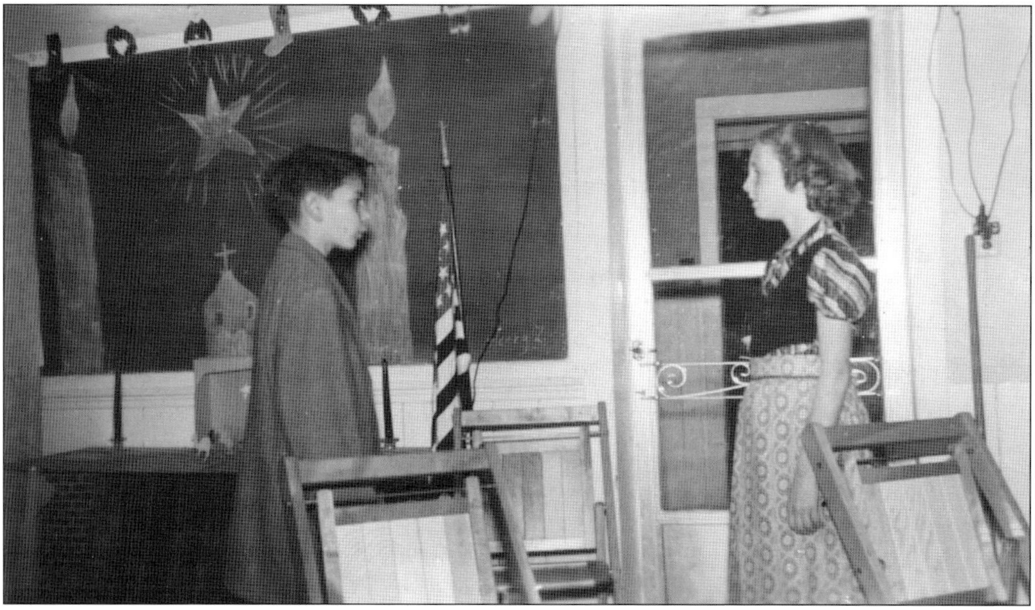

**Interior Shots of District School No. 10.** These photographs show Christmastime at Frankfort Hill School in 1948. Above, reciting their lines for a Christmas play, are Anthony Cacconie and Lillian Jones. Below are, from left to right, (first row) Rose Zakrewski, Mickey Caruso, Glenda Connine, Diane Jones, Linda Leitz, Frank Rockwell, and Anthony Cacconie; (second row) Lillian Jones, Eugene Zakrewski, Wayne Keefe, John Leitz, and Hank Zakrewski (hidden). (Both, courtesy of Keith McNally.)

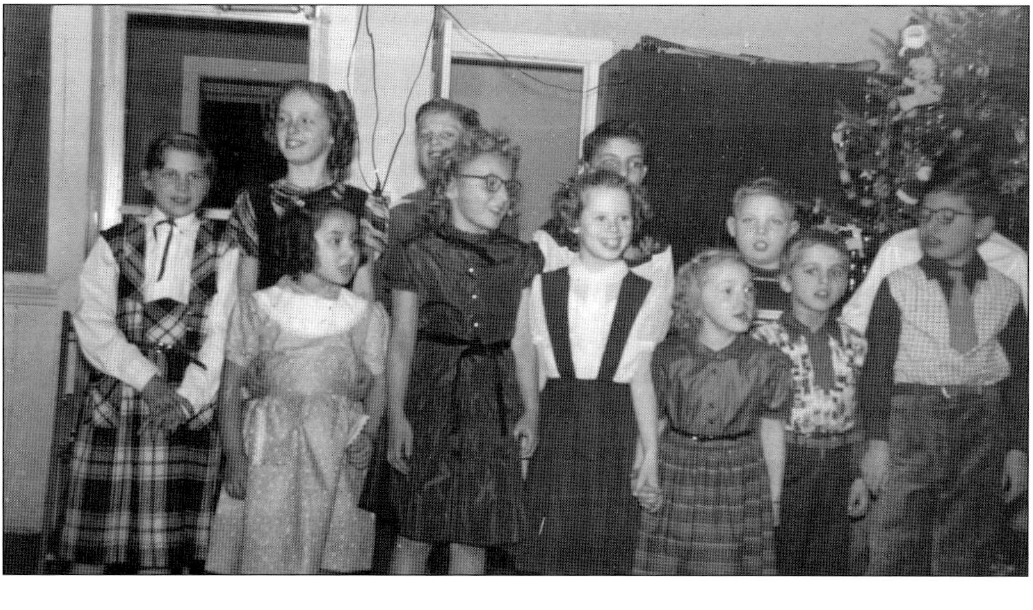

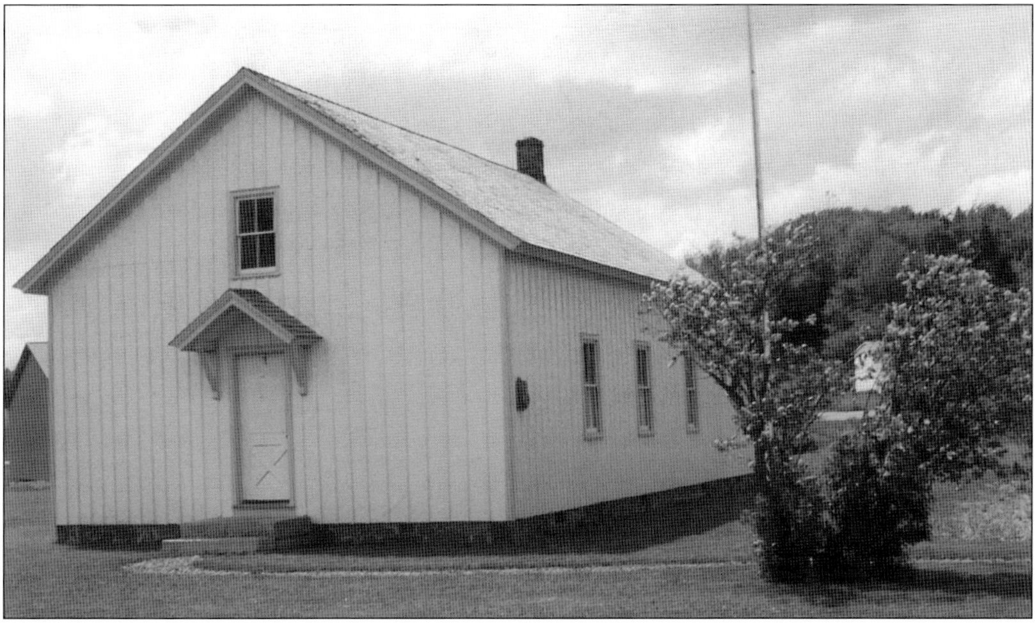

**DISTRICT NO. 10 SCHOOLHOUSE SAVED.** Through the efforts of the Frankfort Hill Historical Society, the only one-room school left in the town of Frankfort was saved. Plans to save it were started in 2005, and in 2007, the schoolhouse was lifted on to its new foundation, 10 feet from its original location, by a crane operated by Rig All, Inc., which donated its services. Jay-K Lumber Co. donated the lumber for the new supports. The building is now a museum representing what one-room schoolhouses looked like. The historical society is working with local schools to bring students on tours for the day and experience what it was like to be educated in a one-room school. The interior is currently being retrofitted to look like 1841, but with 1940s and 1950s–era desks. (Both, courtesy of Keith McNally.)

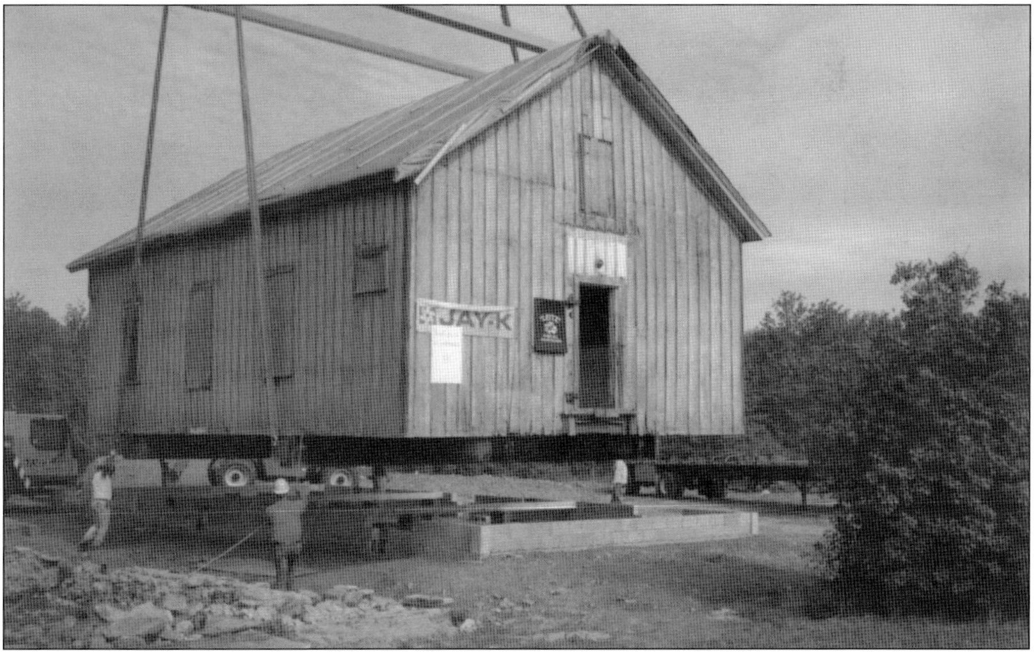

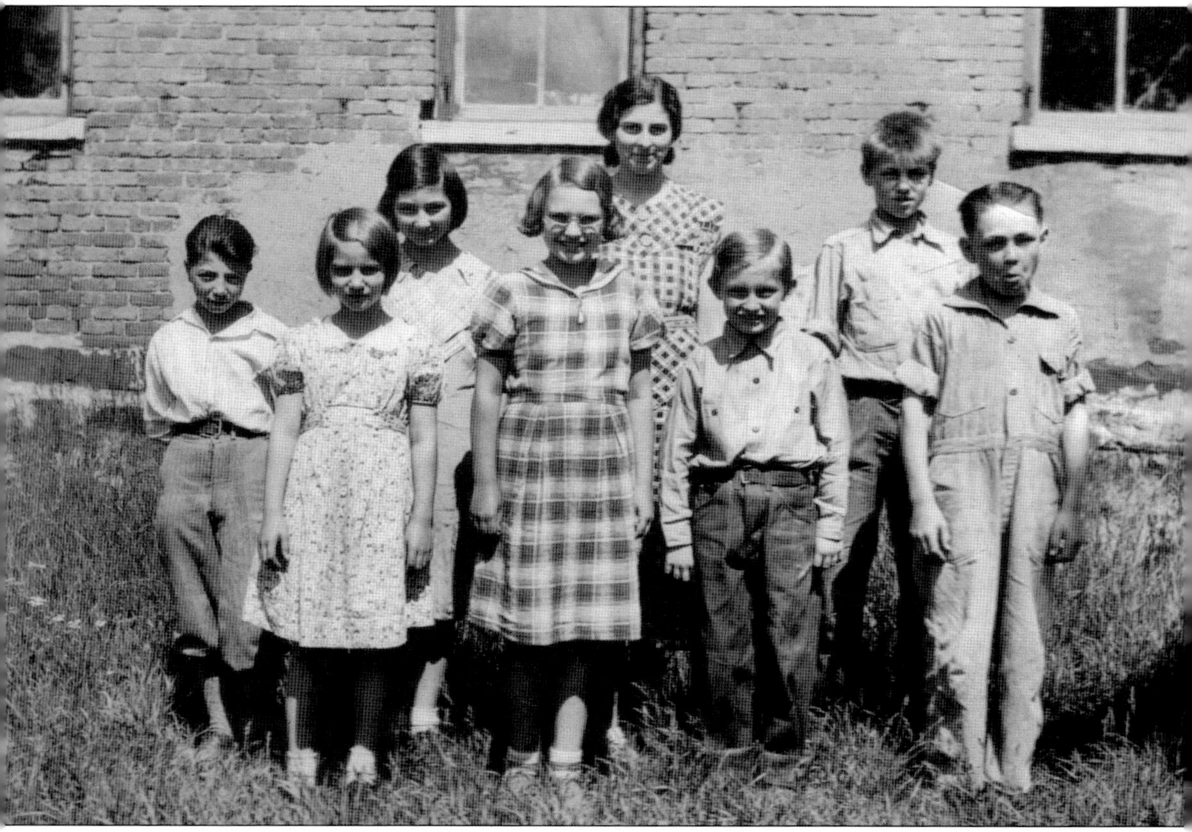

**Furnace Hill School No. 8.** This brick schoolhouse was located at the corner of Coup Hill (Higby) and Bouck Roads. This class photograph was taken in June 1932 by Henry Seeger, an amateur photographer who took school photographs in the area. These students are, from left to right, (first row) Mildred Hamer, Katherina Seeger, Henry Seeger Jr., and Vernon Harvey; (second row) John Gendian, Rose Gendian, teacher Helen Hubbell (1911–1999), and Walter Nelson. Hubbell taught in Frankfort schools for 35 years, in two one-room schools and then at Reese Road Elementary, before retiring in 1973. This building burned down in later years, after it had been turned into a private residence. (Courtesy of William Ferguson.)

# *Five*

# Business and Industry

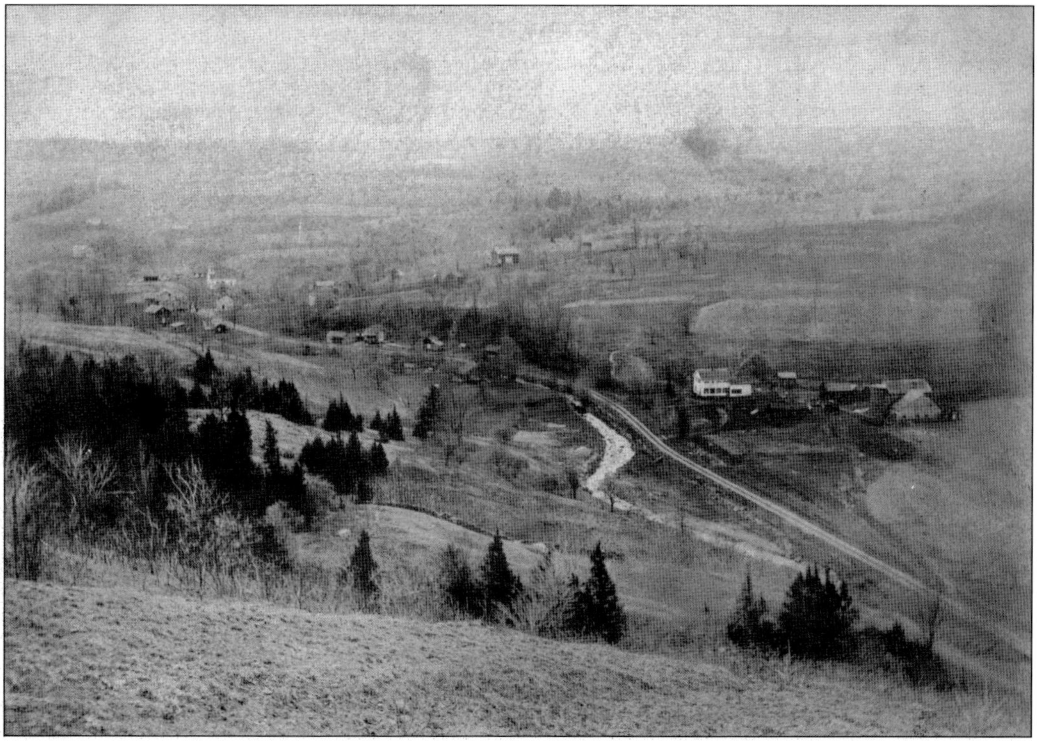

**Rolling Hills and Farming.** Throughout the 1700s and 1800s, farming was the primary livelihood for the majority of the county's residents and an essential part of the local economy. This view of Frankfort Center was taken from a glass-plate negative by Eugene Dougherty around 1900. It shows Center Road and Ferguson Creek meandering through the valley, with the farm of Truman Nicholas (1872–1921) on the right. (Courtesy of Eunice Hanson.)

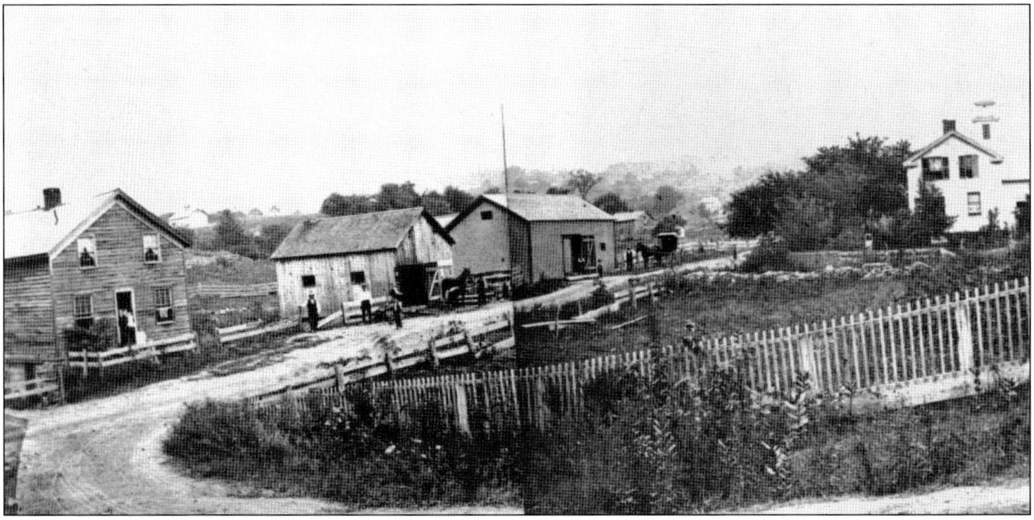

**Hub of Frankfort Center.** Blacksmiths were essential for settlers in the 1700s and 1800s, providing the necessary tools and hardware for agriculture and the shoeing of horses and oxen. The 1875 photograph above shows Center Road at the corner of Gates Road in Frankfort Center. The home of Franklin Pryne (1848–1912) is on the left, as well as the blacksmith shop he operated. The photograph below shows the same area in 1898, with new additions across from the blacksmith shop, which was then operated by Francis Riddell. A new post office and a general store graced the street, the latter of which was operated by James Harvey (1819–1907) and William Tisdale (1825–1902). This location was the site of a store where the neighborhood gathered all the way into the 1940s, when it was finally closed. Fred and Lila Priest were the last proprietors. (Both, courtesy of Eunice Hanson.)

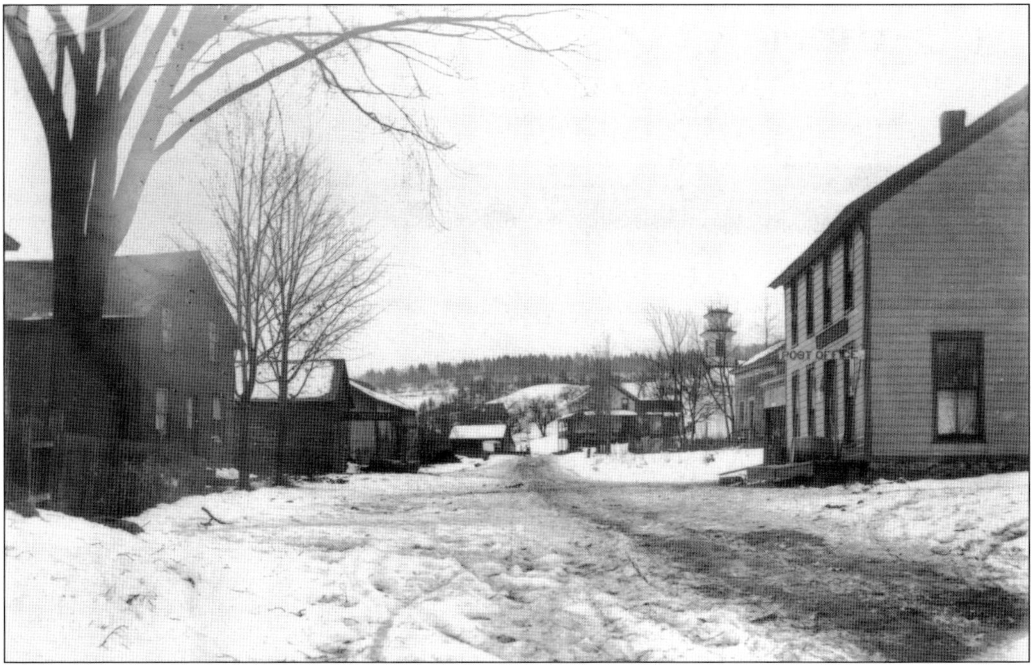

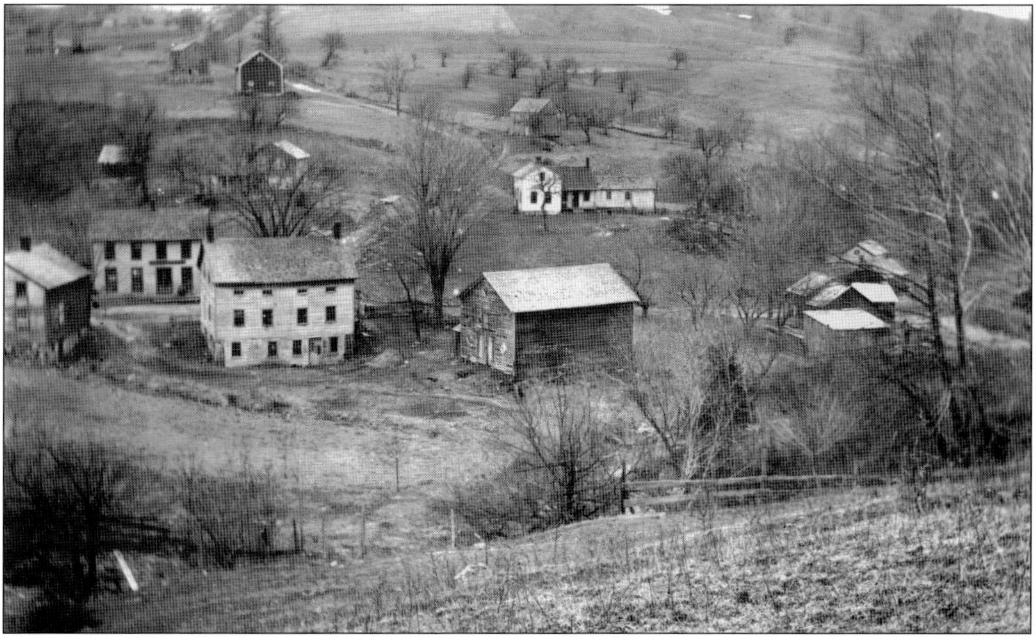

**Frankfort Center Looking Northwest.** This picturesque photograph shows the Harvey/Tisdale store on the far left, facing Center Road on the corner of Gates Road, which curves up the hillside. The building in the center was the home of Porter Dougherty. The right side of the home, made of brick, is the original structure, built by James and Patience Howard, who purchased this land in the early 1800s, when the community was known as Howard's Bush. (Courtesy of Eunice Hanson.)

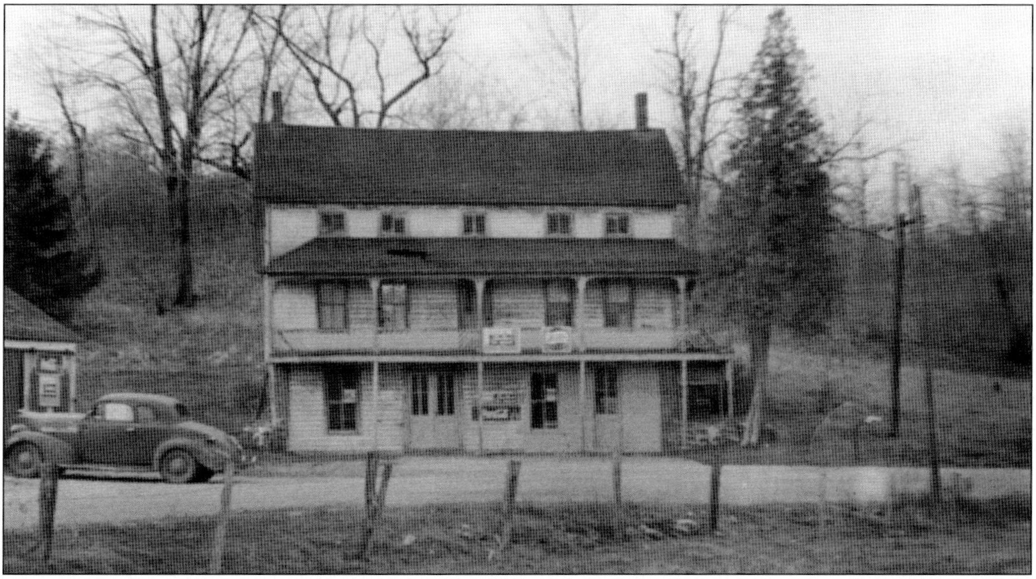

**Frankfort Center Grocery Store.** Frankfort Center once again had a local grocery store when Clinton and Grace Maydole opened one in 1948. They lowered the old structure to two stories, with the store in the basement. They operated for 10 years, selling canned goods, fresh meat, fruits and vegetables, ice cream, and a large candy display. The store closed in 1958. The building is now a private residence. (Courtesy of Eunice Hanson.)

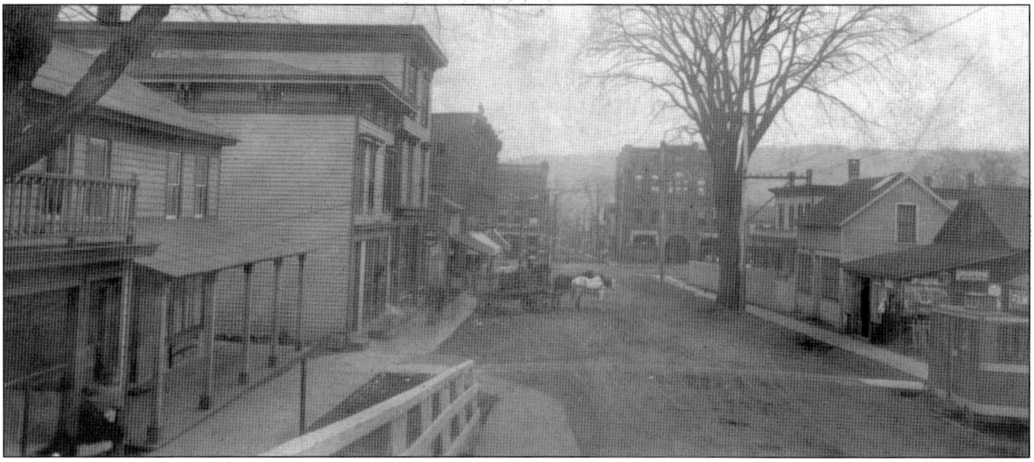

**Looking North on Litchfield Street.** This photograph from around 1907 shows the railing to a bridge over the Erie Canal in the foreground. On the left are the John Swartz bakery, the undertaking rooms of Seymour Holdredge and Horatio Getman, a saloon, the American Express office, and Edward Steele's drugstore. On the right is a cart selling cigars and popcorn. (Courtesy of Chad Wohler.)

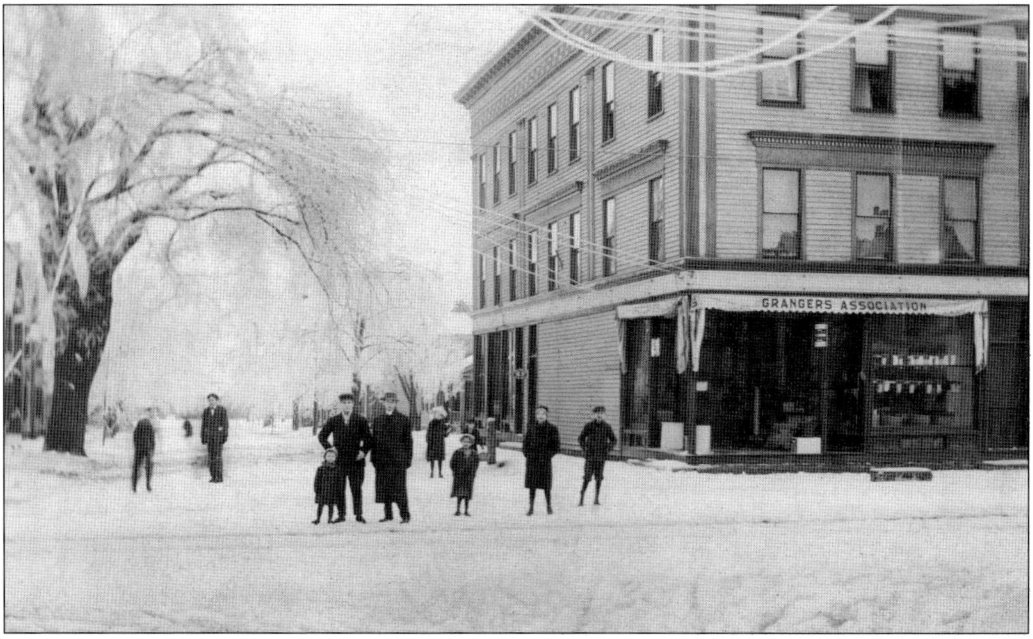


**Grangers Association.** The Grangers Association grocery and farm produce store opened in the Farrell Block, on the corner of East Main and Frankfort Streets, in 1906. It was a cooperative concern organized by farmers and was a leading trading center. Morrell McKennan (1877–1959) managed the store. It relocated across the street in 1921 and was sold to the Blue Ribbon Market Company in 1925. (Courtesy of Chad Wohler.)

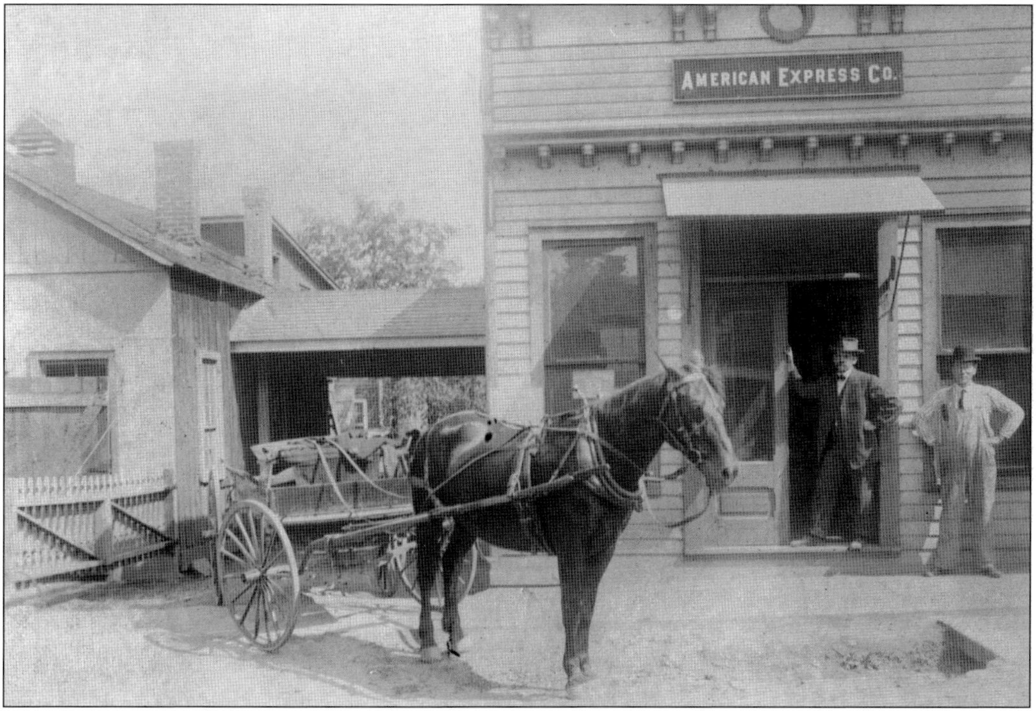


**AMERICAN EXPRESS COMPANY.** This photograph was taken around 1910 of the American Express Company, located on Litchfield Street. Standing in the doorway is William Waterbury (1862–1943), who was a grocer and express agent. He was later an insurance agent and a justice of the peace. Arthur Stone (1876–1949), standing next to him, was the driver for American Express. (Courtesy of the Frankfort Free Library.)

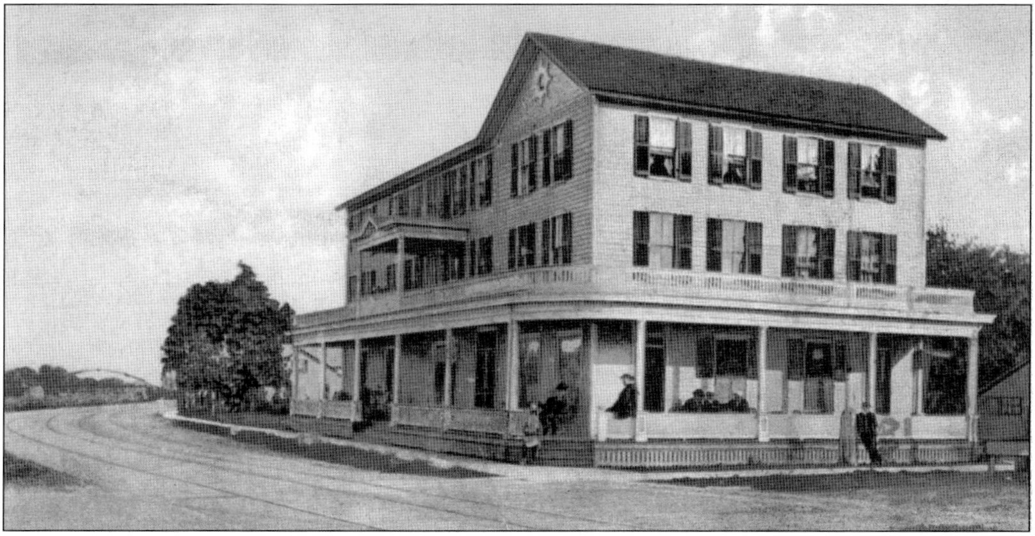

**HOTEL THURSTON.** In 1902, Frank Thurston (1865–1952) purchased this 1850s hotel, located on the corner of Litchfield Street and Pleasant Avenue. It had 22 rooms and a dining area that seated 100. In 1961, Peter Conigilaro added an eight-lane bowling alley and remodeled the first and second floors. On November 26, 1963, it burned to the ground, and it was later rebuilt. The building was auctioned in 2013. (Courtesy of Chad Wohler.)

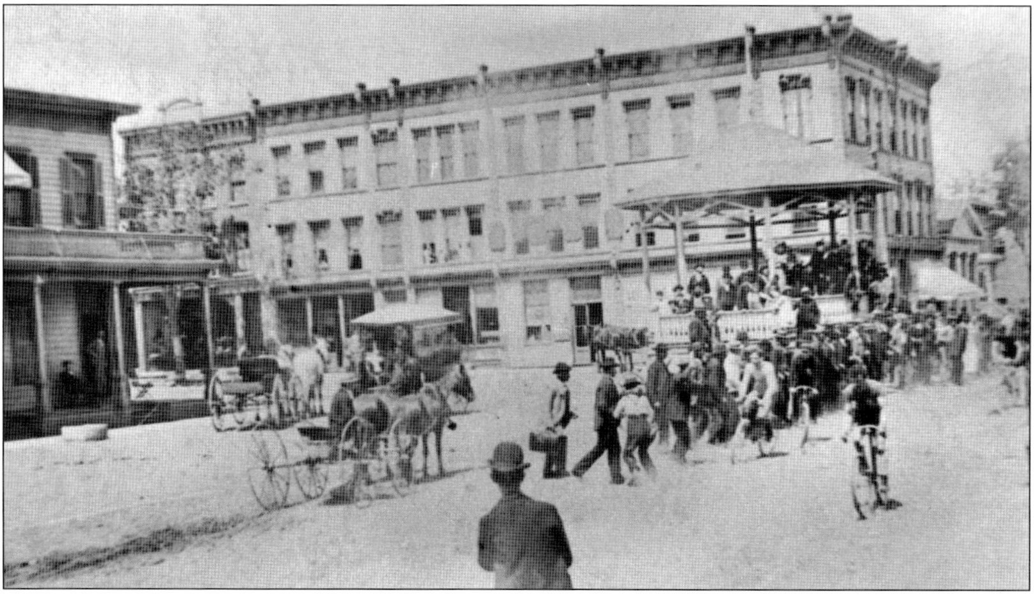

**Joslin Block.** The intersection of Main and Litchfield Streets (above) was the center of village life for many years. Aaron V. Joslin (1836–1905) constructed the largest building in town in 1857. The three-story building had stores on the main floor and offices and living quarters above. He operated a large mercantile business. Seen below on the same side of Main Street, across Litchfield Street, is a portion of the Central Hotel, operated by Henry M. Wood (1842–1896), who served two terms as president of the village. Years later, in 1922, Citizens First National Bank purchased the land and built its bank there. The bank was a consolidation of two banking establishments in the village: First National Bank and Citizens. (Above, courtesy of the Frankfort Fire Department; below, courtesy of Jacquelyn Conners.)

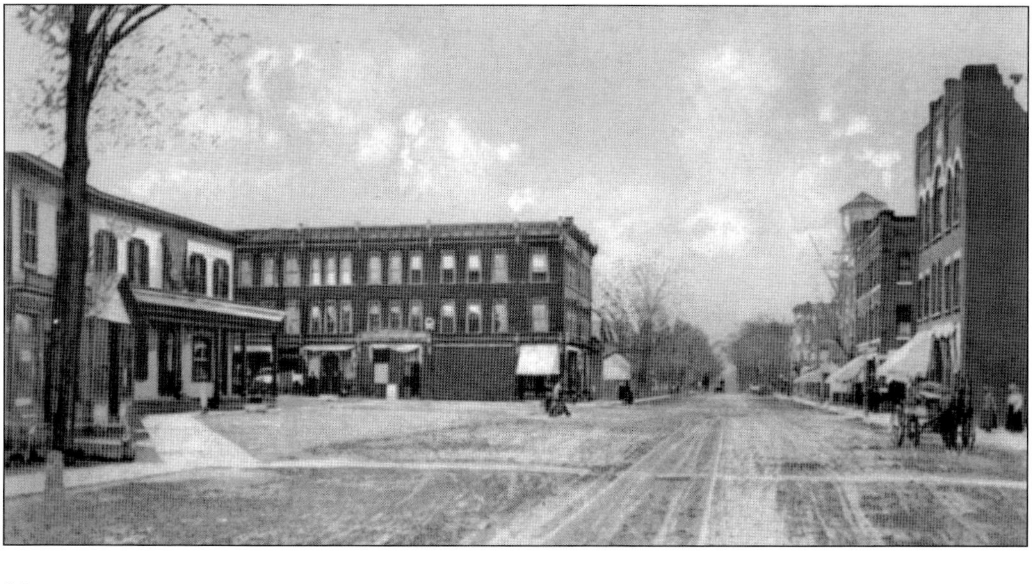

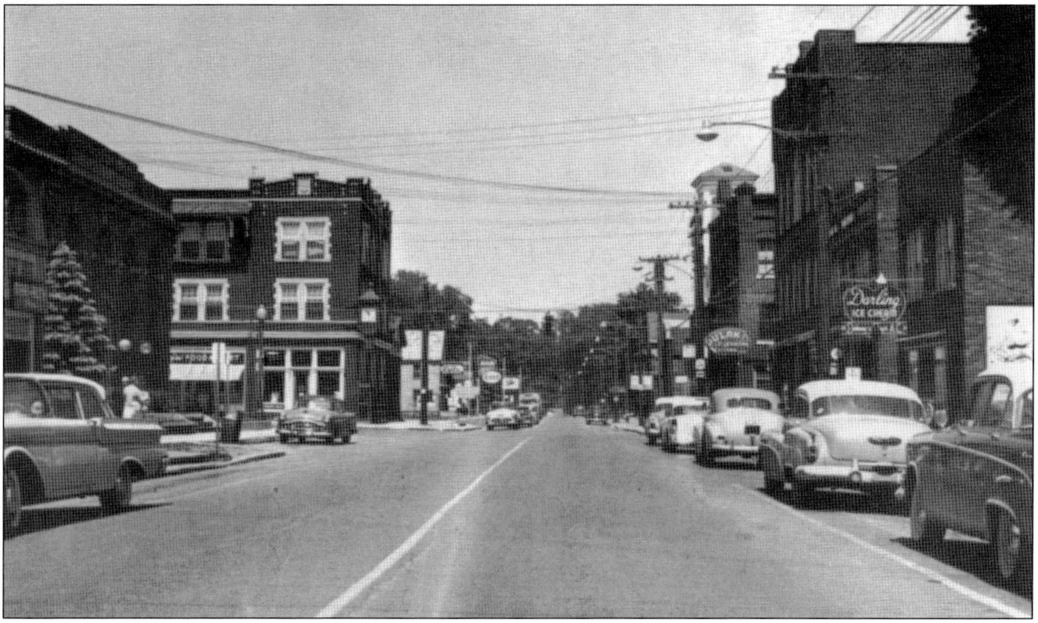

**East Main Street Business Section, 1960.** These photographs of the corner of Main and Litchfield Streets show that this intersection was still the busy hub of the village. The photograph above, looking from East Main Street towards West Main Street, shows that the Joslin Block was replaced with the Union Block, which showcased the Royal Food Market sign, and that the Central Hotel was replaced with Citizens First National Bank. On the other side of the street are Josie's Dinette and the Masonic Block, which featured the Beckwith shop, the Masonic temple, and Dulak Cleaners. Towards the back is Thomas Enea's Esso station. The photograph below looks back towards East Main Street and gives a better view of the Masonic Block and, in the background, the First Methodist Church. (Both, courtesy of Chad Wohler.)

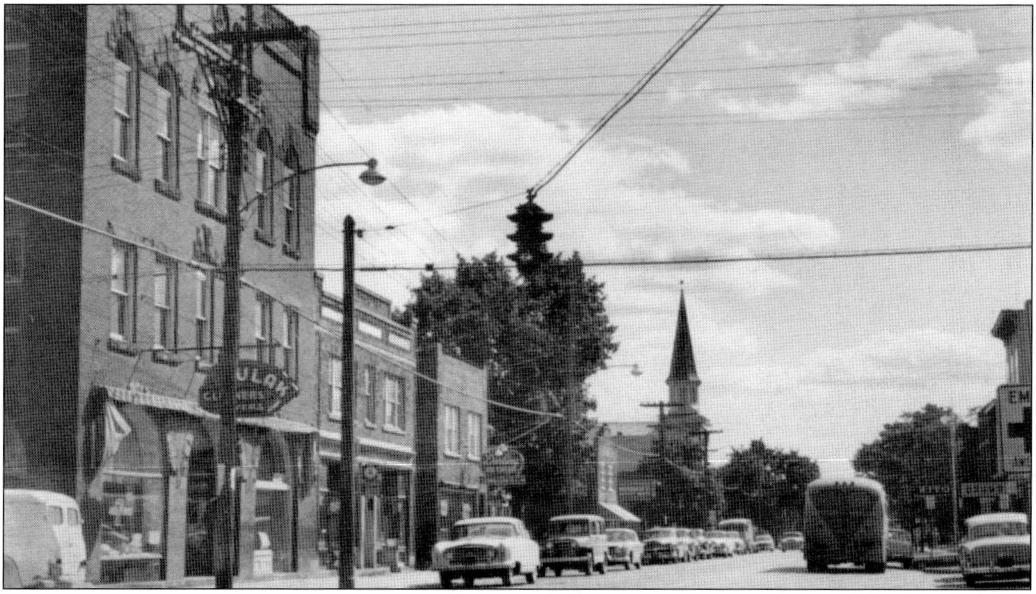

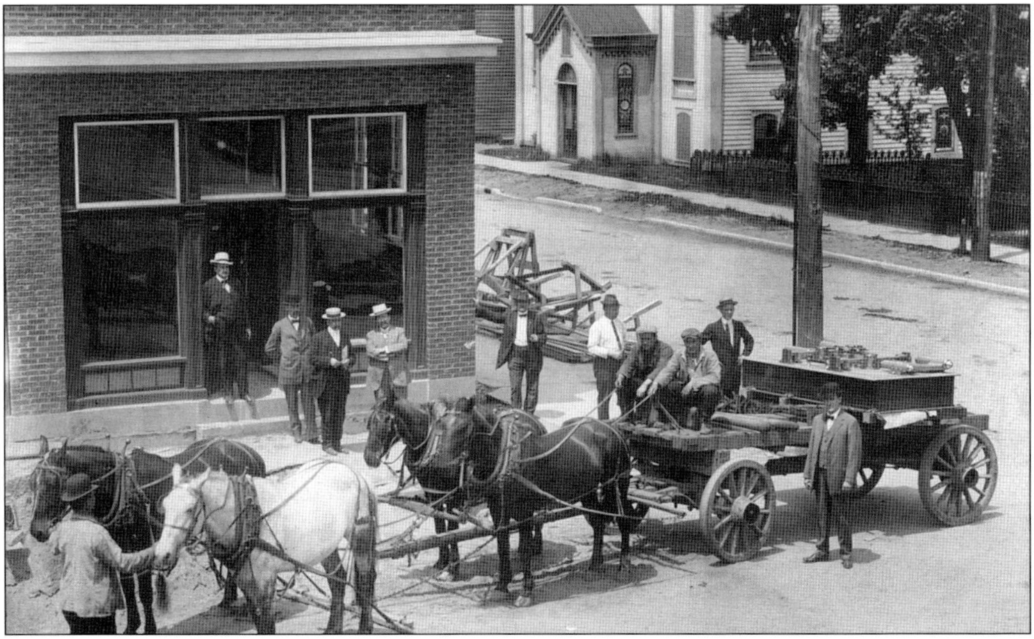

**Citizens National Bank.** This photograph shows the bank vault being delivered to Citizens National Bank, located in the Union Block, on the corner of West Main and Litchfield Streets. The Union Block was built on the site of the Joslin Block, which burned down on February 14, 1912. John Lewis (1837–1926) was one of the organizers and directors of Citizens National Bank, which was organized on December 12, 1912. (Courtesy of Dave Sanders.)

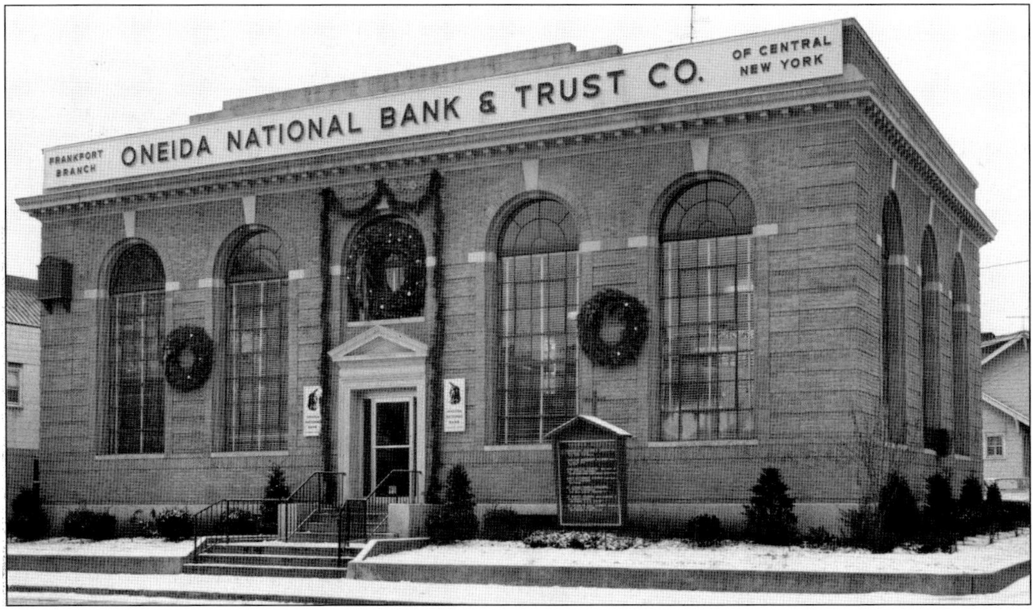


**Oneida National Bank.** Formed in 1959, Oneida National Bank & Trust Company was located on the former site of the Central Hotel, at 100 East Main Street. When the bank was built in 1924, it was first known as Citizens First National Bank, which was formed in 1922 as a merger of First National Bank (1886–1921) and Citizens National Bank (1912–1921). Branck Construction owns the building today.

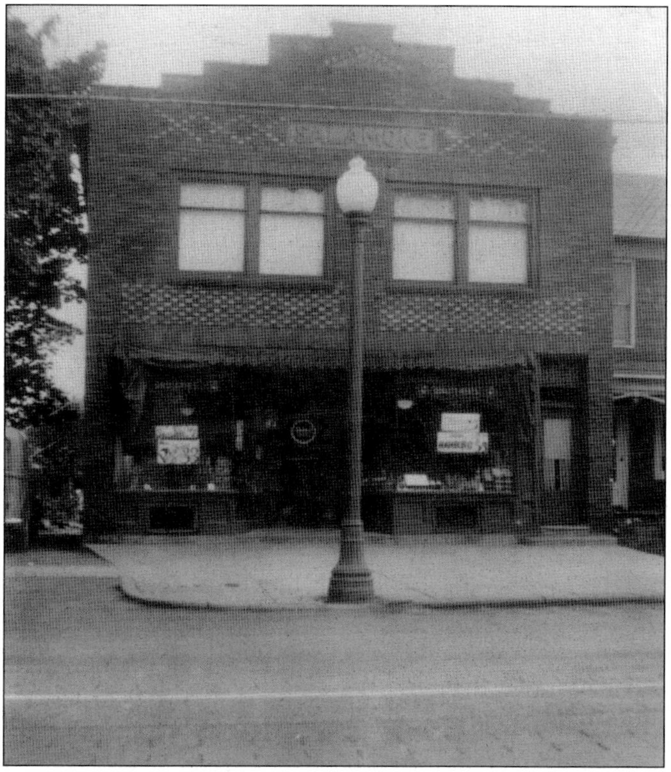

**Salamone Meat and Grocery Market.** Located at 121 East Main Street, this market was operated by John Salamone (1874–1957) from 1919 until 1954. His son Joseph (1915–2005) and Joseph's wife, Regina (1918–2008), ran the business until 1968. After that, it was run as a supermarket by James Lore and then as a Laundromat from 1972 until the early 1990s. Today, it is the site of Big Willy's Pizzeria. (Courtesy of Donald Roberts.)

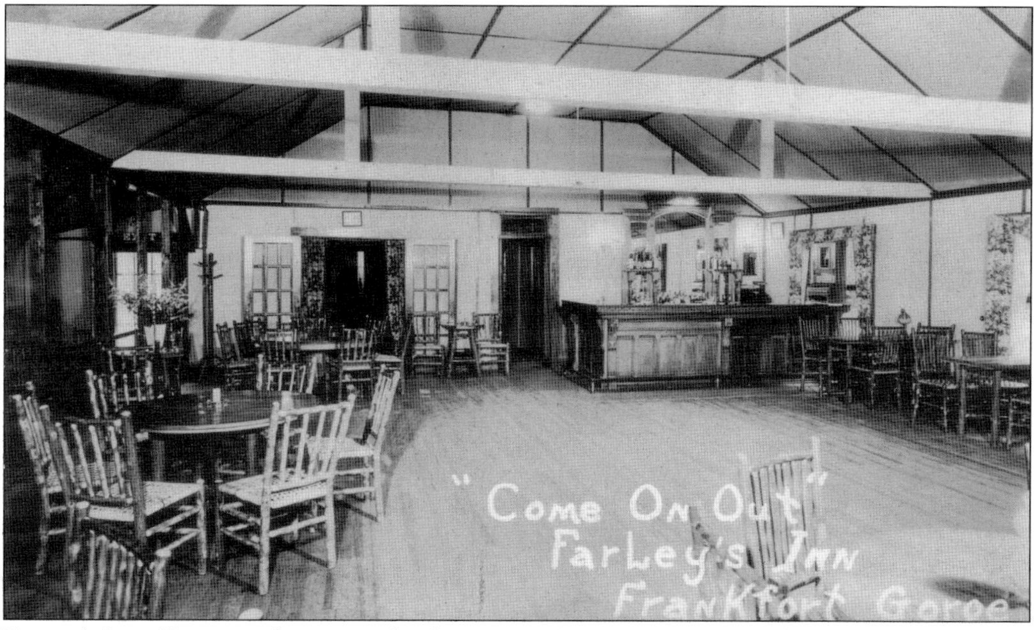


**Farley's Inn.** Known in later years for their Route 5S restaurant in Frankfort, John (1897–1986) and Peg (1903–1994) Farley first ran this quaint inn in Frankfort Gorge from 1924 to 1947. It was then operated by Gordon and Marion Walker from 1947 to 1954 and by Leonard and Doris Smith from 1954 to 1969, when it was known as Smitty's. It was a great venue for dancing, wedding parties, and clambakes. (Courtesy of Lillian Gaherty.)

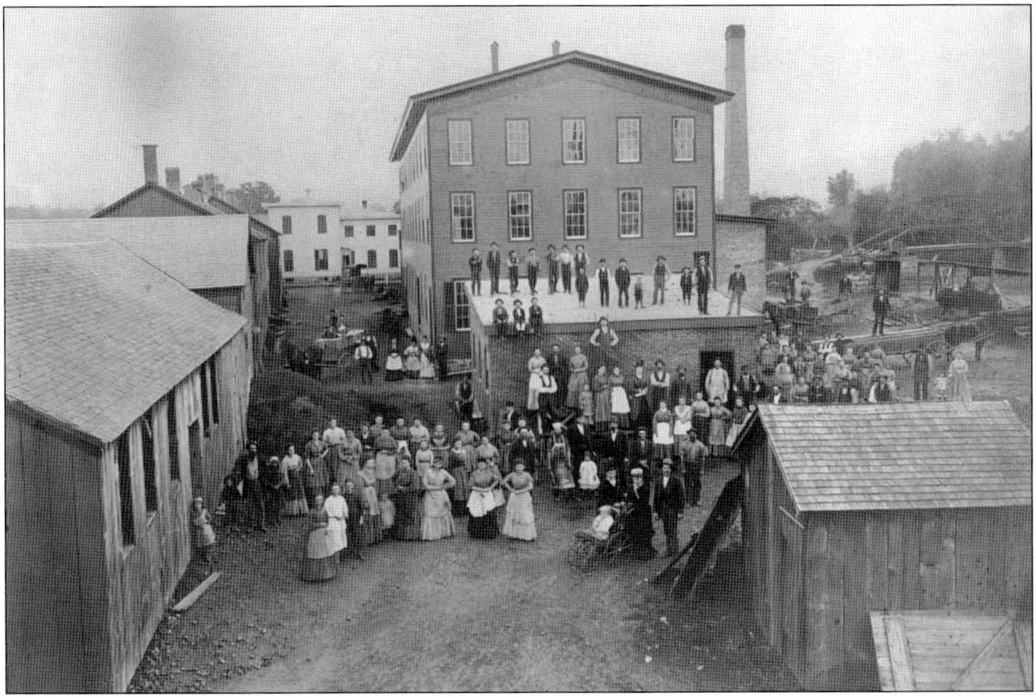

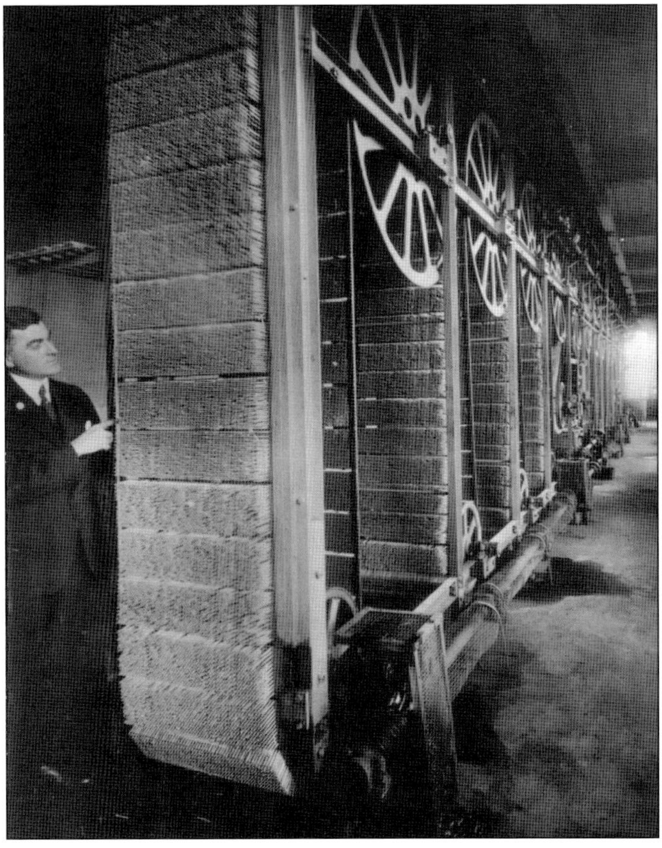

**GATES MATCH FACTORY.** The Gates Match Factory, on South Litchfield Street, was one of the earliest industries in the village. It was founded by William Gates (1808–1877) in 1844. Gates obtained a patent in 1854 for a continuous match-making machine that could manufacture friction matches. Gates bought the land that is now Lehman Park for the expansion of his factory along Moyer Creek. In 1877, his sons William B. (1840–1900), George W. (1843–1918), and Frederick (1848–1942) took over the business. They sold it in 1881 to the Diamond Match Company, which moved to Oswego in 1893. In 1894, Frankfort Linen Manufacturing Company started manufacturing on the site. In November 1956, a monument was dedicated on the site of the Gates Match Factory. (Above, courtesy of the Frankfort Free Library.)

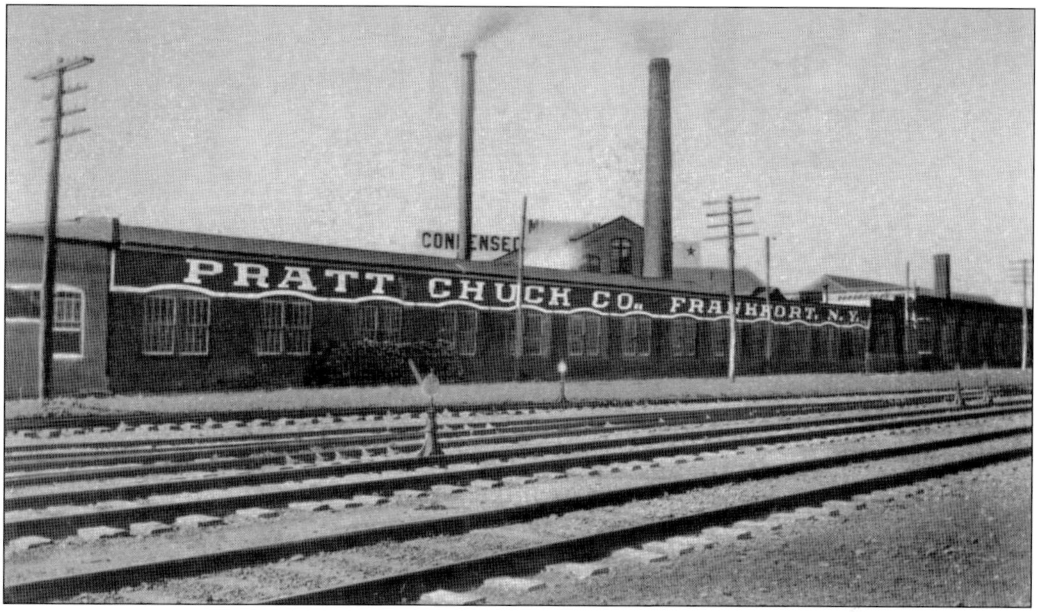


**Pratt Chuck Company.** This company, established by Charles Pratt (1858–1930) in Clayville in 1892, moved to the former blacksmith shop of the West Shore Railroad in Frankfort in 1897. It manufactured Pratt's patent-improved positive-driving drill chucks and Empire Friction chucks, both of which were used by machinists. It expanded in 1912 to make hoes, rakes, and forks. The company was sold in 1953 to Maremont Automotive Products of Chicago. The photograph below shows a motorcar specially designed by Pratt himself. The 75-horsepower, six-wheeled automobile could carry seven passengers and had a wheelbase of 14 feet. The two rear wheels were used to drive, and the remainder were used to steer. He built the car for his own use, but he did patent his invention in 1907. (Above, courtesy of Chad Wohler.)

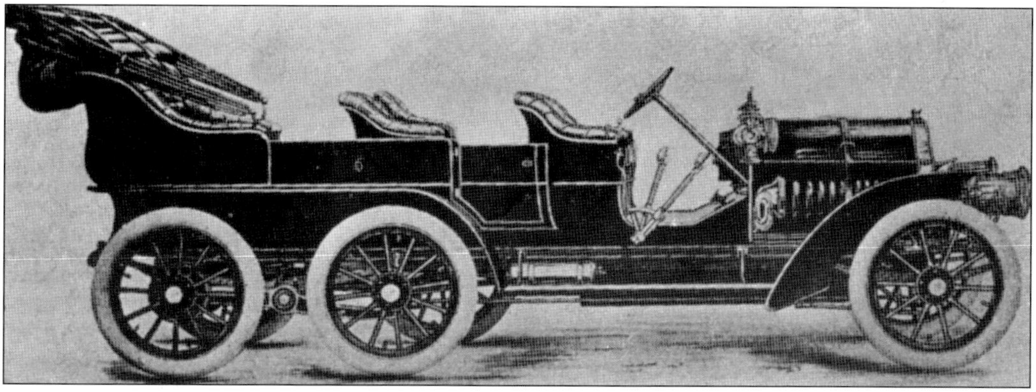

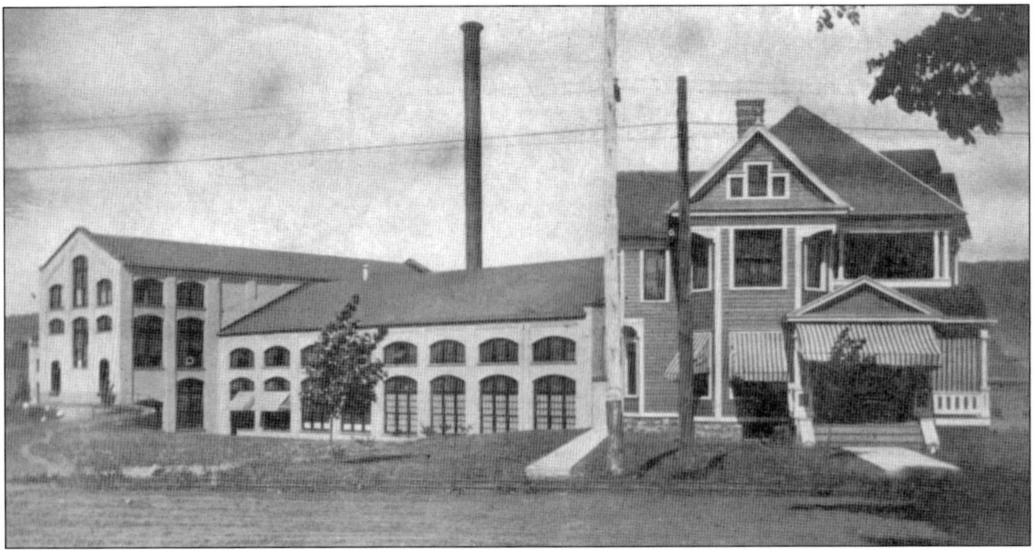

**MICHIGAN CONDENSED MILK COMPANY.** In 1899, the Michigan Condensed Milk Company located a factory in the old West Shore Railroad coach shop, on the corner of East Main Street and Reese Road, in this dairy-rich farm area. Local farmers would bring their milk cans to a community milk stand. The large cans would be loaded onto a farm wagon—and, later, onto trucks—that would haul them to the milk plant in Frankfort. The company aspired to hire 200 people, and, by 1900, it was making about 8,000 quarts of milk daily. The company was sold to the Gail Borden Company in 1902 as part of Borden's expansion to all regions of the country. In 1929, Borden acquired the Casein Company of America in Bainbridge and brought that division to the Frankfort location, manufacturing powdered dairy products. (Both, courtesy of Chad Wohler.)

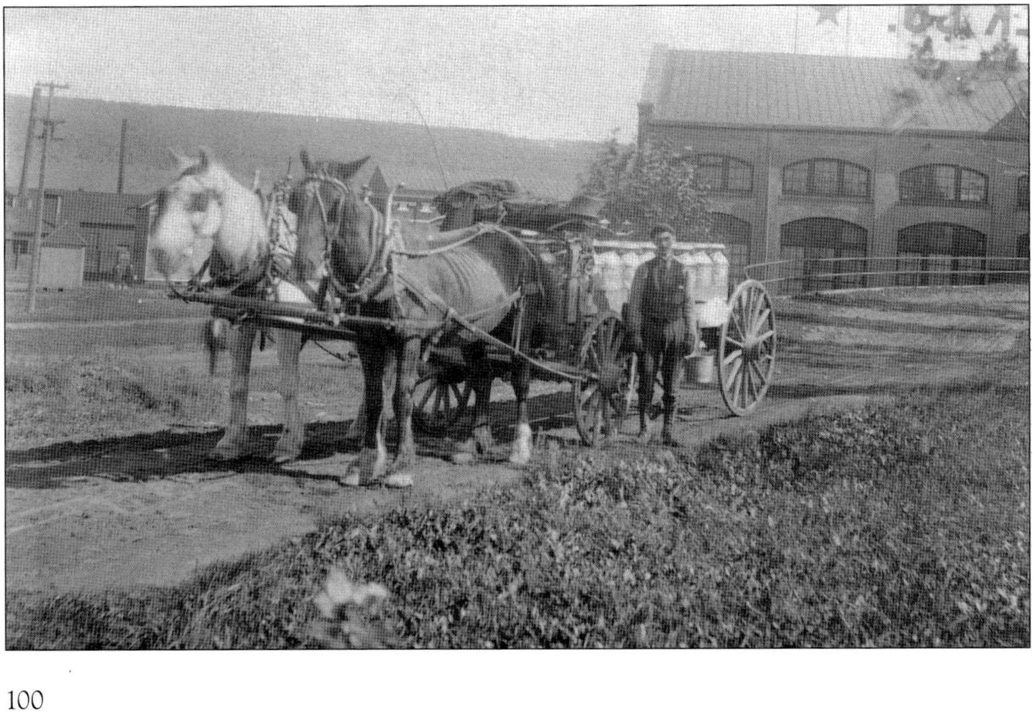

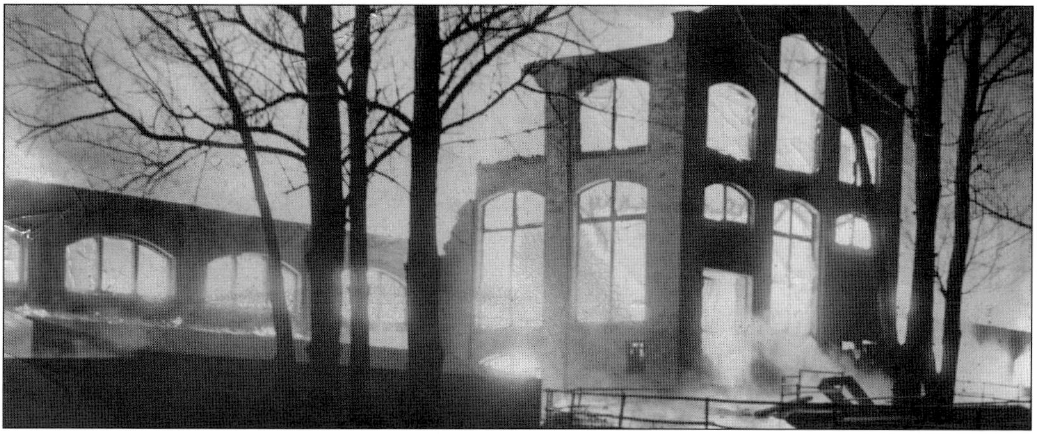

**Western Condensing Company Fire.** The Casein Company leased the building in the 1940s to the Western Condensing Company, which manufactured dry whey from skimmed milk for chicken feed. A fire broke out in December 1943, destroying the plant. Bricks were salvaged from the building to erect a brick church across from the Russian Holy Trinity Monastery. The 150-foot chimney was dynamited in 1952 when Pratt Industries took over the property.

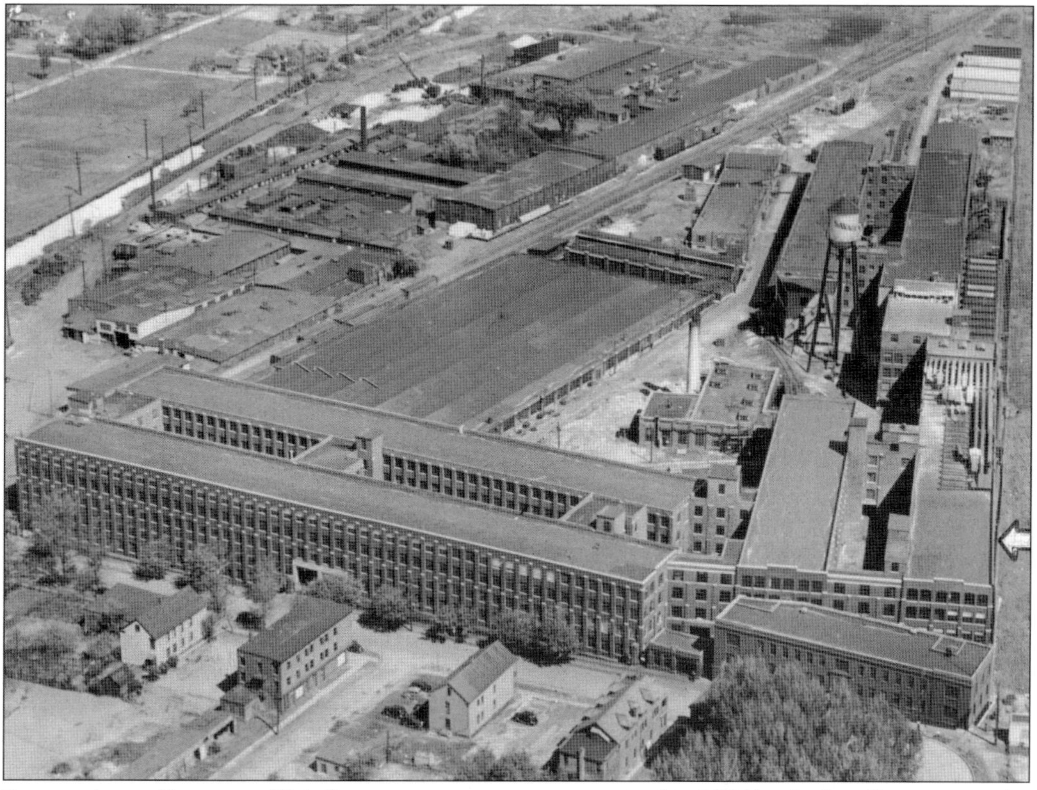

**Savage Arms Company.** This firearms company was organized in 1894 by Arthur Savage to make sporting rifles on Broad Street. As business prospered, it built a larger plant on Turner Street. War contracts during World Wars I and II for machine guns brought more prosperity, and the business employed 8,000 people at its peak. Sperry Univac took over the facility in the 1950s, and in 1982, the buildings were opened as CharlesTown Outlet stores, which closed in 1991.

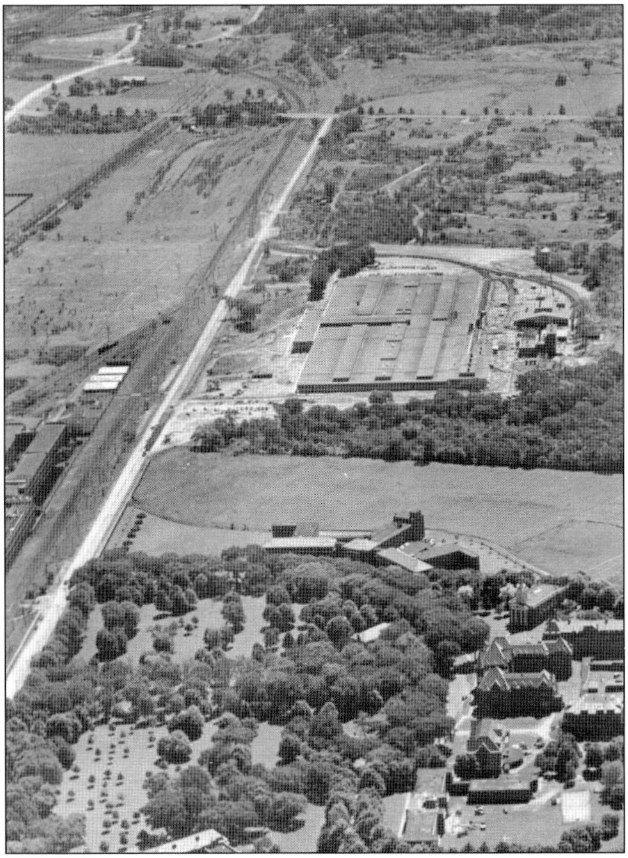

**Chicago Pneumatic Tool Company.** When Chicago Pneumatic built a plant in West Frankfort near the outskirts of Utica, it was the world's largest portable power tool manufacturer. Ground was broken in March 1948, and construction was completed in 1949. A total of 2,000 employees were then hired, with three steady shifts. The company manufactured portable air and electric tools, rock drills, air compressors, diesel engines, and vacuum pumps, many of them designed and developed in the company's laboratories. In the 1960s and 1970s, employment fluctuated with the rise and fall of business, but, by the 1980s, employment had dropped due to economic conditions. On February 27, 1996, Chicago Pneumatic announced it would close its Utica headquarters and relocate the company to South Carolina. Today, the buildings house DeIorio's, which makes dough products and par-baked pizzas.

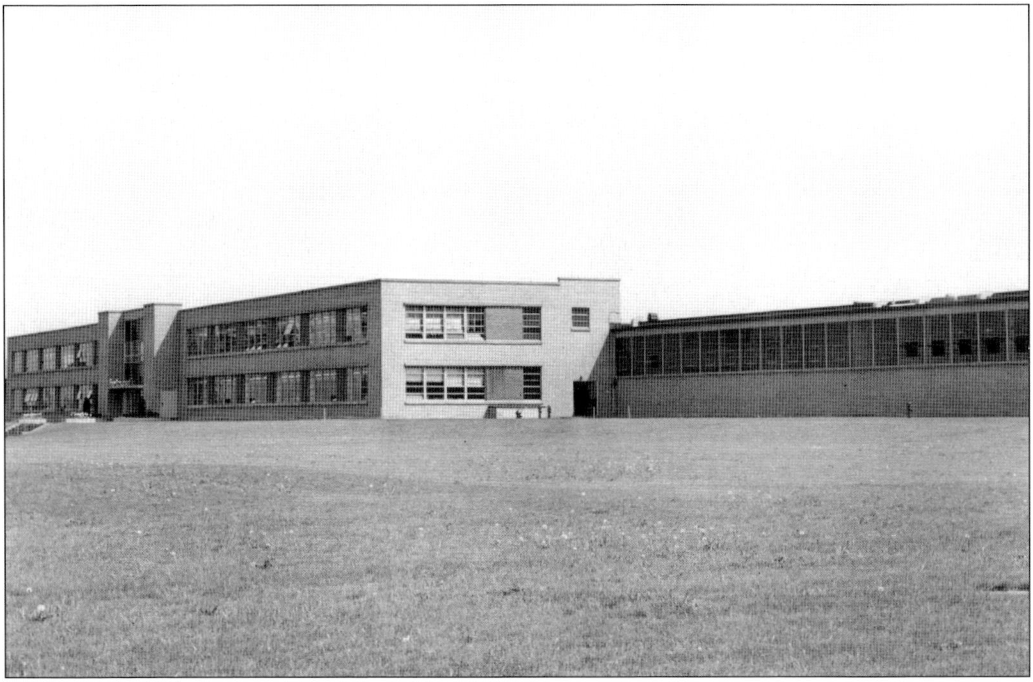

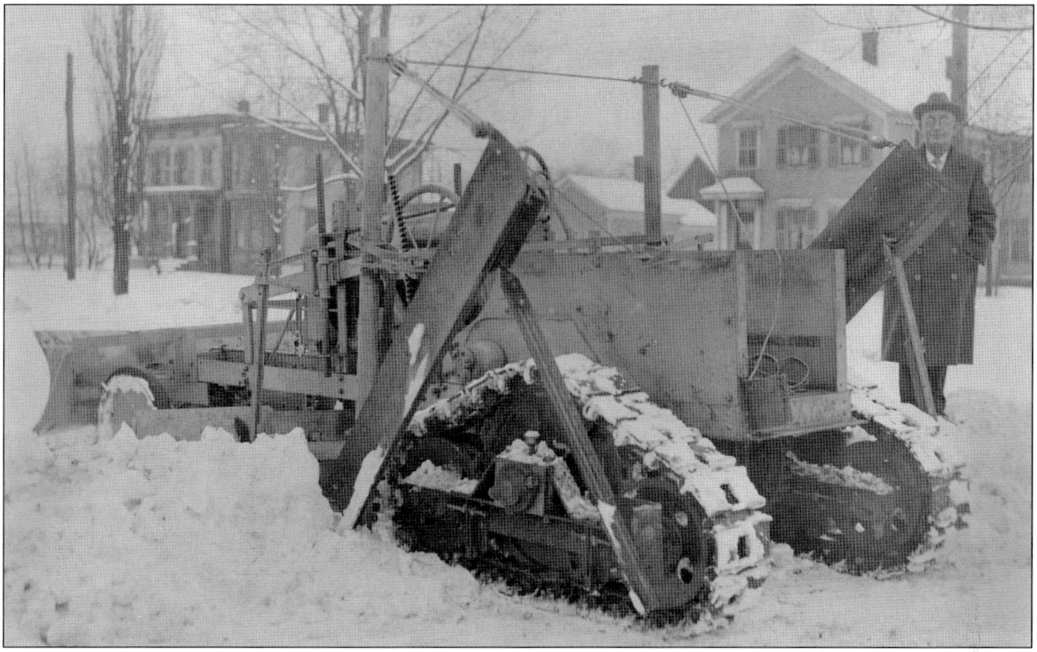

**ACME ROAD MACHINERY COMPANY.** This company was organized on January 4, 1900, by brothers David Cook Sr. (1872–1956) and Walter Cook (1861–1922) on land leased from the West Shore Railroad Shop committee. The main building was on East Main Street. The company manufactured road-making machinery and prospered, shipping road equipment to 52 countries. The photograph above, dated December 29, 1926, shows David Cook standing next to an Acme snowplow. Cook received a patent for the snowplow on February 12, 1929. During World War II, he was a consultant for the government on the construction of heavy machinery. The interior photograph below shows road rollers being assembled. In 1912, the Cooks expanded their property with the construction of additional buildings on the 10-acre site.

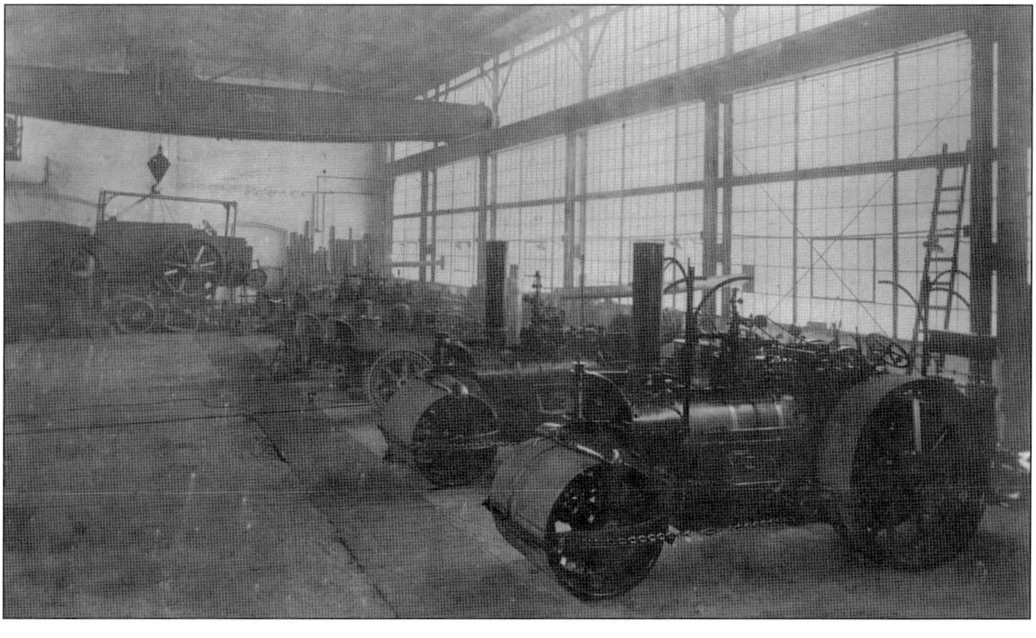

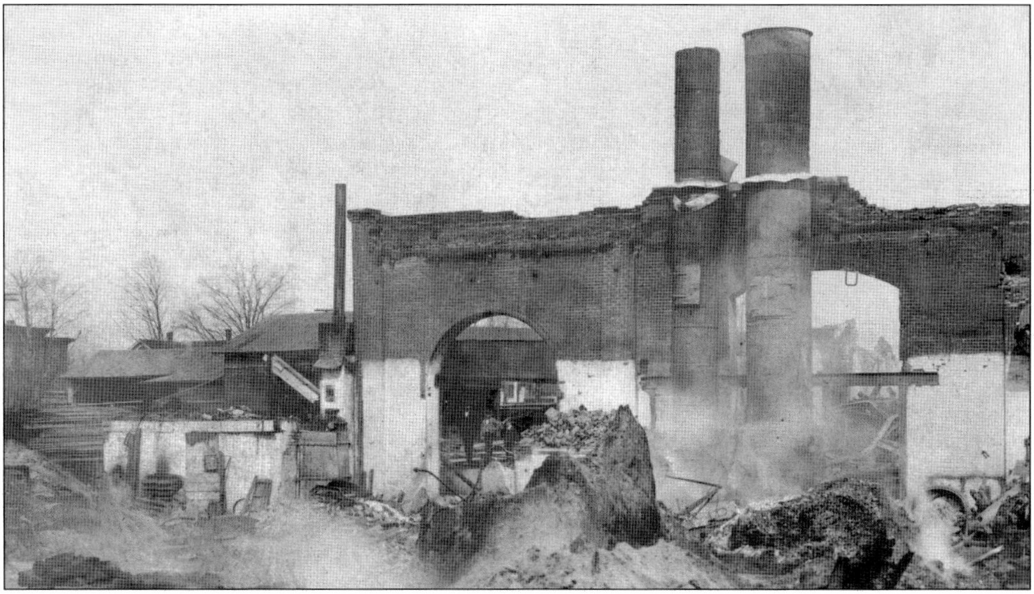

**ACME BUILDING FIRES.** In 1907, the company had a major fire that destroyed its original building, the aftereffects of which can be seen in this photograph. Acme rebuilt and continued to have a prosperous business. In 1961, it suffered another major fire that burned down the plant. All that was saved was the office, holding the company records, and the pattern room. (Courtesy of Chad Wohler.)

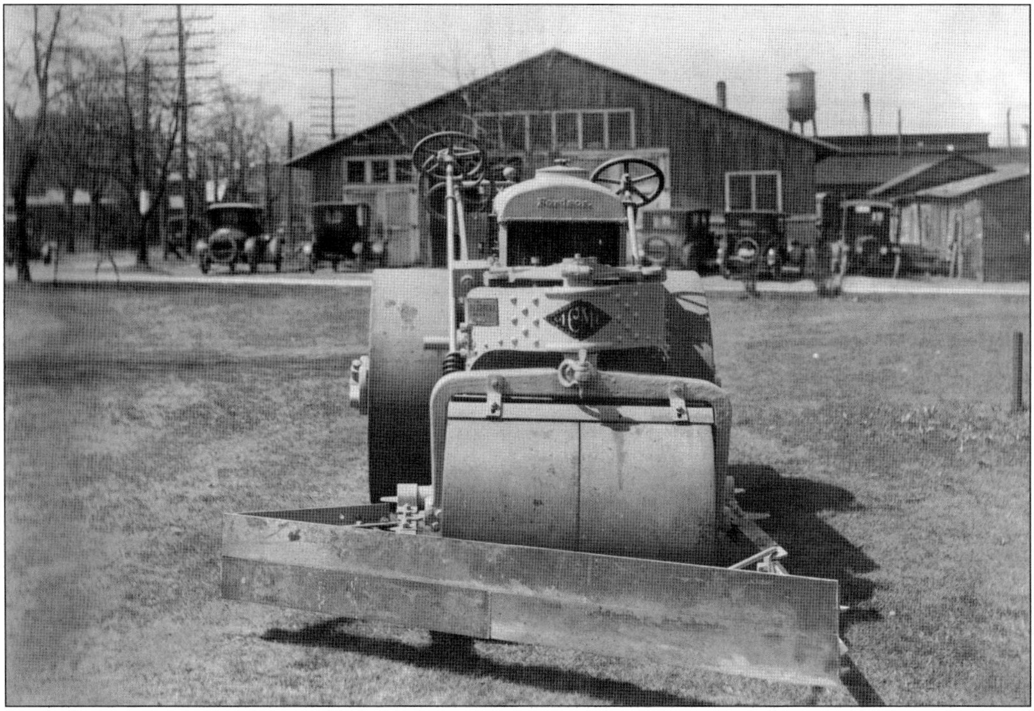

**ACME ROAD EQUIPMENT.** This photograph was taken on April 29, 1924. It shows one of the road rollers made by Acme. Gas rollers and steamrollers were manufactured by the company. In the background is the water tower of the Union Fork & Hoe Company.

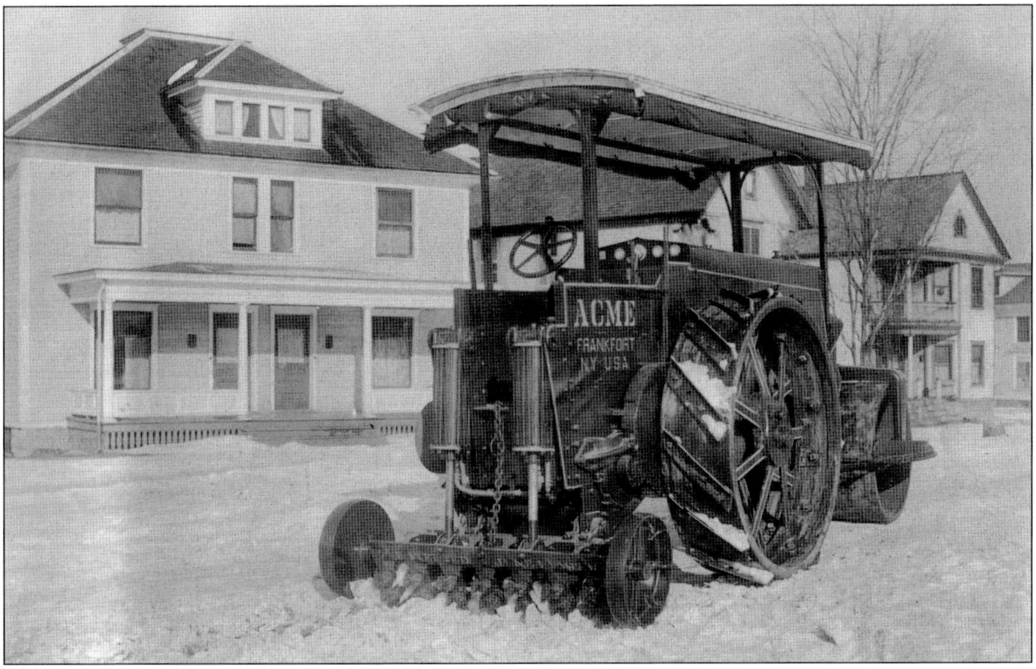


**ACME ROAD GRADER.** This photograph, dated January 9, 1924, shows an Acme grader. The Herkimer County Historical Society collection includes a photograph album that features a number of images of road equipment made by the company in the 1920s.

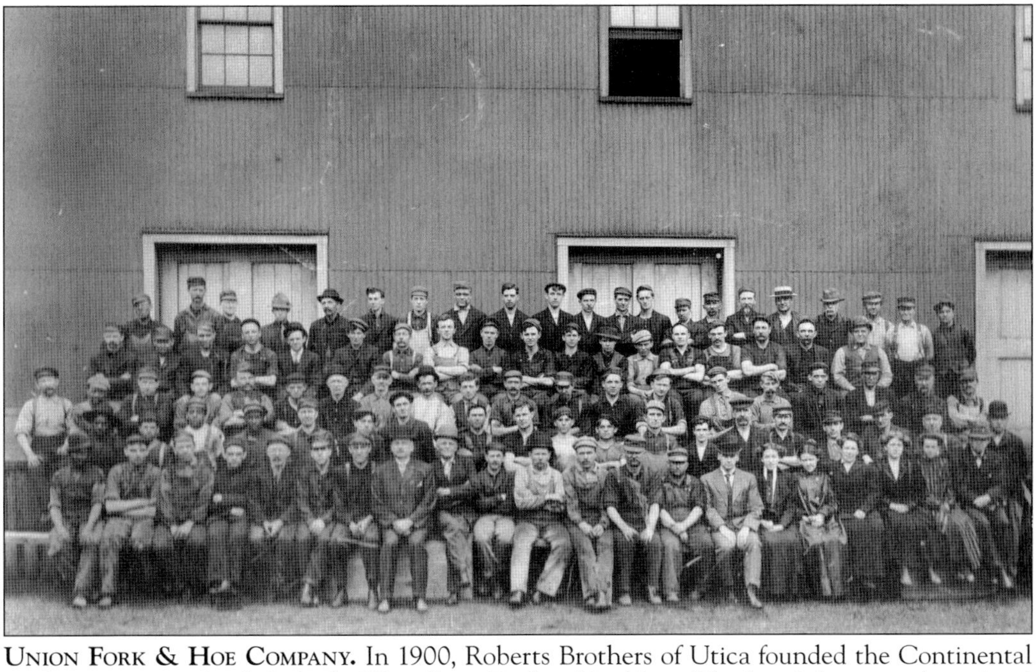

**UNION FORK & HOE COMPANY.** In 1900, Roberts Brothers of Utica founded the Continental Tool Company and refurbished a West Shore Railroad building. The first fork was made in April of that year. The company merged with the United States Hoe & Tool Company of Columbus, Ohio, in 1907 through the efforts of George Durell, and Union Fork & Hoe Company came into being. This photograph of company employees was taken around 1915.

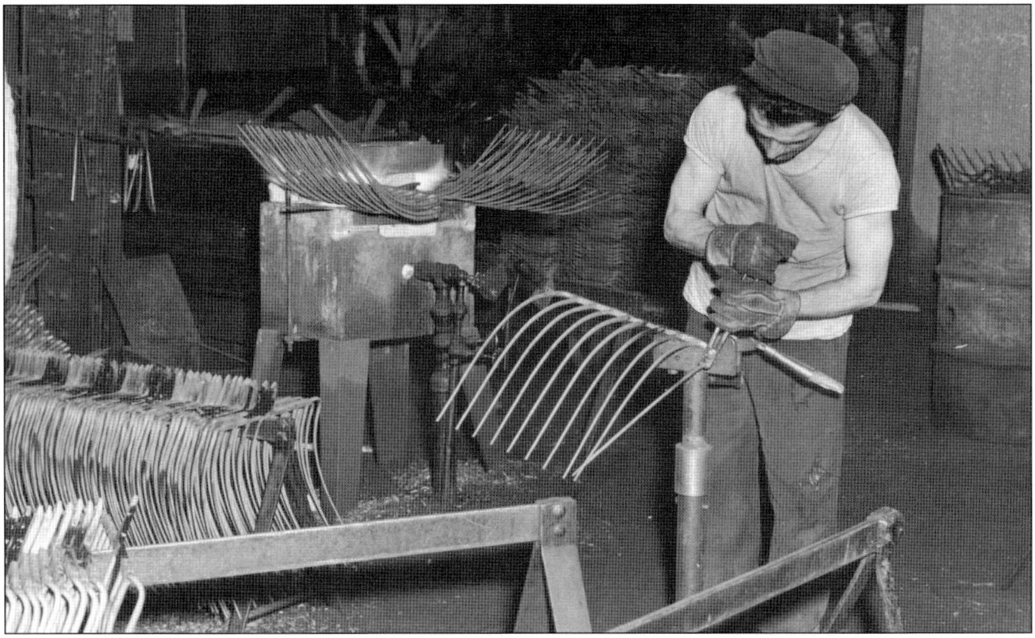

**Farm and Garden Tools.** As farming became more intensive, a demand for patterned hoes for cultivating led to their increased production. The need for a universal small tool led to the production of rakes, hoes, spades, and forks for homes. The company expanded its facilities to 40 acres between the old West Shore Railroad tracks and East Main Street, including the purchase of a building from the Pratt Chuck Company in 1918. Production during the war years was booming, as the armed forces had a need for hand tools and shovels for building roads and airfields. Above, Stanley Mroz is in the process of "ear turning," or bending of ends of the fork head to increase its load-holding abilities. The photograph below shows how the shovels are shaped. The operator on the left is Steve Rizzo, and Anthony Riente is on the right.

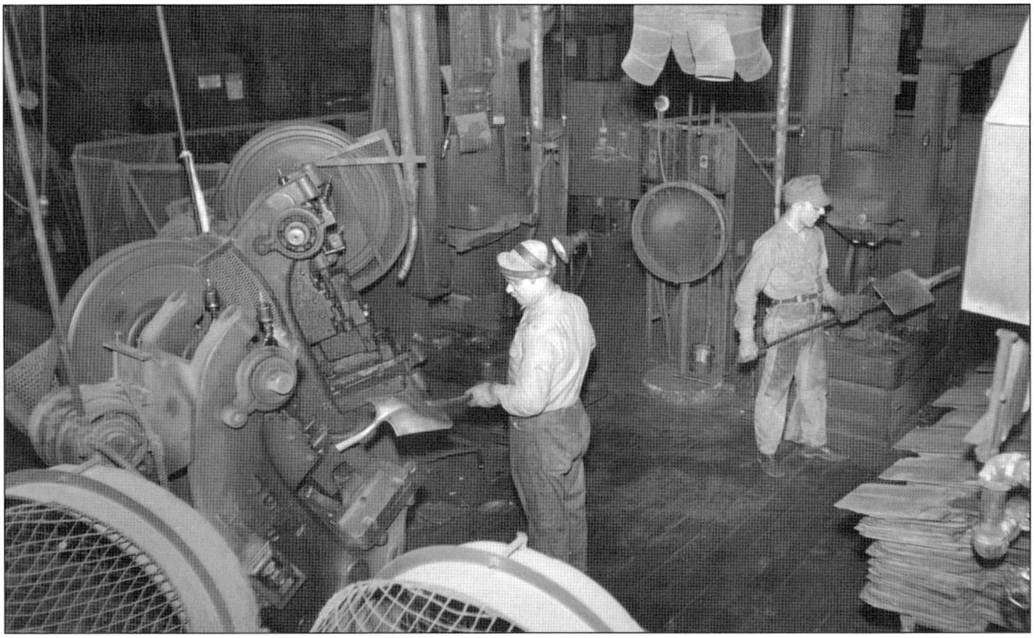

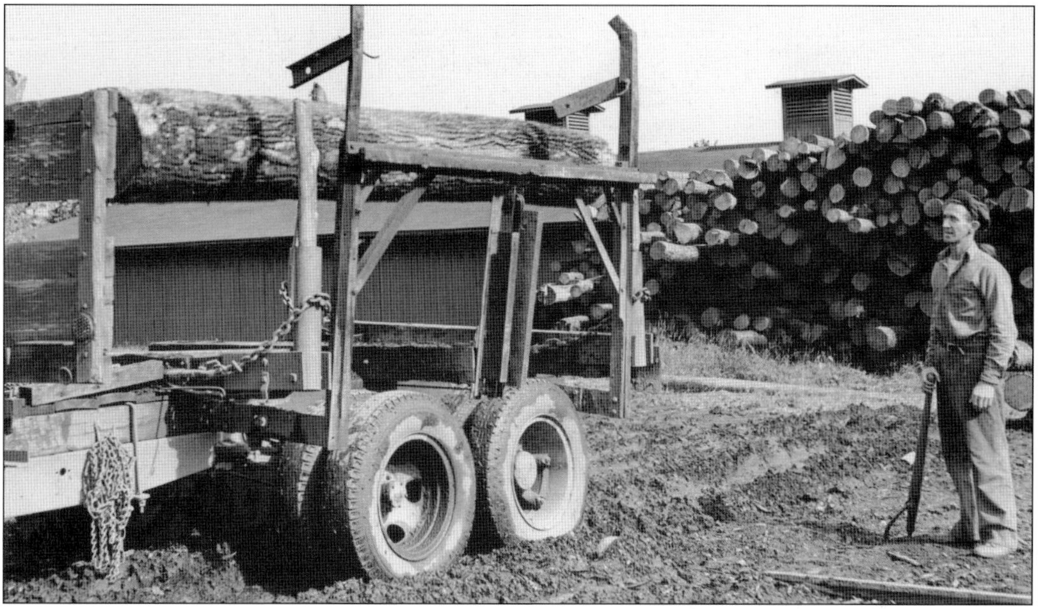

LUMBERING OPERATIONS. The company had its own lumbering operations to manufacture handles for garden, farm, and small utility tools. Seen here in 1949 is Harvey Eckler, who invented the "timber tosser," which would deposit a log on the bed of the truck on which the device was attached. At the time, it was mainly used to transport logs from yard to yard, but it came to be used in other operations at the plant.

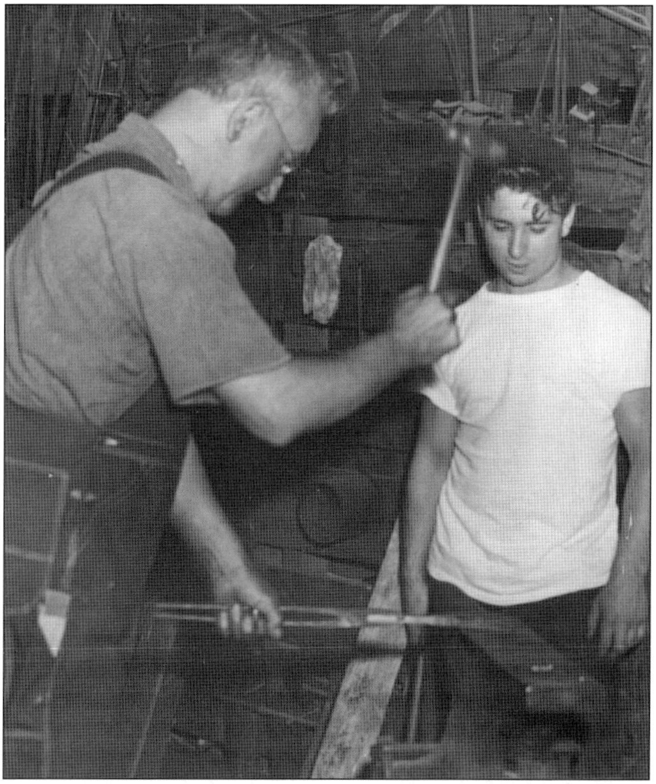

BLACKSMITHING. This 1952 photograph shows Joseph Bellino (right) studying the work of Harry Doodson, a blacksmith at the Union Fork & Hoe Company. Bellino, who was 24 at the time, had been apprenticing under Doodson in order to master the many aspects of the trade and meet the state requirements for becoming a certified blacksmith.

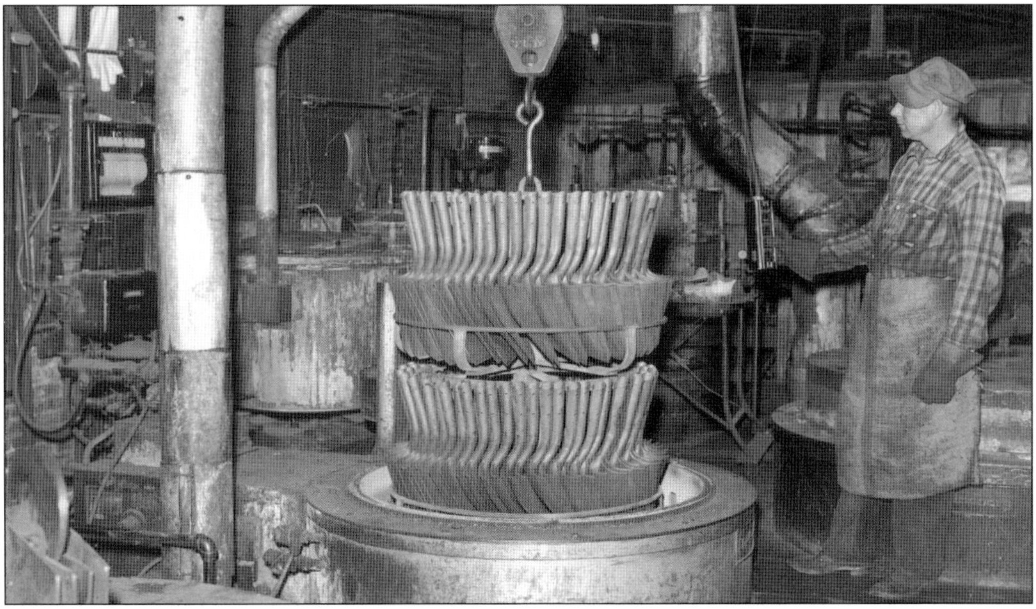

**How Shovels Were Made.** This photograph at the Union Fork & Hoe Company shows a rack of shovels being withdrawn from the Lindberg draw furnace by employee Stanley Rasmussen (1914–1964).

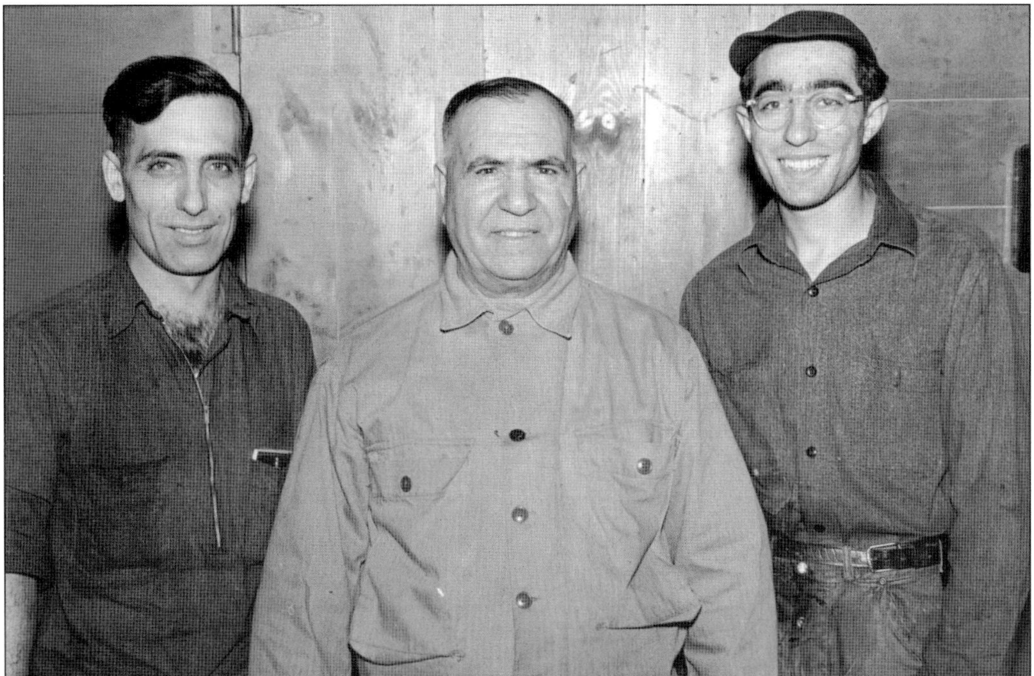

**Families Worked Here.** Union Fork & Hoe employed many people from the community, including family members, like the Rolchigos, seen here. Philip Rolchigo (1883–1961, center) came to Frankfort from Italy and was employed by the company as a fireman for 15 years. His son Vito (1909–1987, left) worked in the stamping department for 47 years. Vito's cousin, also named Philip Rolchigo (right), worked as a polisher.

**WATER TANK.** The Union Fork & Hoe Company water tank, located on the site of the former Liberty Works, could be seen from all corners of Frankfort and was considered a landmark for many years. The 73,000-gallon tank, however, had ended its days of service and needed to be taken down. In 1952, the water tank was sold and the complicated dismantling operation began.

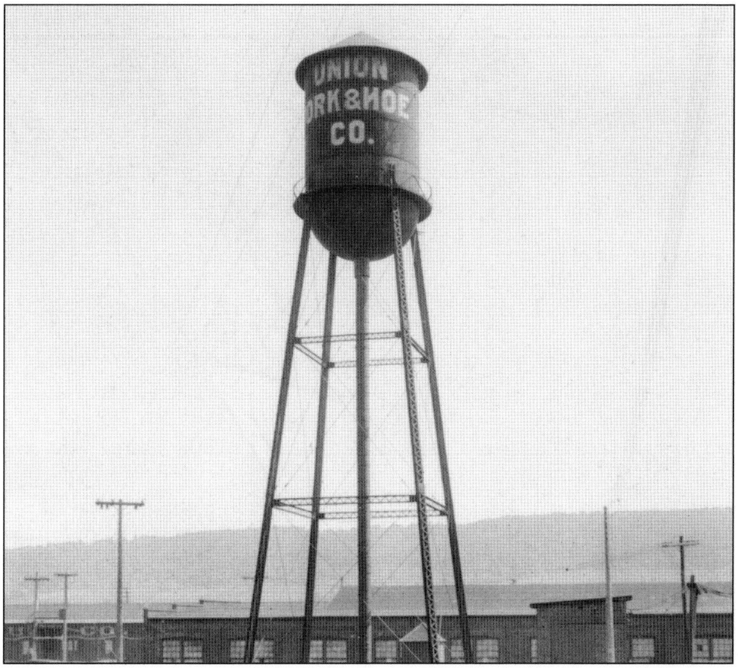


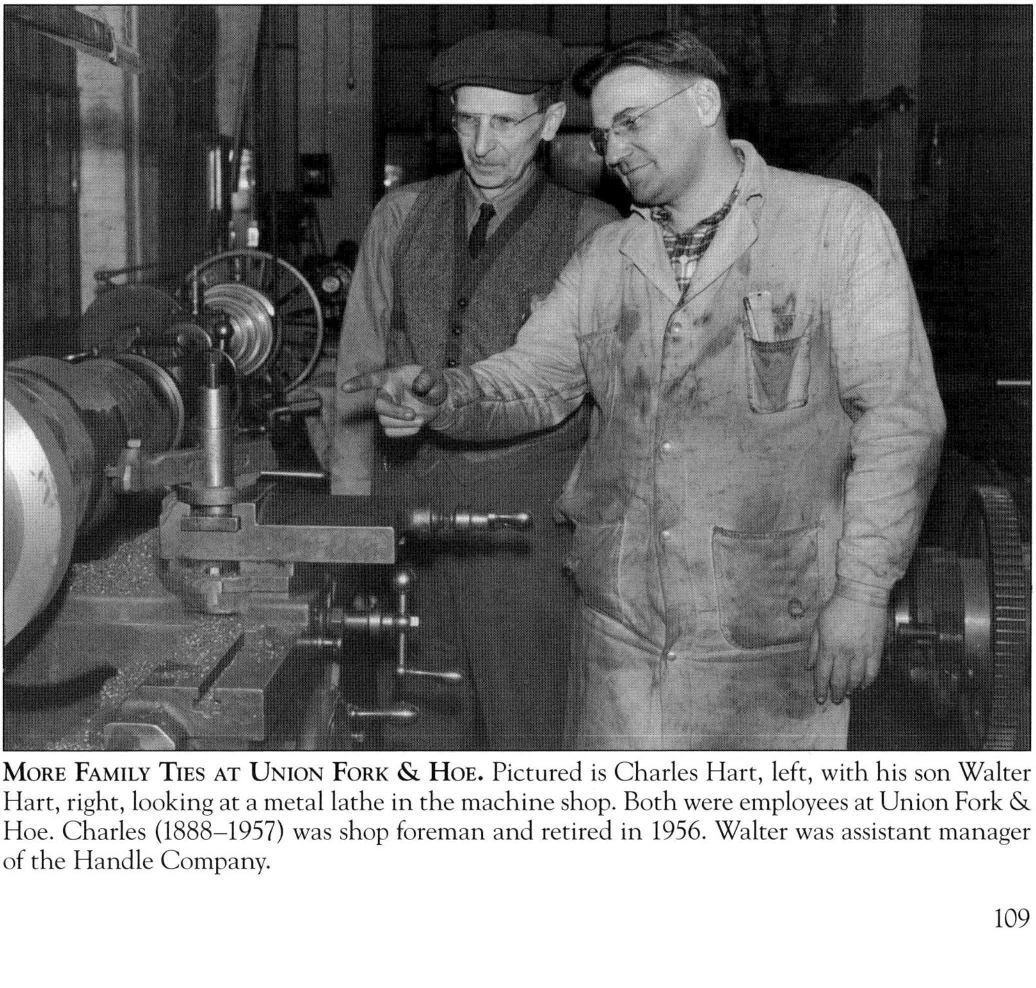

**MORE FAMILY TIES AT UNION FORK & HOE.** Pictured is Charles Hart, left, with his son Walter Hart, right, looking at a metal lathe in the machine shop. Both were employees at Union Fork & Hoe. Charles (1888–1957) was shop foreman and retired in 1956. Walter was assistant manager of the Handle Company.

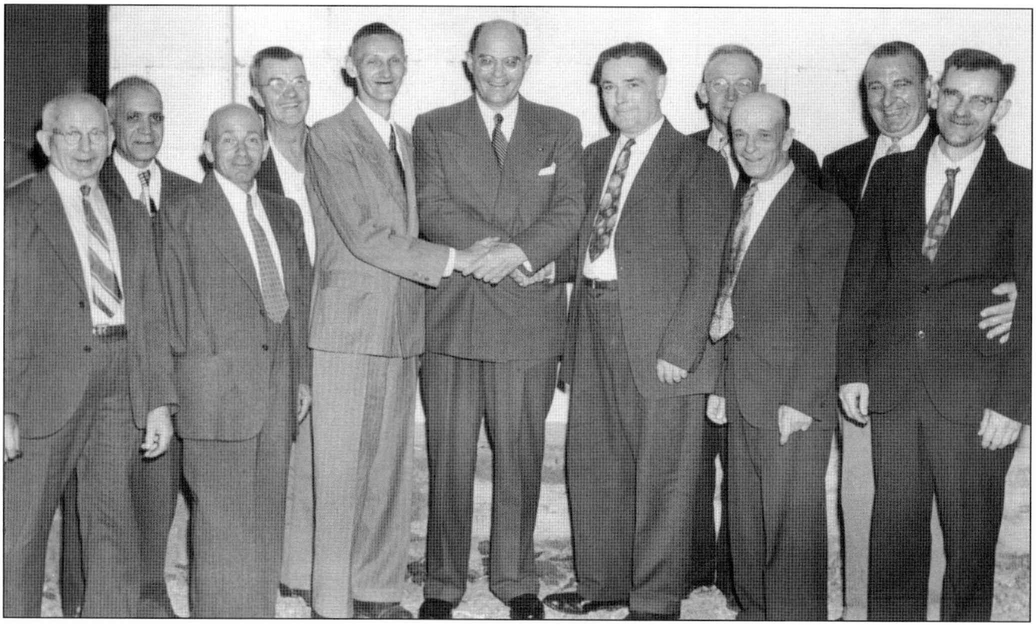

**Employees Honored.** This photograph, taken on June 22, 1949, at the annual meeting of the New York Chapter of the Diamond Service Club, shows Edward Durell, the president of the Union Fork & Hoe Company, congratulating members who have reached new service milestones. They are, from left to right, Leonard Weiss, Frank Egitto, Michael DePalma, Bert Jones, Richard Parker, Durrell, Frederic Collins, Seymour Thompson, Arthur Walker, Ralph Bouck, and William Graves.

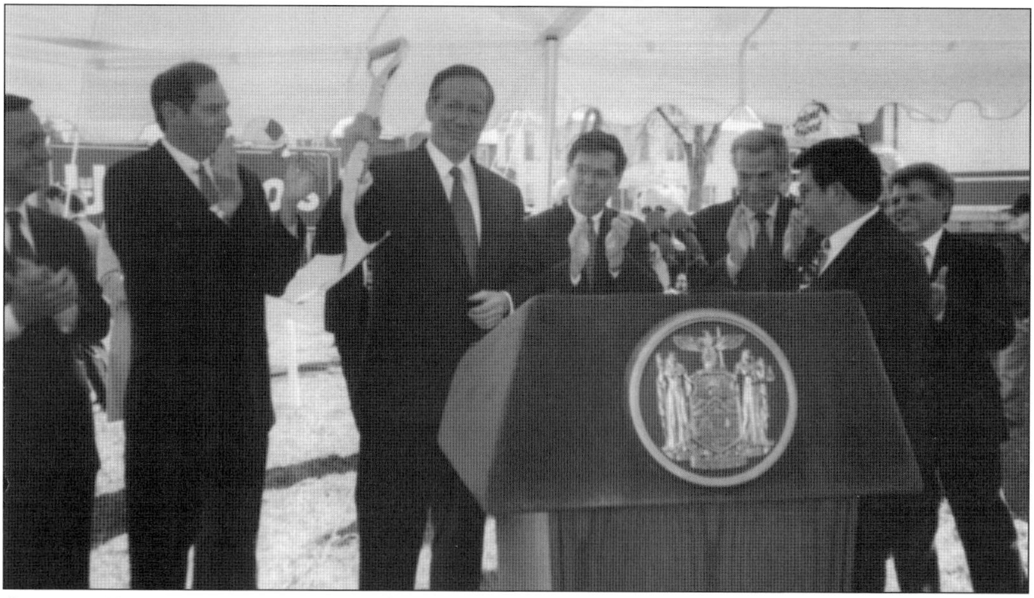

**Ground-Breaking Ceremony.** The Durell family sold the company in 1987 to American European Associates, and the name was changed to Union Tools. This photograph shows a ground-breaking ceremony on April 8, 1999, for a $3-million expansion for new equipment and building renovations. From left to right are Sen. Raymond Meier, assemblyman Marc Butler, Gov. George Pataki (holding the gold shovel), Sen. James Seward, two unidentified men, and Frankfort mayor Fred Pumilio.

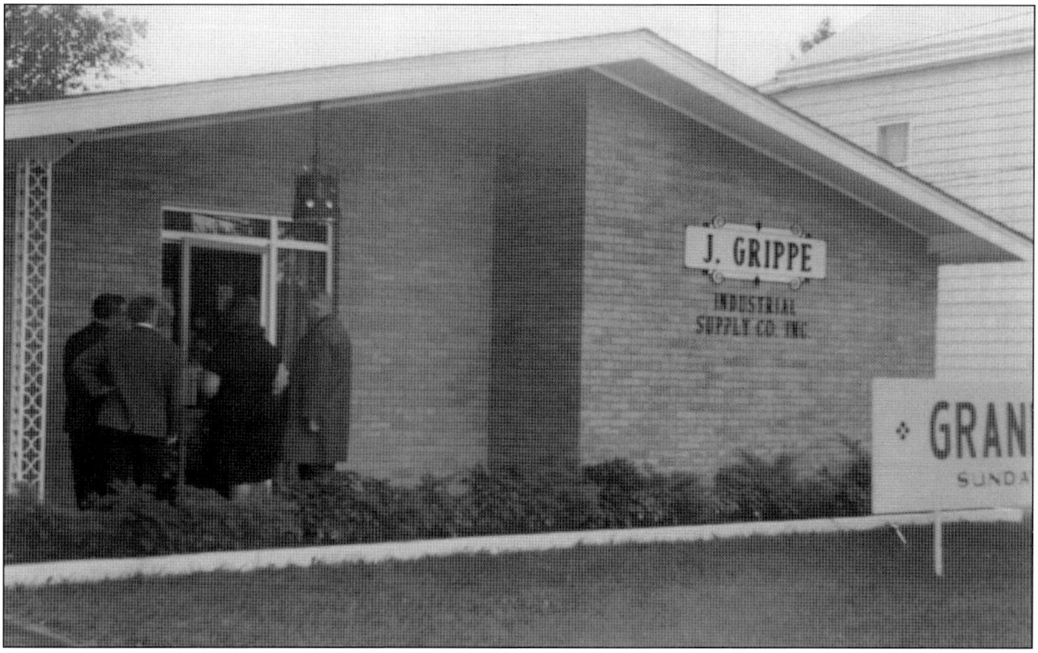


**J. Grippe Industrial Supply Co.** A family-operated business to this day, this company was started in the family basement by Joseph Grippe (1924–2010), with the assistance of his wife, Mary Alice (1927–2008), in 1962. It supplied all types of quality cutting tools to local and national industries and was one of the original industrial supply companies in New York State. Located at 4160 Acme Road, the company continues to have a large customer base, including automotive manufacturers, gun manufacturers, machine shops of all sizes, aircraft manufacturers, and educational institutions. The photograph below shows the business decorated for the Christmas season, a tradition at the company that drew spectators from all over the area. (Both, courtesy of the estate of Joseph J. and Mary Alice Grippe.)

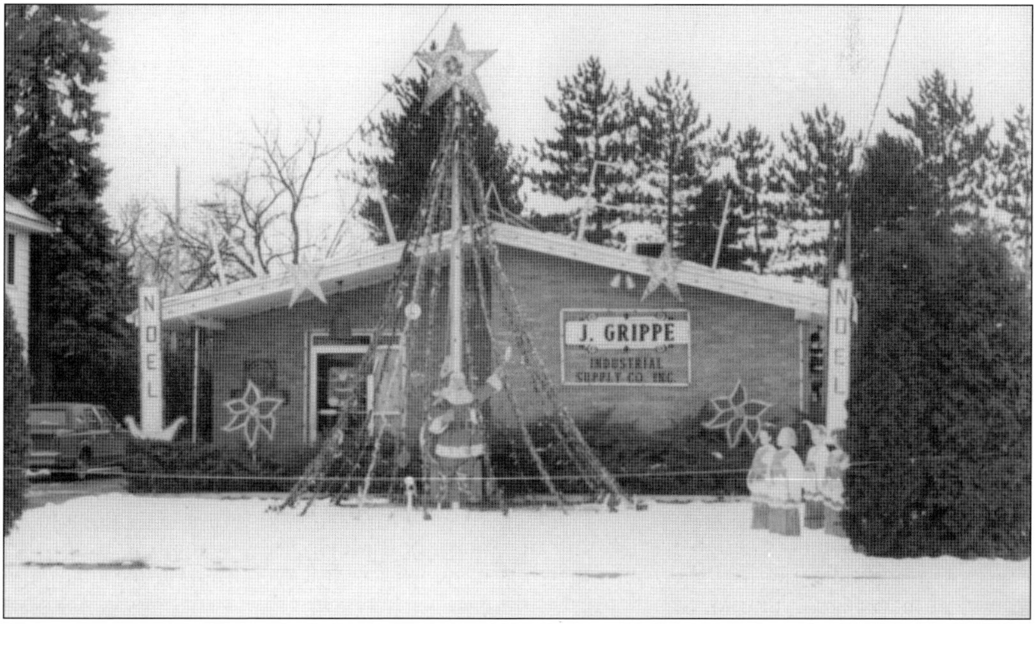

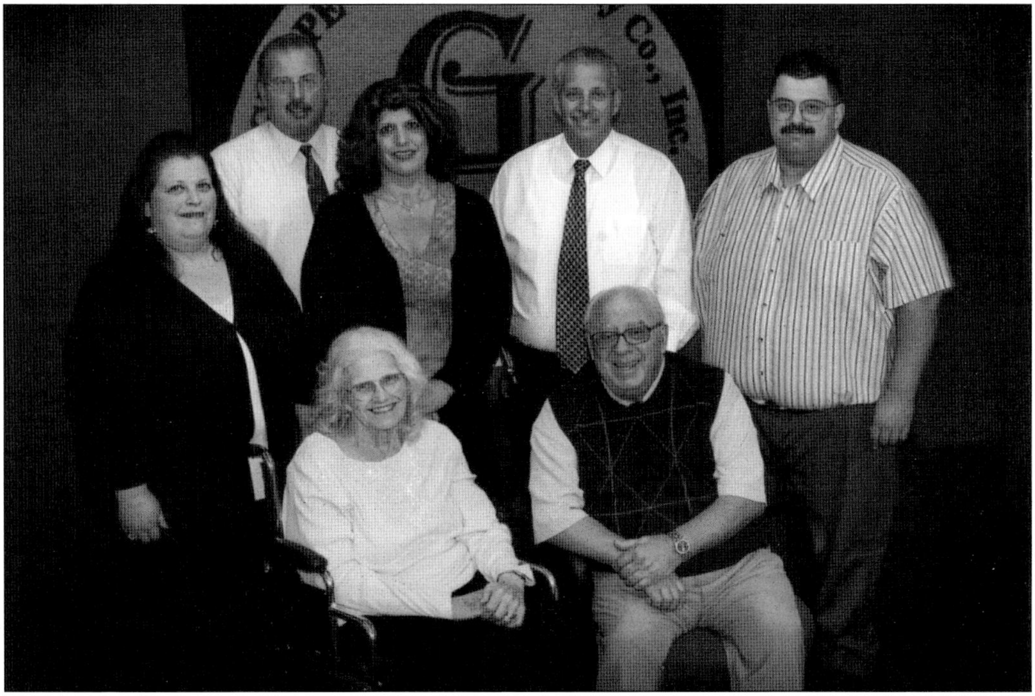

**Family Employees.** This 1985 photograph shows family employees at J. Grippe Industrial Supply Co. Sitting in front are parents Mary Alice (Cobb) Grippe and Joseph J. Grippe. Standing in the back are their children, from left to right, Karen Grippe Rumrill, Jack Grippe, Bridget Grippe Foti, Jody Grippe, and Brian Grippe. (Courtesy of the estate of Joseph J. and Mary Alice Grippe.)

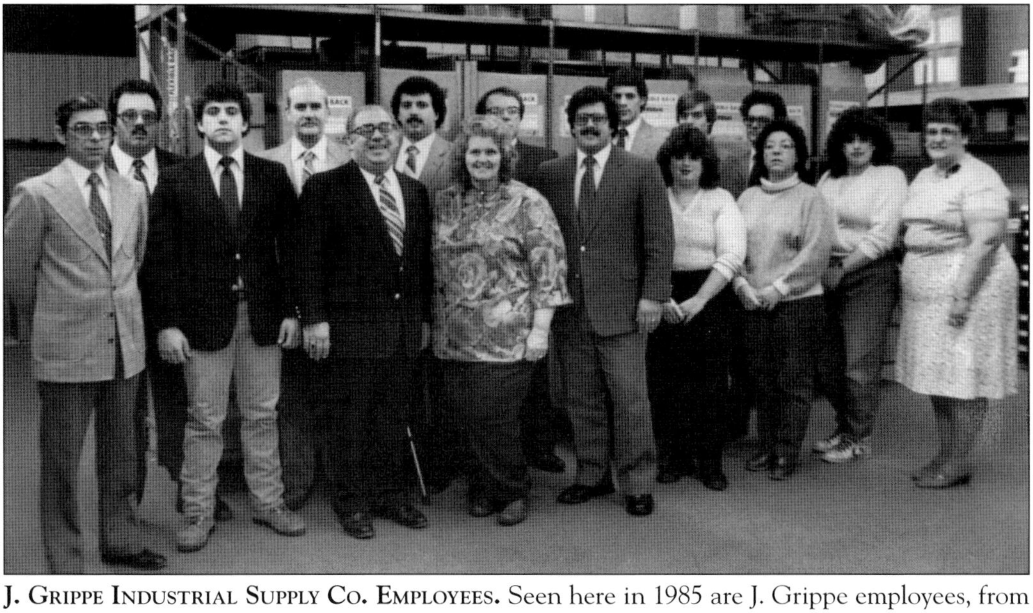

**J. Grippe Industrial Supply Co. Employees.** Seen here in 1985 are J. Grippe employees, from left to right, (first row) Peter Biando, Brian E. Grippe, Joseph J. Grippe, Mary Alice Grippe, Jody T. Grippe, Mary Grippe, Mary Ellen Fucchi, Bridget Grippe Foti, and Becky Eaker; (second row) Gary Grippe, Dave Gage, Jack Grippe, Pat Reed, Joe Loiacano, Jeff Miagza, and Bill Pickles. Not pictured is Karen Grippe Rumrill. (Courtesy of the estate of Joseph J. and Mary Alice Grippe.)

# *Six*

# TRANSPORTATION

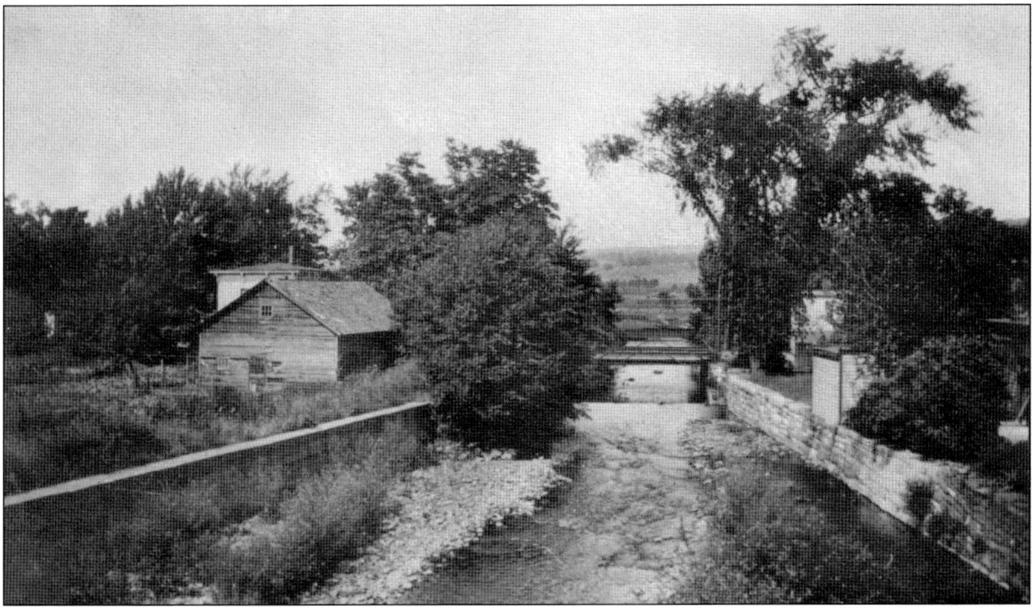

**ERIE CANAL.** The Erie Canal opened in 1825, after the section between Utica and Little Falls was completed in 1823. This view from the canal looks north from the aqueduct to Main Street, where the canal crossed Moyer Creek. The dwellings on the left belonged to Dr. William Budlong (1826–1914) on West Main Street. The first bridge is on West Main Street, and the one beyond it is the railroad bridge.

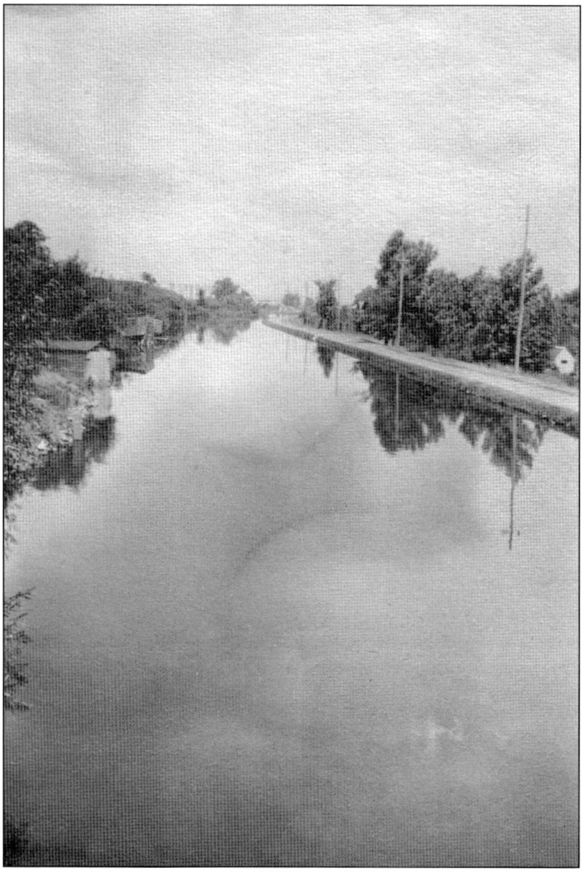

**The Towpath.** This view of the Erie Canal looks west from the bridge at Cemetery Street. The towpath, on the right, was a path alongside the canal used by horses towing boats by rope. The Erie Canal was transformed into the Barge Canal system between 1903 and 1918.

**Frankfort Aqueduct.** The postcard below shows Moyer Creek and the Erie Canal aqueduct in the background. The aqueduct was located between the Cemetery Street Bridge and Lock No. 45. This bridge-like structure carried the canal and its towpath across the creek.

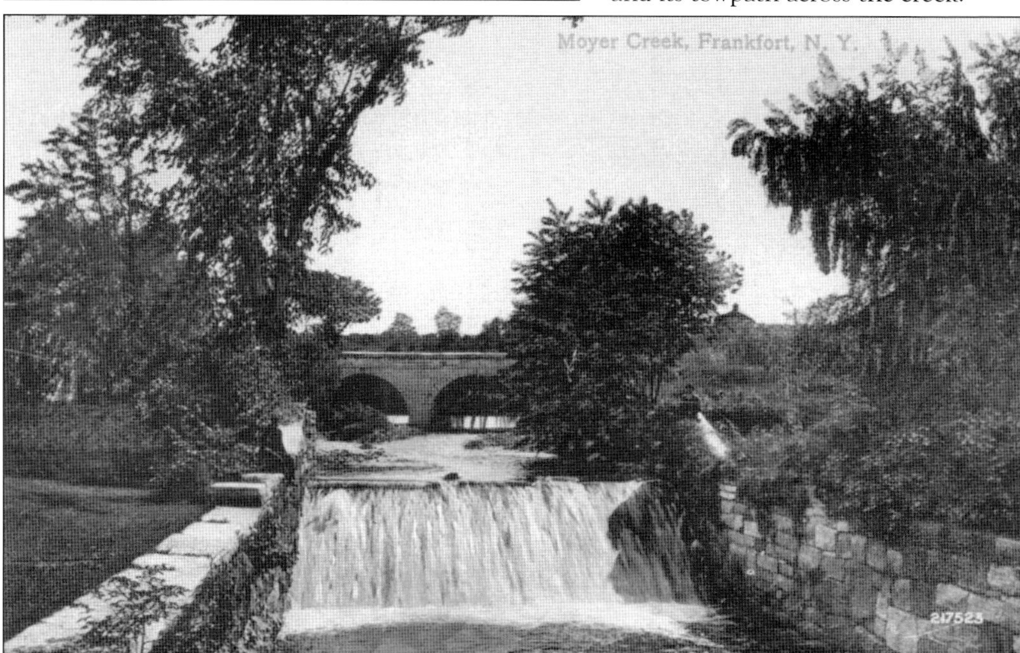

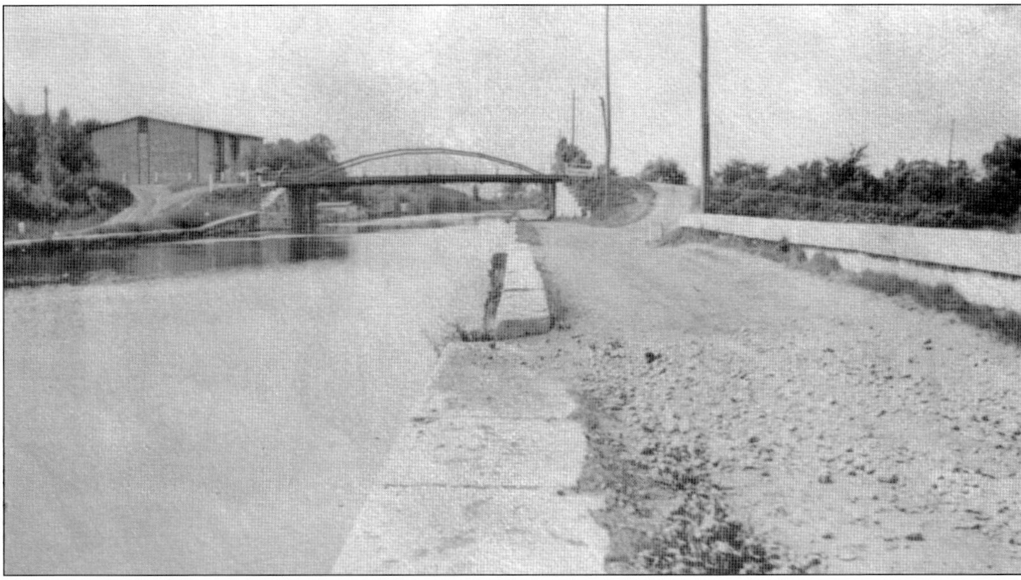

**Cemetery Street Bridge.** This view looks west from the Erie Canal to the Cemetery Street Bridge. The 77-foot-long bridge, the first iron-truss bridge in America, was constructed by Earl Trumbull (c. 1810–1851) of Little Falls. On the right is the towpath. On the left is the icehouse owned by Bertram Owen (1868–1926).

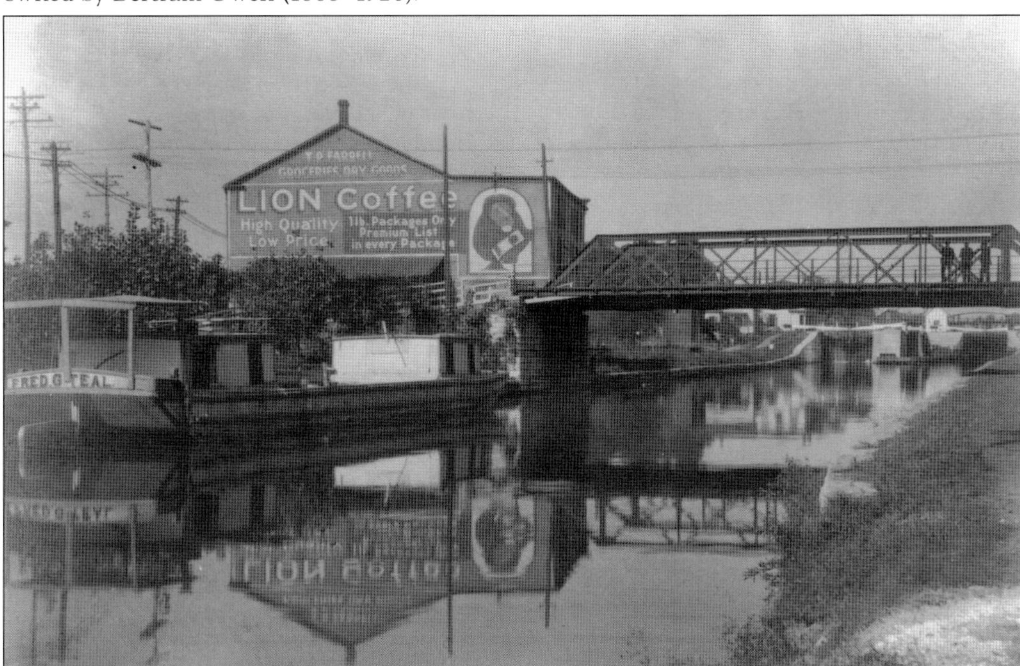


**Businesses along the Canal.** Thomas Farrell (1843–1900) emigrated from Ireland with his parents to Frankfort. He operated a dry goods business and owned canal boats and a coal yard near the Erie Canal at 44 Litchfield Street. The business was torn down for the parking lot of the town hall in 1924. The Litchfield Street Bridge is in the center, with Lock No. 45 just behind it. (Courtesy of Chad Wohler.)

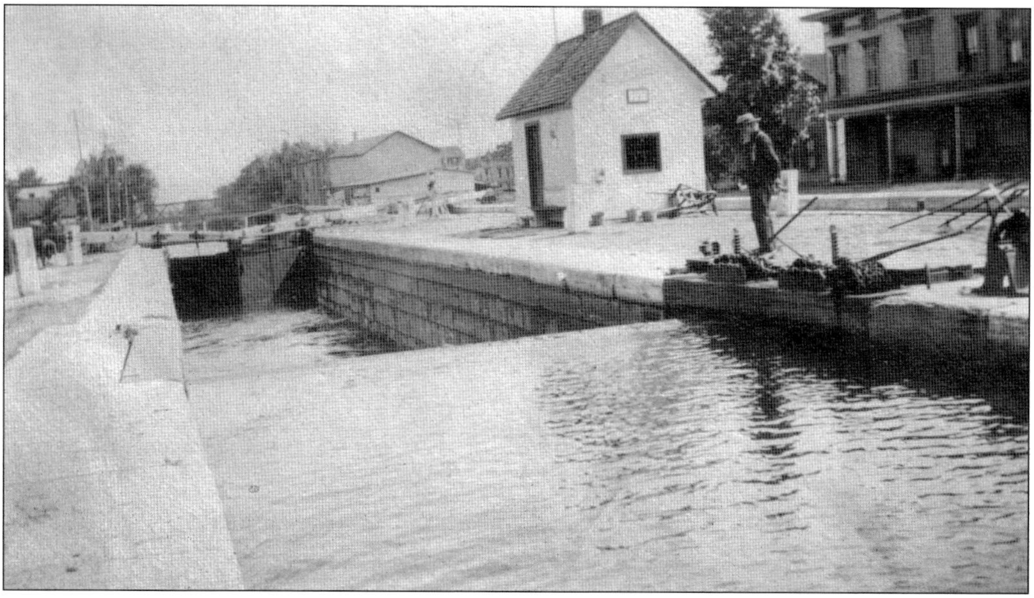

**Erie Canal Lock No. 45.** Seen above are Lock No. 45 and the lock-tenders' house. The lock had a lift of 10.949 feet. The Erie Canal Grocery, operated by Jacob Dieffenbacher (1845–1927), is on the far right. The lock was a prime location for stores, as it provided ready customers because people had extra time while waiting for their boats to go through the lock. Two stores were on the north bank and one was on the south. Below is a view of the lock seen from Cemetery Street looking east. Moyer Creek crosses the lock, and the Litchfield Street Bridge is in the far background.

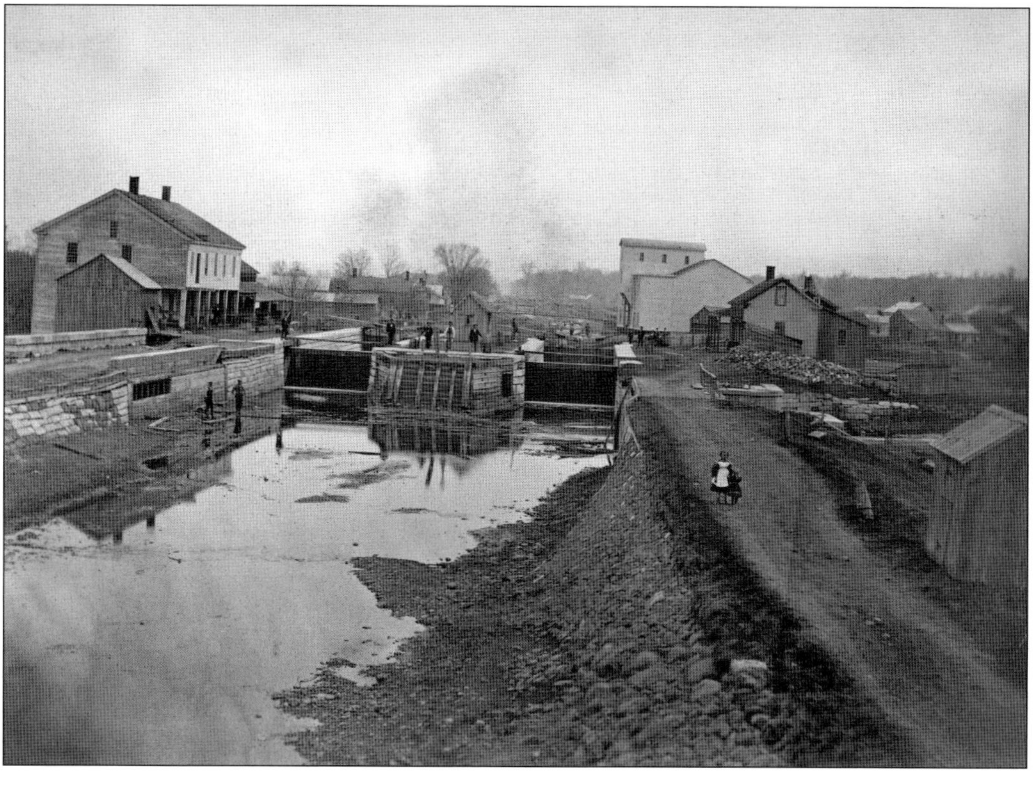

**Moyer Creek.** This view of Moyer Creek looks north from the West Main Street Bridge. The railroad bridge is in the background. Moyer Creek flows in a north-northeasterly direction from the town of Litchfield through the town of Frankfort before emptying into the Mohawk River near the village of Frankfort. It is approximately 11.5 miles in length.

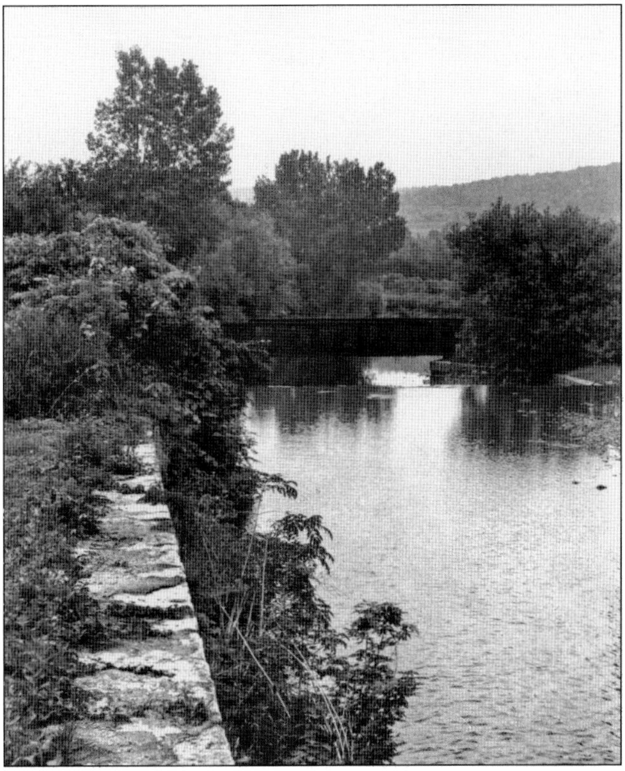

**Trolley Line.** In 1872, track was laid for the single-line Herkimer, Mohawk, Ilion & Frankfort Electric Railway, which served local traffic to its western terminus at Main and Litchfield Streets. In 1902, the Utica & Mohawk Valley Railway built a double-track extension running along Pleasant Avenue, providing trolley service from Rome to Little Falls, a total of 37 miles. On the left is the Masonic temple. (Courtesy of Dave Sanders.)

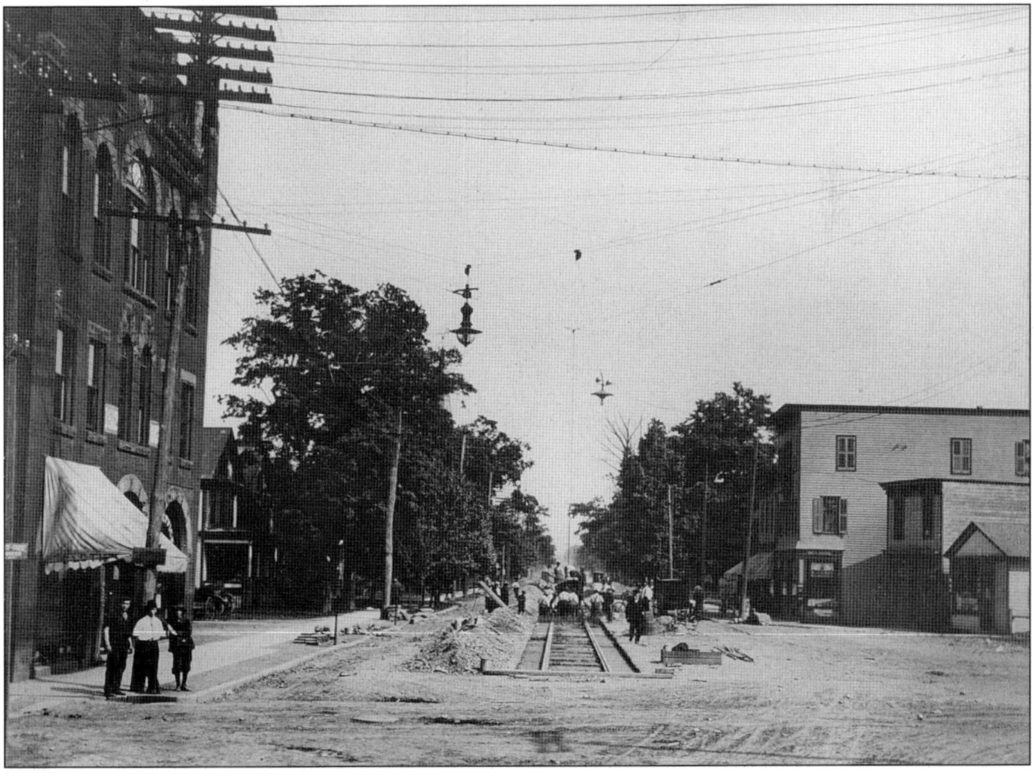

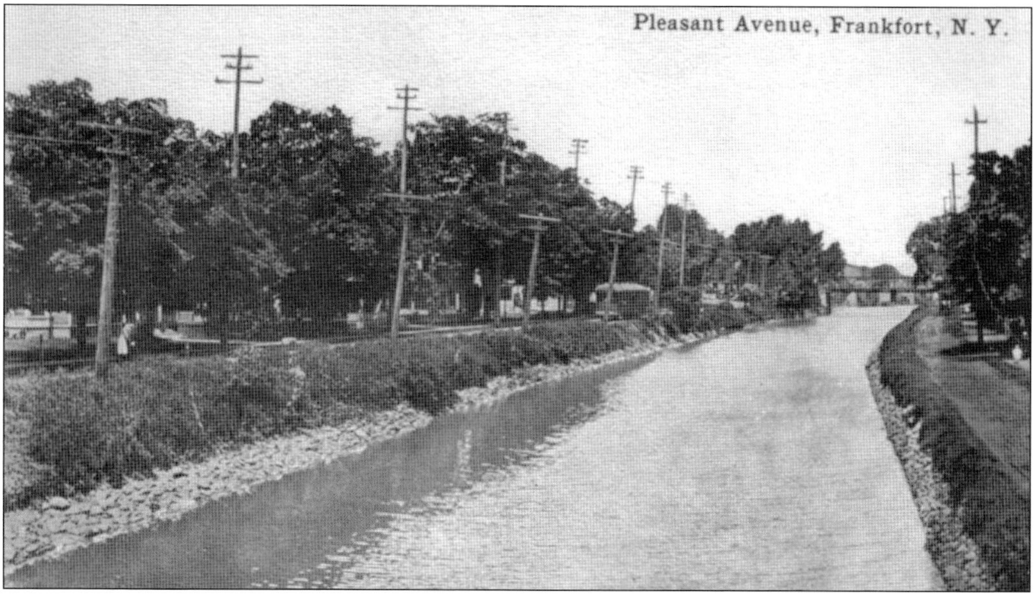


**PLEASANT AVENUE TROLLEY LINE.** This postcard shows the trolley line that ran along Pleasant Avenue and the Erie Canal. It was double-tracked and provided service every half hour. The street railway prospered until 1927, when it had its first operating losses. The line finally closed in 1933.

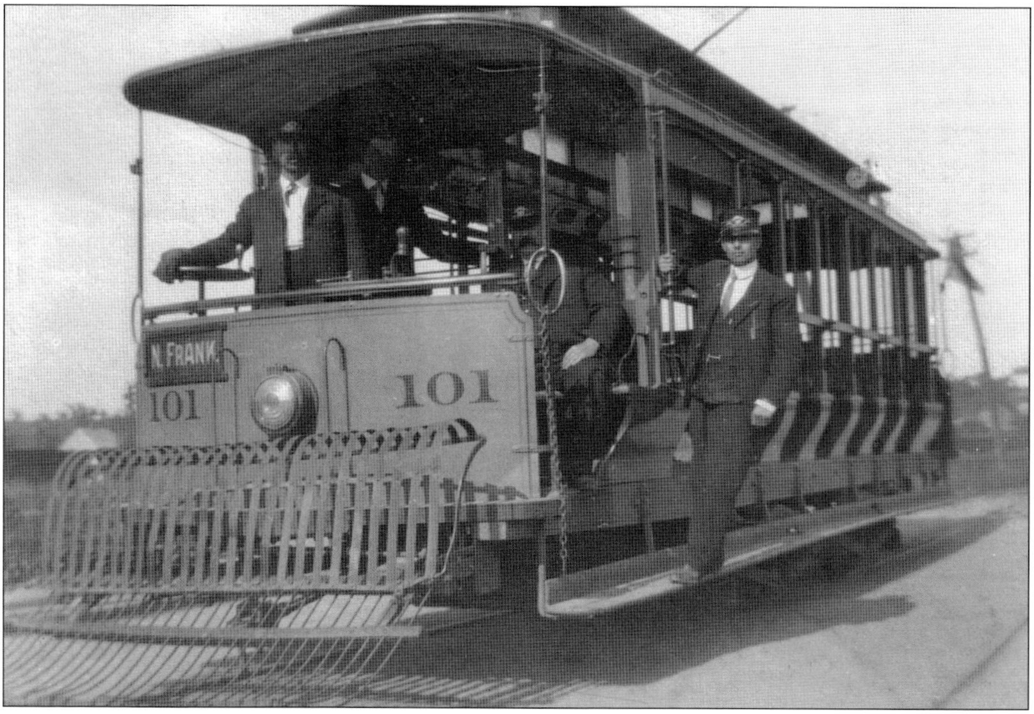


**NORTH FRANKFORT TROLLEY CAR.** The trolleys were double-end cars with a trolley pole at each end for contact with the overhead power wire. A control box at either end raised and lowered the "cow-catcher," or guard. The Short Line, on the north side of the canal, ran between Frankfort and Herkimer, and the Main Line, south of the canal, extended from Rome to Little Falls. (Courtesy of Chad Wohler.)

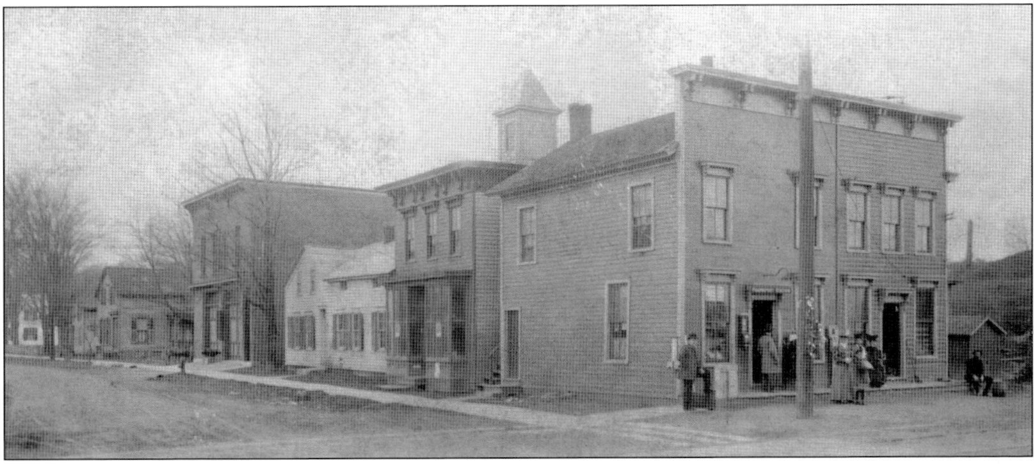

**Frankfort Trolley Station.** In 1904, this property, on the corner of Pleasant Avenue and Litchfield Street, was acquired as a depot for the trolley line. John Watkins (1869–1950) was the station agent, and he and his family lived upstairs. When the line closed, Watkins operated the building as a confectionery and newsstand. The building was razed to provide room for the Frankfort community fair. (Courtesy of the Frankfort Fire Department.)

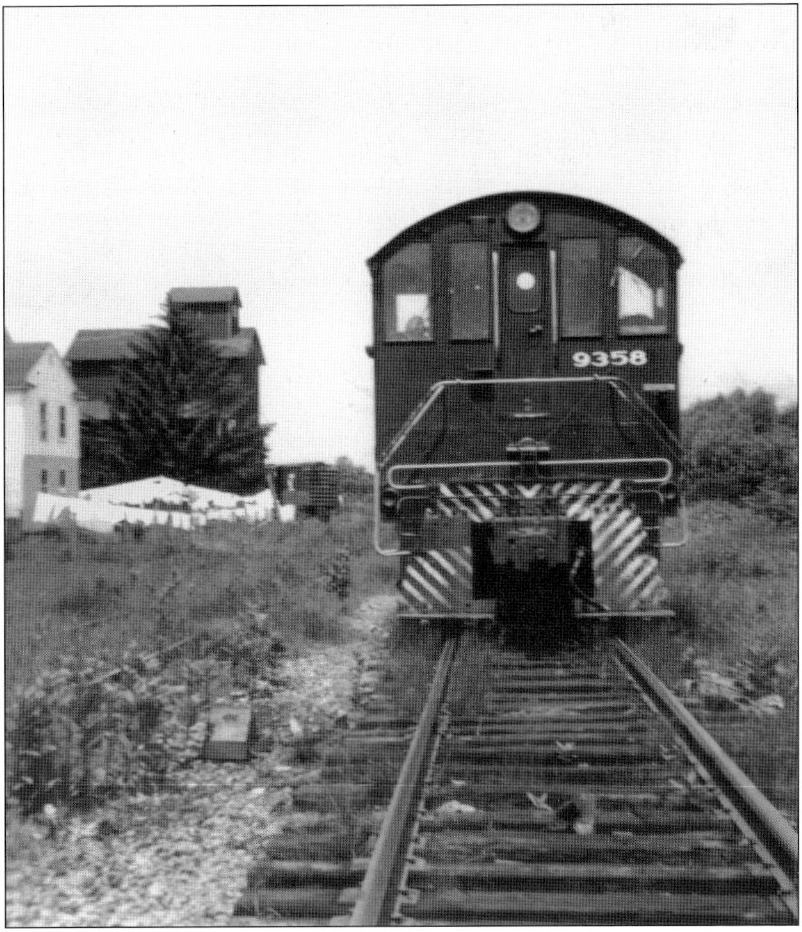


**West Shore Railroad.** In 1881, the New York, West Shore & Buffalo Railroad began construction on a line that ran along the western shore of the Hudson River and the southern shore of the Mohawk River. By 1884, bankruptcy led to its sale and lease to the New York Central Railroad. There were stations in Little Falls, Mohawk, Ilion, and Frankfort. By 1947, only a milk train traveled the double-tracked line. (Courtesy of Donald Roberts.)

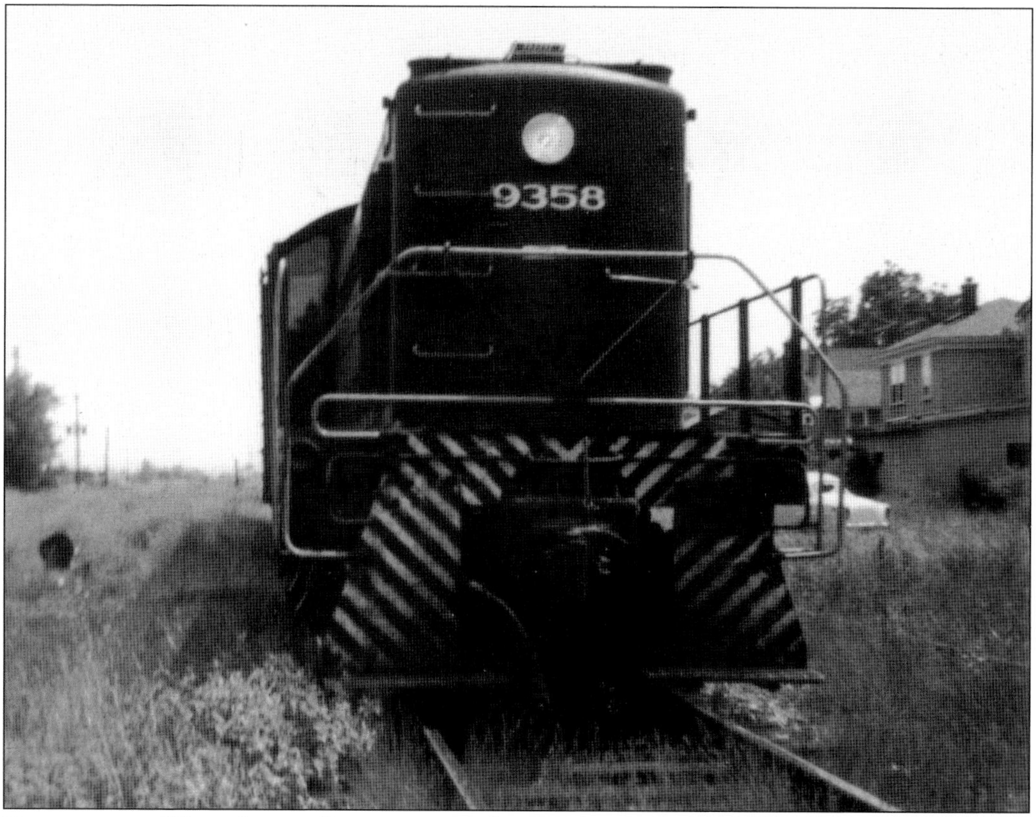


**Remnants of West Shore.** Passenger travel in Herkimer County ended after World War II, and freight travel ceased in 1966. The Frankfort freight house closed in 1959. The path of the West Shore can still be seen in some communities and is now used as a hiking and biking trail. The City of Little Falls built a trail along the roadbed behind Lock No. 17 in 1988. (Courtesy of Donald Roberts.)

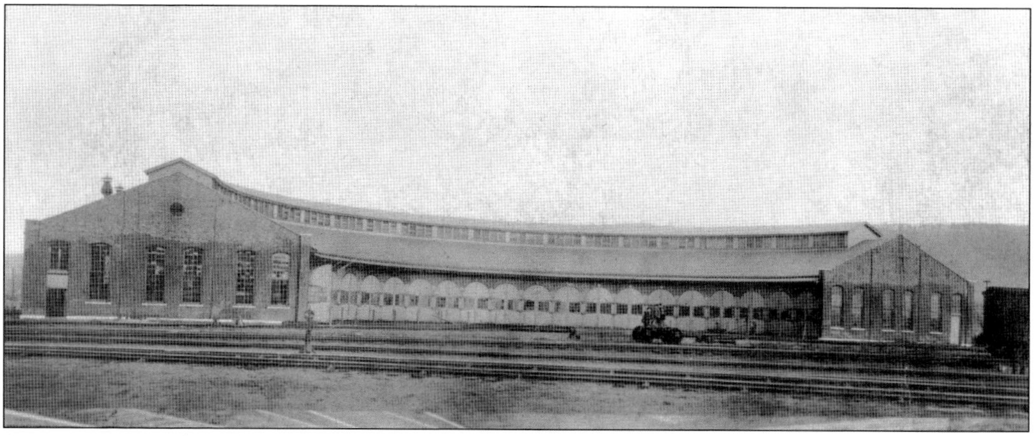

**Roundhouse.** The old roundhouse on the site of the West Shore Railroad repair shop was built in 1883. It had the capacity to service 22 locomotives at a time. The building was abandoned when the repair shop was closed in 1897 and was demolished in 1927. The other buildings on site were repurposed at different times for the Michigan Condensed Milk Company, Continental Tool Company, and the Pratt Chuck Company. (Courtesy of Chad Wohler.)

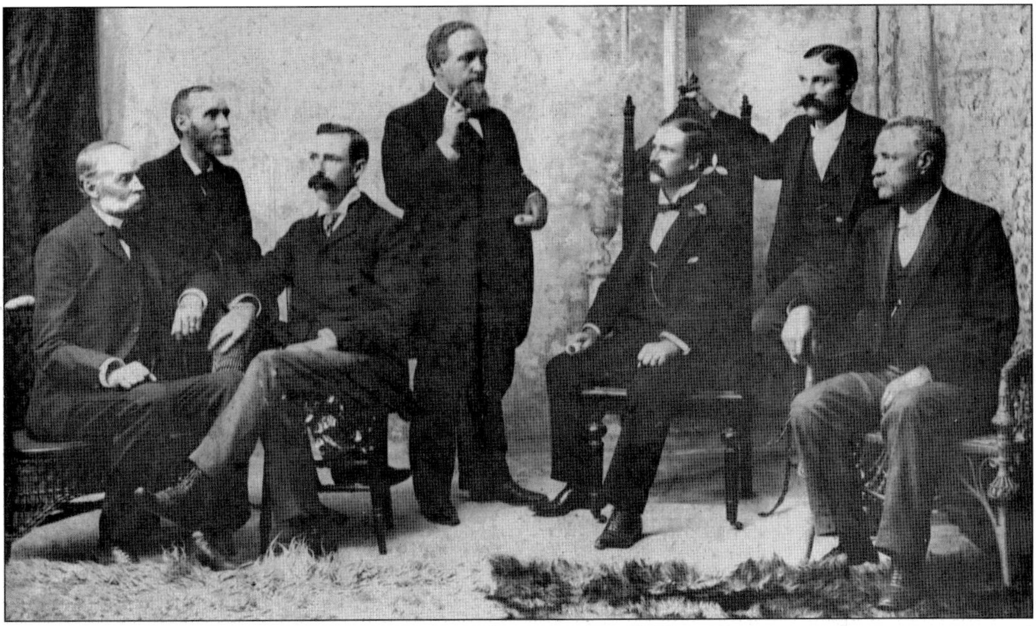

**West Shore Railroad Shops.** The West Shore Railroad Shop Committee was instrumental in bringing the repair facility to Frankfort in 1883. The community raised enough money to convey a large tract of land on the eastern end of the village. The committee members seen above are, from left to right, George Watson (1843–1920), Dr. Gilbert Lehr (1857–1938), Dr. Seymour Richards (1860–1926), Joseph Dudleston (1838–1913), Alonzo Lints (1856–1904), George Seaman (1850–1907), and Hamilton Ingham (1842–1920). Work at the shops attracted families to Frankfort seeking employment. The buildings included the roundhouse, a blacksmith shop, a planing mill, a storehouse, a boiler shop, a foundry, and an erecting shop. Expert machinists and mechanics were placed at work, and the village prospered. When the shops closed in 1897, an arrangement was made with the New York Central Railroad to lease the shops with the right to obtain manufacturing plants. (Both, courtesy of Frankfort Free Library.)

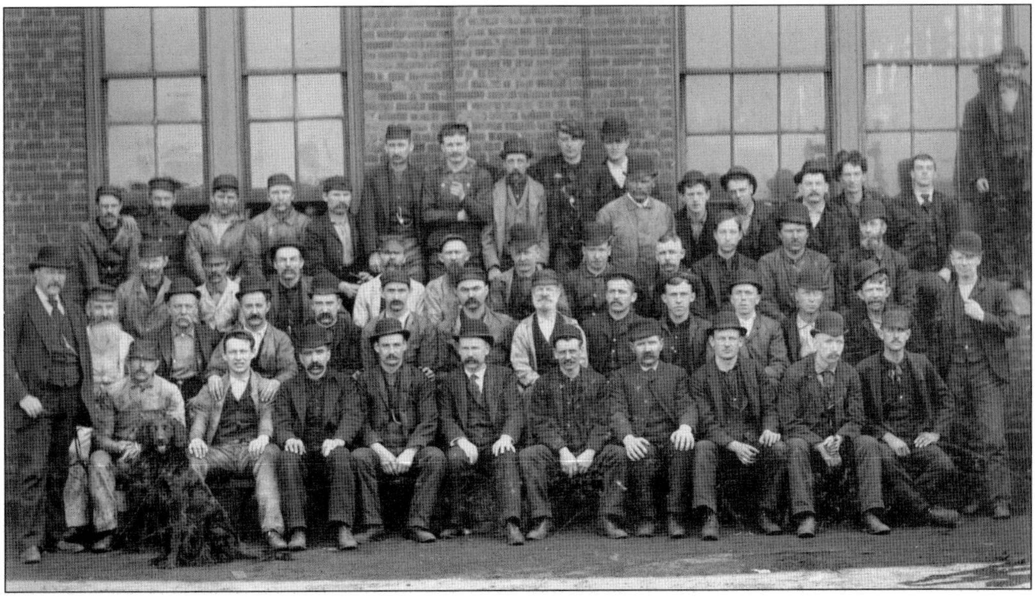

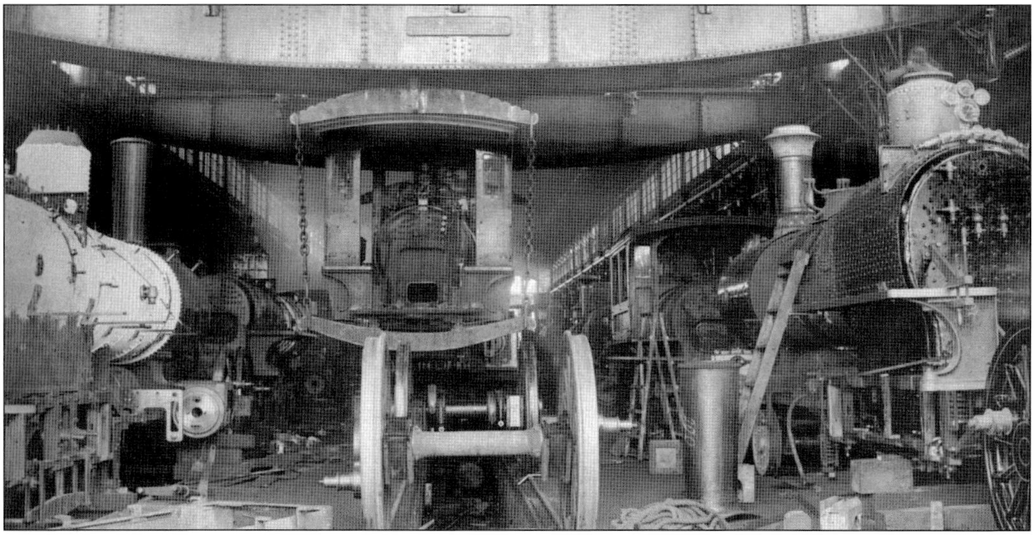

**Interior, West Shore Railroad Shops.** This photograph shows the interior of the erecting shop, located west of the turntable in front of the roundhouse. A railroad track ran through the center of the building. On each side were sidetracks running parallel to the main track. A traveling crane was used to lift heavy machinery or cars from the track and deposit it on one of the sidetracks. (Courtesy of Frankfort Free Library.)

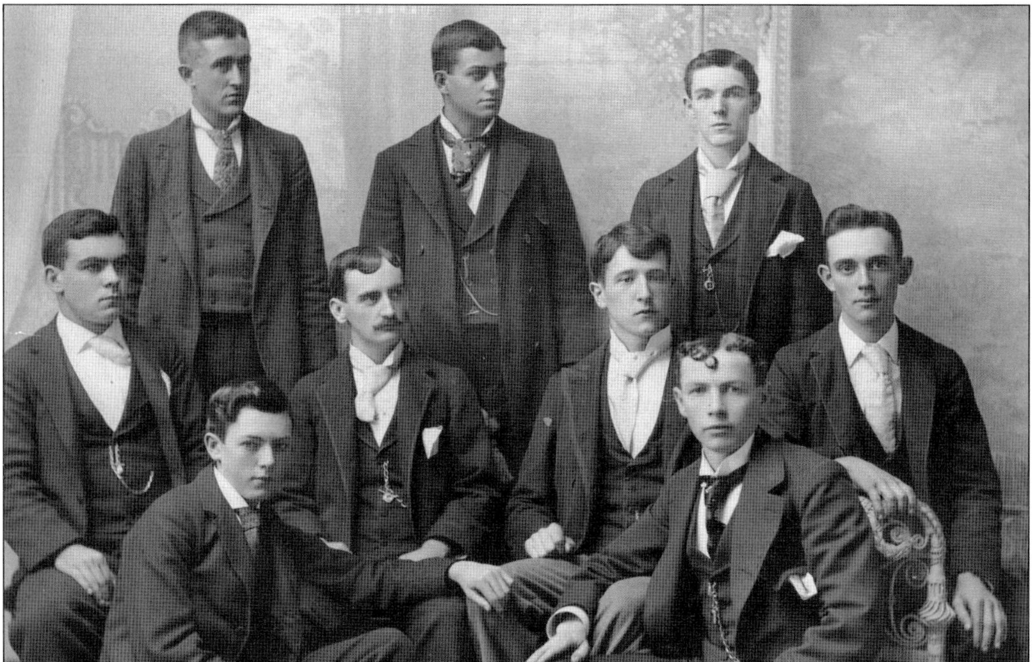

**The Albermarle Club.** The Albermarle Club was formed in Albany in 1884 for the purpose of social and intellectual enjoyment. The young men affiliated with the West Shore Railroad Shops formed a club in Frankfort. Seen here in 1894 are members Starkey Whitney (1874–1953), kneeling on the left, John Frazer, Frank Piper (1875–?), Samuel Williams (1874–1928), Bert Sterling (1873–1936), George Marshal, George Bennett, James Kerivan (1874–1901), and Warren Carder (1875–1943).

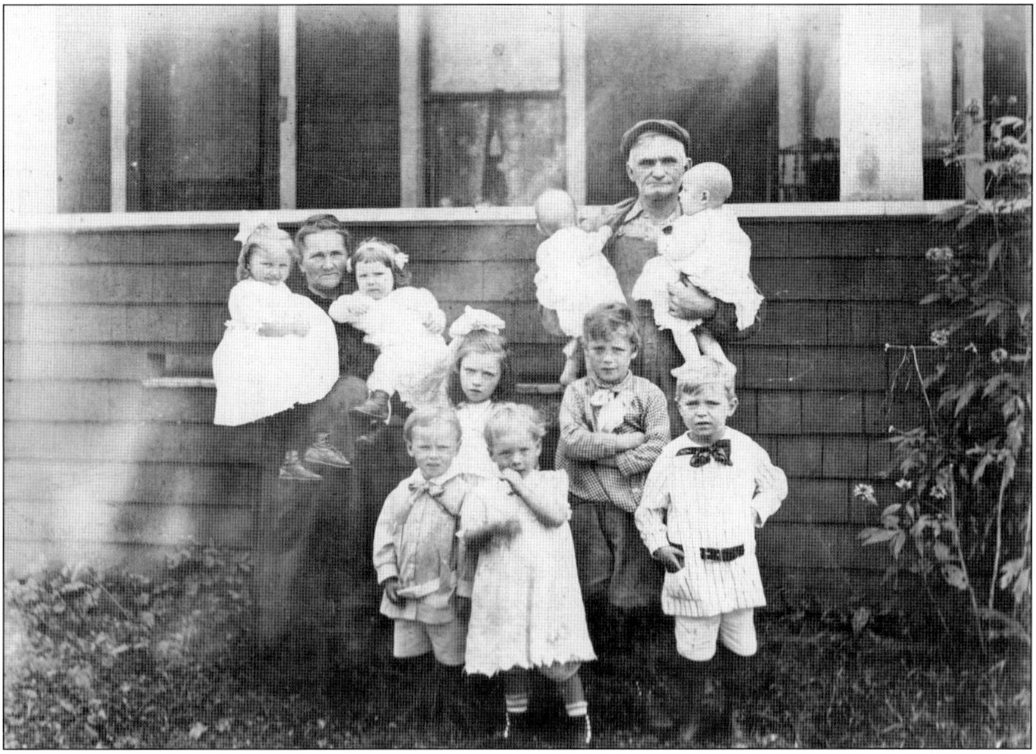

**West Shore Shops Brings New Families.** John Farley (1862–1938) and wife Mary (1865–1942) moved from Amsterdam to Frankfort in 1885 and worked for the railroad until the shops closed in 1897. They remained in Frankfort, where they raised their family, and John became a well-known contractor, the first one to used a motor truck instead of teams. Pictured with John and Mary are their grandchildren. (Courtesy of Mary Haefele.)

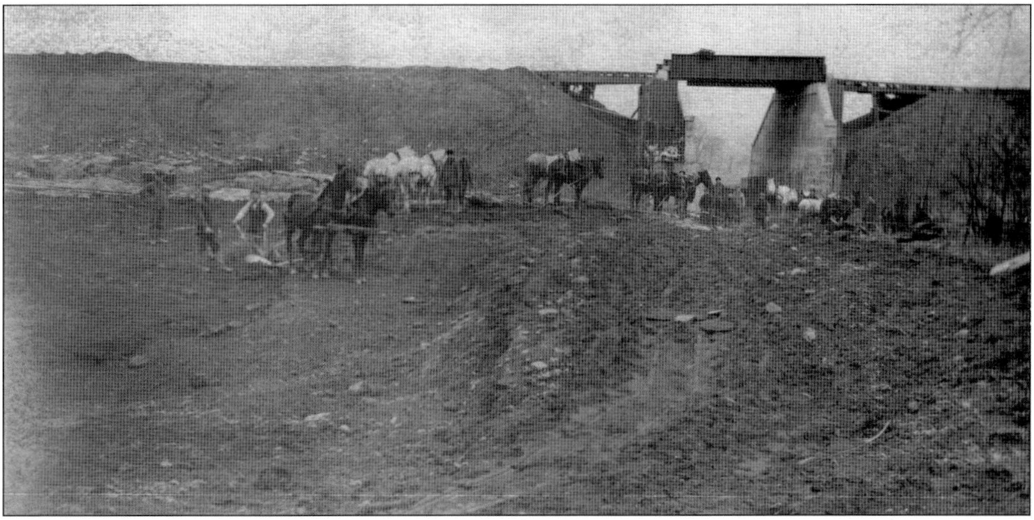

**Dyke Road Crossover.** The photograph above shows the 1914 construction of the West Shore Railroad spur just off of Dyke Road, which connected to the railroad crossover above old Route 5S in West Frankfort. After the stones were loaded into a stone-crusher, they were hauled away by horse and wagon.

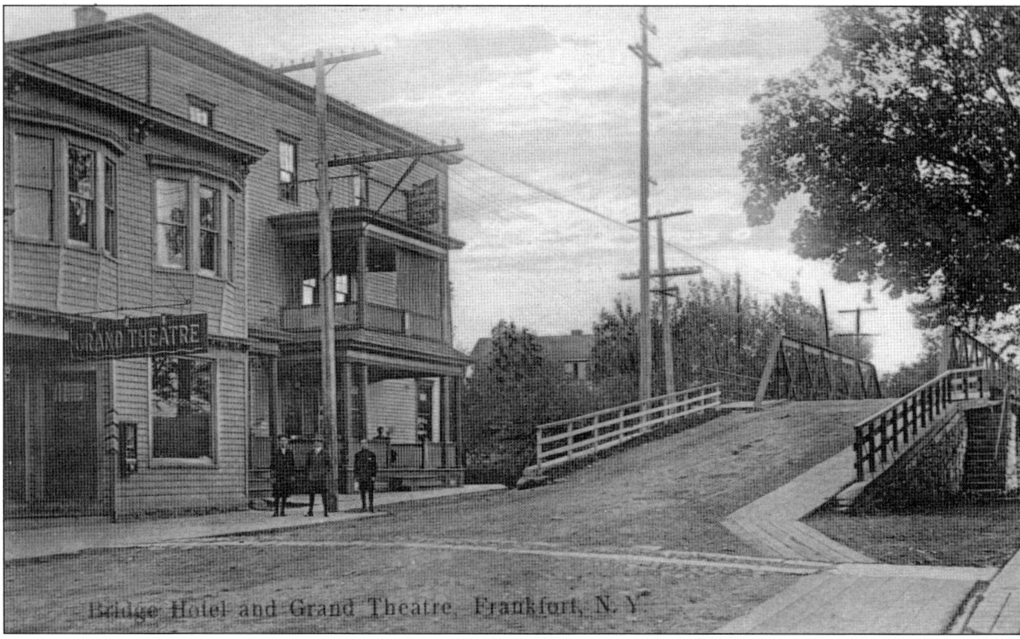


**Litchfield Street Bridge.** This postcard shows the Litchfield Street Bridge going over the Erie Canal. The Grand Theatre and the Bargy & Carder Bridge Hotel are on the corner. The theater was operated by George Loomis (c. 1844–1964) in 1912. The hotel was run by Warren Carder (1875–1943) and Willard Bargy (1863–1938) from 1906 to 1918. It remained a hotel into the 1970s. (Courtesy of Chad Wohler.)

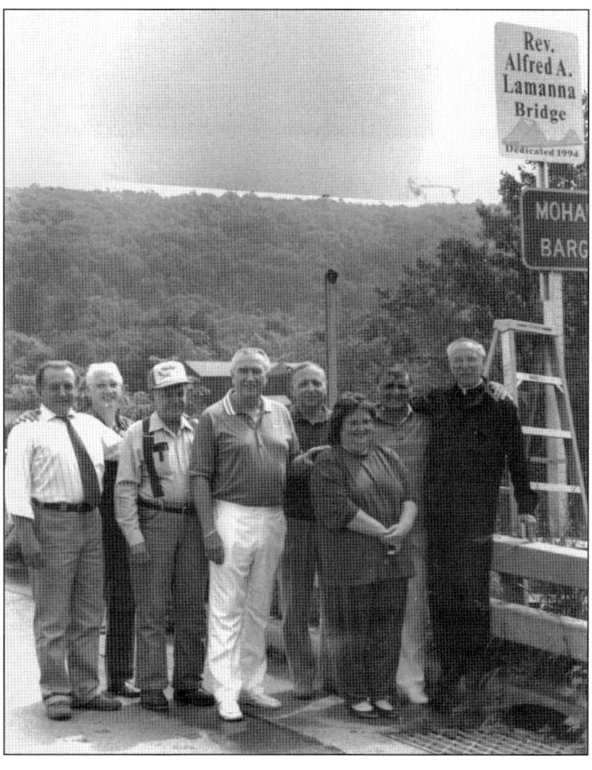


**Rev. Alfred A. Lamanna Bridge.** The $2.8-million North Frankfort Bridge over the railroad tracks and the Mohawk River–Barge Canal was opened on October 22, 1980. In 1994, the bridge was dedicated to Rev. Alfred Lamanna in honor of his efforts to replace the previous, unsafe structure. Seen here in 1994 are, from left to right, Joseph Kinney, Joseph Maneen, Anthony Rella, Hank Brown, Robert VanDusen, Dorothy Luther, Raymond DeLuke, and Reverend Lamanna. (Courtesy of Rev. Alfred Lamanna.)

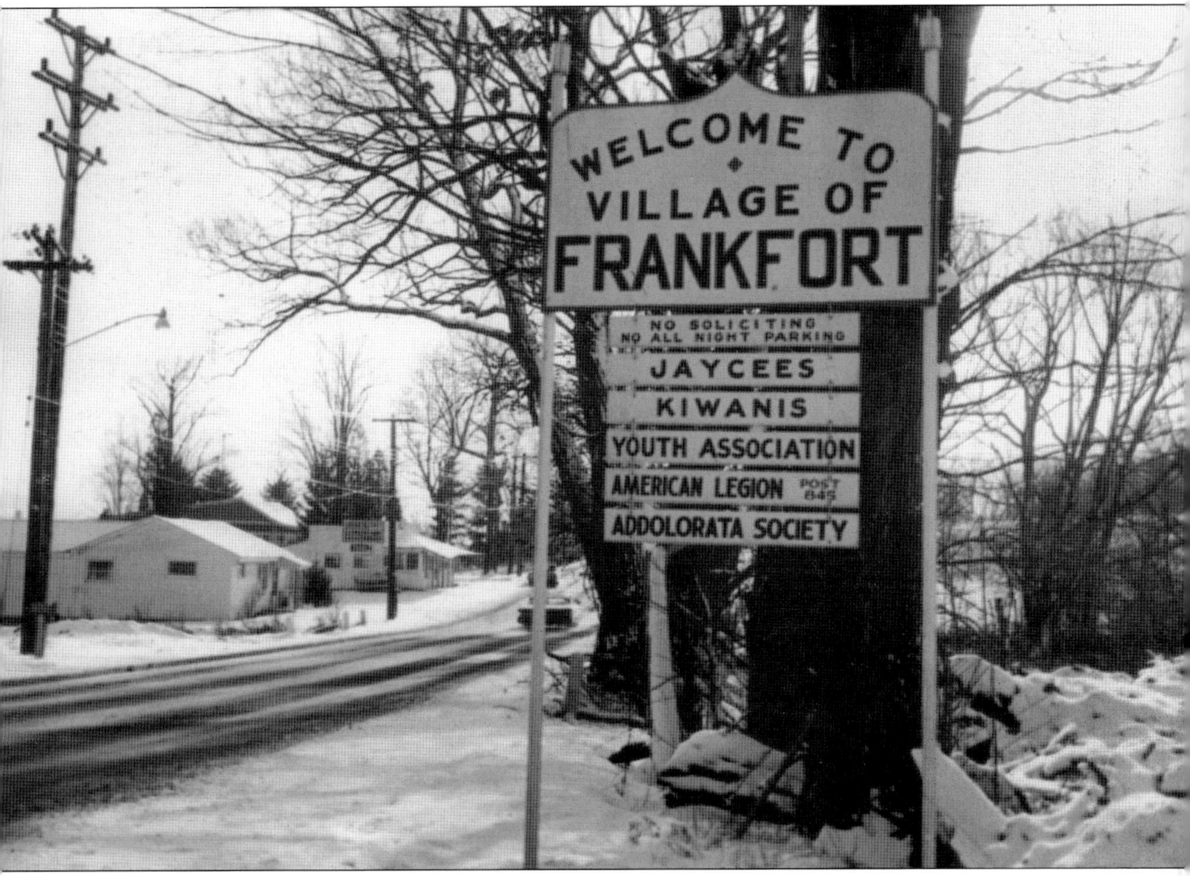


**The Town and Village of Frankfort, 2013.** The Town of Frankfort was established on February 5, 1796. Today, the town supervisor is Joseph P. Kinney, and the council members are Darlene Abbatecola, Joseph Tamburro, Michael Testa, and John Wallace. The town clerk is Gina Bellino, and the deputy town clerk is Dorri DeRollo. The town offices are located at 140 South Litchfield Street in the village of Frankfort. This was a very special year for the village of Frankfort, as it celebrated its sesquicentennial in 2013. The village was established on May 4, 1863. The mayor of the village of Frankfort is Frank M. Moracco, and the village trustees are Richard Adams, Michael Entwistle, Anthony Fumarola, and Mark Harris. The village clerk is Karlee Tamburro, and the village treasurer and deputy village clerk is Doreen Fiorentino. The village offices are housed in a refurbished school building at 110 Railroad Street.

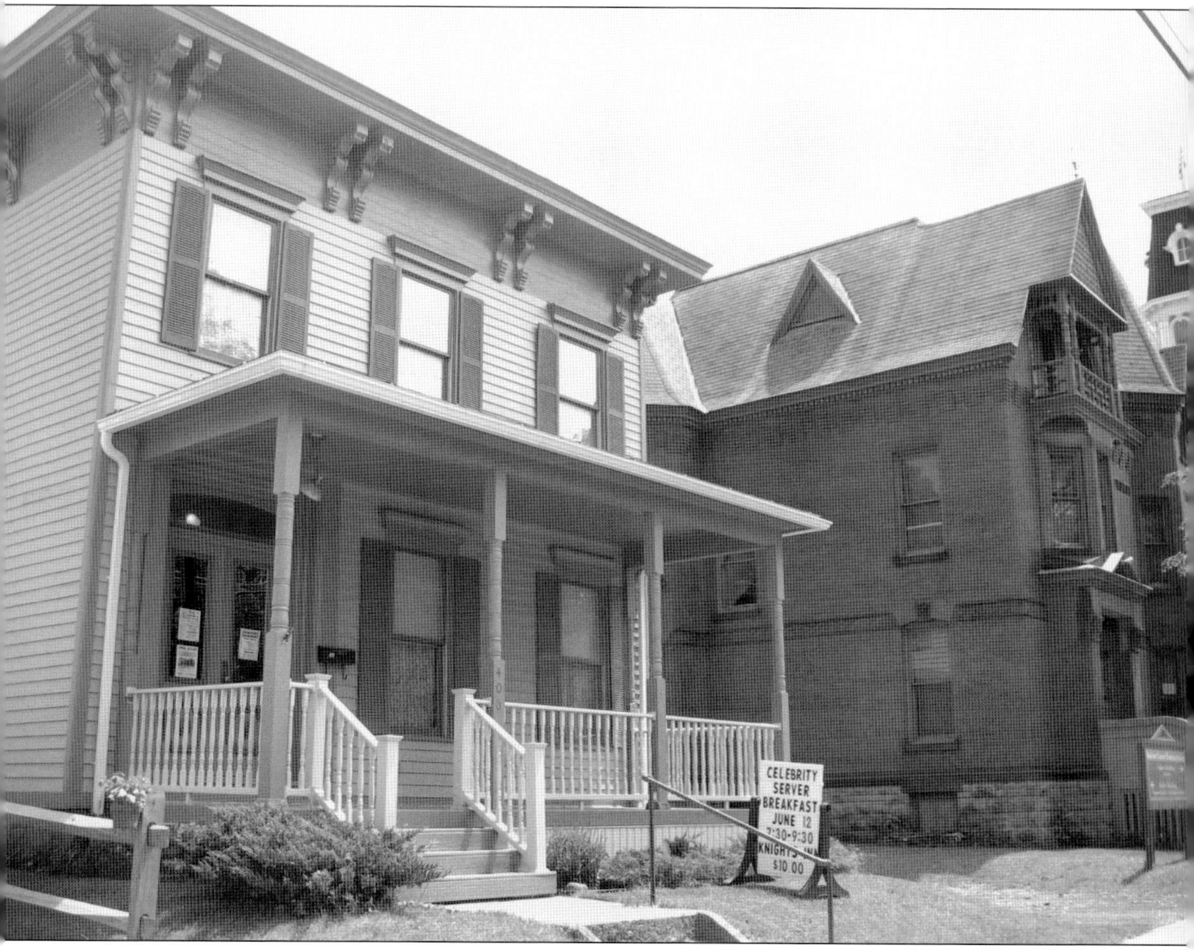


**HERKIMER COUNTY HISTORICAL SOCIETY.** Located at 400–406 North Main Street in Herkimer, the Herkimer County Historical Society is open Monday through Friday from 10:00 a.m. to 4:00 p.m. and on Saturdays in July and August from 10:00 a.m. to 3:00 p.m.

# About the Herkimer County Historical Society

Since 1896, the Herkimer County Historical Society has been a nonprofit organization discovering, collecting, preserving, and publishing information pertinent to the county's history. With the donation of the Suiter Memorial Building in 1925, the society has had a permanent headquarters where exhibits are displayed and a library where people can research their genealogy and local history.

In 2000, the society moved its library, gift shop, and offices into the renovated Eckler Building, which neighbors the Suiter Building on Main Street. The Suiter Building still contains a museum with displays open to the public, the society's vast collection, and the Daughters of the American Revolution Room, which features genealogical material. Both buildings are handicapped accessible with an adjoining link.

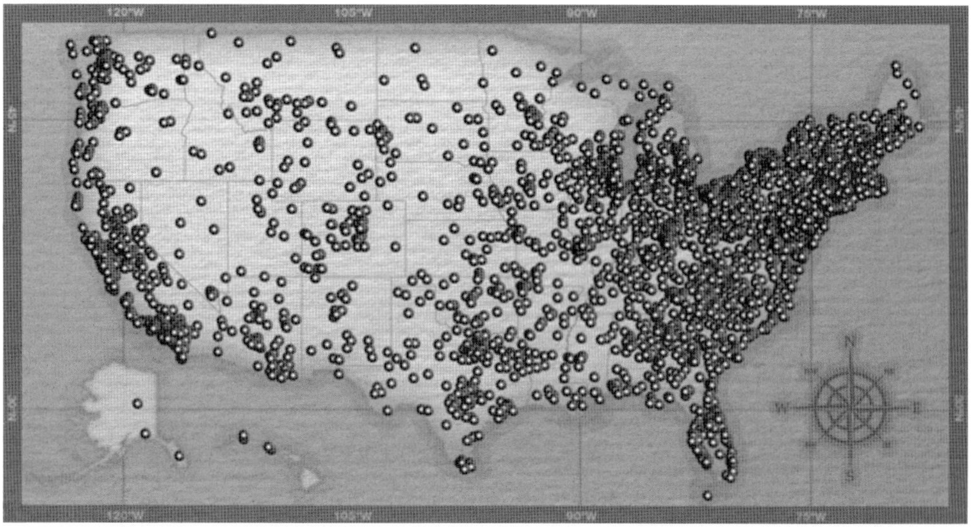



Consistent with our mission to preserve history on a local level, this book was printed in South Carolina on American-made paper and manufactured entirely in the United States. Products carrying the accredited Forest Stewardship Council (FSC) label are printed on 100 percent FSC-certified paper.

MADE IN THE USA